CHANGING MEDIA, CHANGI

1-37
202-224

CHANGING MEDIA, CHANGING CHINA

Edited by Susan L. Shirk

OXFORD
UNIVERSITY PRESS

2011

OXFORD
UNIVERSITY PRESS

Oxford University Press, Inc., publishes works that further
Oxford University's objective of excellence
in research, scholarship, and education.

Oxford New York
Auckland   Cape Town   Dar es Salaam   Hong Kong   Karachi
Kuala Lumpur   Madrid   Melbourne   Mexico City   Nairobi
New Delhi   Shanghai   Taipei   Toronto

With offices in
Argentina   Austria   Brazil   Chile   Czech Republic   France   Greece
Guatemala   Hungary   Italy   Japan   Poland   Portugal   Singapore
South Korea   Switzerland   Thailand   Turkey   Ukraine   Vietnam

Published by Oxford University Press, Inc.
198 Madison Avenue, New York, New York 10016

www.oup.com

Oxford is a registered trademark of Oxford University Press

Library of Congress Cataloging-in-Publication Data
Changing media, changing China / edited by Susan L. Shirk.
p.   cm.
Includes bibliographical references and index.
ISBN 978-0-19-975198-3; 978-0-19-975197-6 (pbk.)
1. Mass media—China. 2. Mass media and culture—China.
I. Shirk, Susan L.
P92.C5C511   2010
302.230951—dc22
2010012025

1 3 5 7 9 8 6 4 2

Printed in the United States of America
on acid-free paper

Contents

Changing Media, Changing China

Susan L. Shirk

[handwritten marginalia: Liberalization Compare to Brazil, Mexico, Taiwan contrast to USSR — mimeos + Nazis — radios Jacob the Liar]

O VER THE PAST thirty years, the leaders of the Chinese Communist Party (CCP) have relinquished their monopoly over the information reaching the public. Beginning in 1979, they allowed newspapers, magazines, and television and radio stations to support themselves by selling advertisements and competing in the marketplace. Then in 1993, they funded the construction of an Internet network. The economic logic of these decisions was obvious: requiring mass media organizations to finance their operations through commercial activities would reduce the government's burden and help modernize China's economy. And the Internet would help catapult the country into the ranks of technologically advanced nations. But less clear is whether China's leaders anticipated the profound political repercussions that would follow.

This collection of essays explores how transformations in the information environment—stimulated by the potent combination of commercial media and Internet—are changing China. The essays are written by Western China experts, as well as by pioneering journalists and experts from China, who write from personal experience about how television, newspapers, magazines, and Web-based news sites navigate the sometimes treacherous crosscurrents between the market and CCP controls. Although they involve different types of media, the essays share common themes and subjects: the explosion of information made available to the public through market-oriented and Internet-based news sources; how people seek credible information; how the population—better informed than ever before—is making new demands on government; how officials react to these demands; the ambivalence of the leadership as to the benefits and risks of the free flow of information, as well as their instinctive and strenuous efforts to shape public opinion by controlling content; and the ways in which journalists and Netizens are evading and resisting these controls.

Following a brief retrenchment after the Tiananmen crackdown on student demonstrators in June 1989, the commercialization of the mass media picked up steam in the 1990s.[1] Today, newspapers, magazines, television stations, and news Web sites compete fiercely for audiences and advertising revenue. After half a century of being force-fed CCP propaganda and starved of real information about domestic and international events, the Chinese public has a voracious appetite for news.

This appetite is most apparent in the growth of Internet access and the Web,[2] which have multiplied the amount of information available, the variety of sources, the timeliness of the news, and the national and international reach of the news. China has more than 384 million Internet users, more than any other country, and an astounding 145 million bloggers.[3] The most dramatic effect of the Internet is how fast it can spread information, which in turn helps skirt official censorship. Because of its speed, the Internet is the first place news appears; it sets the agenda for other media. Chinese Internet users learn almost instantaneously about events happening overseas and throughout China. Thanks to the major news Web sites that compile articles from thousands of sources, including television, newspapers and magazines, and online publications like blogs, and disseminate them widely, a toxic waste site or corruption scandal in any Chinese city or a politician's speech in Tokyo or Washington becomes headline news across the country. Other complementary technologies, such as cell phones, amplify the impact of the Internet. Millions of people get news bulletins text messaged automatically to their cell phones.

China is nonetheless still a long way from having a free press. As of 2008, China stood close to the bottom of world rankings of freedom of the press—181 out of 195 countries—as assessed by the international nongovernmental organization (NGO) Freedom House.[4] Freedom House also gives a low score to China's Internet freedom—78 on a scale from 1 to 100, with 100 being the worst.[5] The CCP continues to monitor, censor, and manufacture the content of the mass media—including the Web—although at a much higher cost and less thoroughly than before the proliferation of news sources.

During President Hu Jintao's second term, which began in 2007, the party ramped up its efforts to manage this new information environment. What at first looked like temporary measures to prevent destabilizing protests in the lead-up to the 2008 Olympics and during the twentieth anniversary of the Tiananmen crackdown and other political anniversaries in 2009 now seem to have become a permanent strategy. Apparently the CCP will do whatever it takes to make sure that the information reaching the public through the commercial media and the Internet does not inspire people to challenge party rule.

Information management has become a source of serious friction in China's relations with the United States and other Western countries. In 2010, Google, reacting to cyber attacks originating in China and the Chinese government's intensified controls over free speech on the Internet, threatened to pull out of the country unless it was allowed to operate an unfiltered Chinese language search engine.[6] (Beijing had required Google to filter out material the Chinese government considers politically sensitive as a condition of doing business in China.) Nine days later, Secretary of State Hillary Clinton, in a speech about the Internet and freedom of speech that had been planned before Google's announcement and that did not focus on China or the Google controversy, articulated Internet freedom as an explicit goal of American foreign policy.[7]

The Chinese government was stunned and alarmed by the Google announcement. Google's challenge did not just sully China's international reputation; it also threatened to mobilize a dangerous domestic backlash. A senior propaganda official I interviewed expressed dismay that Google executives had made a high-profile threat instead of using the "good relationship" the Propaganda Department had established with company executives. A Beijing academic heard a senior official say that the government was treating the Google crisis as "the digital version of June 4," referring to the Tiananmen crisis, which almost brought down Communist Party rule in 1989.

In the first twenty-four hours after Google's dramatic statement, angry and excited Netizens crowded into chat rooms to applaud Google's defense of free information. Google has only a 25–30 percent share of the search engine business in China—the Chinese-owned Baidu has been favored by the government and most consumers—but Google is strongly preferred by the members of the highly educated urban elite.[8] To prevent the controversy from stirring up opposition from this influential group, the Propaganda Department went to work. Overnight, the dominant opinion appearing on the Internet turned 180 degrees against Google and the United States.[9] The pro-Google messages disappeared and were replaced by accusations against the U.S. government for colluding with Google to subvert Chinese sovereignty through its "information imperialism," thereby creating suspicions that many of the new postings were bogus. The Propaganda Department asked respected Chinese academics to submit supportive newspaper essays, and provided ghostwriters. Online news portals were required to devote space on their front pages to the government's counterattacks. To defend itself against the threat of a large-scale movement of Google devotees, the CCP fell back on anti-American nationalism. In March 2010 Google followed through on its threat and moved its search engine to Hong Kong; as a result, the Chinese government and not Google now does the filtering. Despite the unique features of the Google case, international as well as domestic conflicts over censorship are likely to be repeated as the party struggles to shape an increasingly pluralistic information environment.

In her book *Media Control in China*, originally published in 2004 by the international NGO Human Rights in China, journalist He Qinglian lambasts the CCP for its limits on press freedom. She describes Chinese journalists as "dancing in shackles." Yet she also credits commercialization with "opening a gap in the Chinese government's control of the news media."[10] Indeed, the competition for audiences provides a strong motivation for the press to break a news story before the propaganda authorities can implement a ban on reporting it—and it has provided an unprecedented space for protest, as was seen in the initial wave of pro-Google commentary. Caught between commercialization and control, journalists play a cat and mouse game with the censors, a dynamic that is vividly depicted in the case studies in this book.

Even partially relinquishing control of the mass media transforms the strategic interaction between rulers and the public in authoritarian political systems like China. Foreigners tend to dwell on the way the Chinese propaganda cops are continuing to censor the media, but an equally important part of the story is the exponential expansion of the amount of information available to the public and how this is changing the political game within China. That change is the subject of this book.

OFFICIAL AMBIVALENCE

As journalist Qian Gang and his coauthor David Bandurski argue in chapter 2, Chinese leaders have a "deep ambivalence" toward the commercial media and the Internet: they recognize its potential benefits as well as its risks. Xiao Qiang, in chapter 9, uses the same term to describe the attitude of Chinese authorities toward the Internet.

By choosing to give up some degree of control over the media, the rulers of authoritarian countries like China make a trade-off. Most obviously, they gain the benefit of economic development; the market operates more efficiently when people have better information. But they also are gambling that they will reap political benefits; that relinquishing control of the media will set off a dynamic that will result in the improvement of the government's performance and ultimately, they hope, in strengthening its popular support. The media improve governance by providing more accurate information regarding the preferences of the public to policymakers. National leaders also use media as a watchdog to monitor the actions of subordinate officials, particularly at the local level, so they can identify and try to fix problems before they provoke popular unrest. Competition from the commercial media further drives the official media and the government itself to become more transparent; to preserve its credibility, the government must *SARS* release more information than it ever did before. In all these ways, the transformed media environment improves the responsiveness and transparency of governance. Additionally, a freer press can help earn international approval.

On the other hand, surrendering control over information creates severe political risks. It puts new demands on the government that it may not be able to satisfy, and it could reveal to the public the divisions behind the facade of party unity. Diminished control also provides an opening for political opposition to emerge. What most worries CCP leaders—and what motivates them to continue investing heavily in mechanisms to control media content—is the potential that a free information environment provides for organizing a challenge to their rule. The Chinese leaders' fear of free-flowing information is not mere paranoia; some comparative social science research indicates that allowing "coordination goods" like press freedom and civil liberties significantly reduces the odds for authoritarian regimes to survive in power.[11]

What is the connection between information and antigovernment collective action? The more repressive a regime, the more dangerous it is to coordinate and engage in collective action to change that regime. Each individual dares to participate only if the risk of participating is outweighed by the potential benefits. One way to minimize the risk is the anonymity afforded by large numbers. Standing on Tiananmen Square carrying an antiregime sign is an act of political suicide if you are alone. It only makes sense to demonstrate if you know that a crowd will turn out.

Even before the Internet was created, news stories could create focal points for mobilizing mass protests. Cell phones and the Internet are even more useful for coordinating group action as they provide anonymity to the organizers and facilitate two-way communication of many to many. In April 1999, approximately ten thousand devotees of the Falun Gong spiritual sect used cell phones and the Internet to secretly organize a sit-in that surrounded the CCP and government leadership compound in Beijing. A decade before, the fax machine was the communication technology that made it possible for students to organize pro-democracy protests in Beijing's Tiananmen Square and more than 130 other cities. As the chapters in this book detail, in recent years a combination of newspaper reports, Internet communication tools, and cell phones has enabled student protests against Japan, demonstrations against rural land seizures, and protests against environmentally damaging industrial projects. The political possibilities of the latest social networking technologies like Twitter (a homegrown Chinese version is FanFou), Facebook (a Chinese version is Xiaonei), or the video-sharing program YouTube (a Chinese version is Youku) have yet to be fully tested in China.[12]

As Michael Suk-Young Chwe points out in his book *Rational Ritual*, media communication and other elements of culture make coordination possible by creating "common knowledge" that gives each person the knowledge that others have received the same message.[13] When all news was communicated through official media, it was used to mobilize support for CCP policies: hence, the CCP had few worries about popular opposition. Thomas Schelling made this point with a characteristically apt analogy: "The participants of a square dance may all be thoroughly dissatisfied with the particular dances being called, but as long as the caller has the phone, nobody can dance anything else."[14] As the number and va[ ] microphones have increased, so have the force of public opinion risk of bottom-up mass action. The CCP propaganda authorities may [ ] been reading Schelling: A June 2009 *People's Daily* commentary titled "The Microphone Era" says, "In this Internet era, everyone can be an information channel and a principal of opinion expression. A figurative comparison is that everybody now has a microphone in front of him."[15]

Examples like the 2009 antigovernment protests in Iran and the so-called color revolutions in former Soviet states, as well as their own experiences, make Chinese politicians afraid that the free flow of information through the new media could threaten their rule. But it is worth considering the other possibility, namely, that the Internet might actually impede a successful revolutionary movement because venting online is a safer option than taking to the streets; and the decentralized nature of online communication splinters movements instead of integrating them into effective revolutionary organizations.[16] Nevertheless, China's leaders are too nervous to risk completely ceding control of information.

MASS MEDIA IN TOTALITARIAN CHINA

In the prereform era, China had no journalism as we know it, only propaganda. Highly conscious of public opinion, the CCP devoted a huge amount of resources to managing popular views of all issues.[17] In CCP lingo, the media were called the "throat and tongue" of the party; their sole purpose was to mobilize public support by acting as loudspeakers for CCP policies.[18] The Chinese public received all of its highly homogenous information from a small number of officially controlled sources.

As of 1979, there were only sixty-nine newspapers in the entire country, all run by the party and government.[19] The standard template consisted of photos and headlines glorifying local and national leaders on the front page, and invariably positive reports written in formulaic, ideological prose inside. Local news stories of interest such as fires or crimes were almost never reported. What little foreign news was provided had to be based on the dispatches of the government's Xinhua News Agency. People read the *People's Daily* and other official newspapers in the morning at work— offices and factories were required to have subscriptions. The 7 P.M. news on

China Central Television (CCTV) simply rehashed what had been in the *People's Daily.*[20] Newspaper editorials and commentaries were read aloud by strident voices over ubiquitous radio loudspeakers and then used as materials for obligatory political study sessions in the workplace.

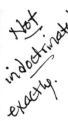

Not, indoctrinated exactly.

A steady diet of propaganda depoliticized the public. As political scientist Ithiel de Sola Pool observed, "When regimes impose daily propaganda in large doses, people stop listening."[21] CCP members, government officials, and politically sophisticated intellectuals, however, had to remain attentive. To get the information they needed to do their jobs—and to survive during the campaigns to criticize individuals who had made ideological mistakes that periodically swept through the bureaucracies—the elite deciphered the coded language of the official media by reading between the lines. Sometimes this esoteric communication was intended as a signal from the top CCP leaders to subordinates about an impending change in the official line.[22] Kremlinology and Pekinology developed into a high art not only in foreign intelligence agencies, but also within Soviet and Chinese government circles themselves. In chapter 8, Daniela Stockmann describes survey research that she completed which shows that government officials and people who work with the government continue to read the official press to track policy trends.

A diet consisting solely of official propaganda left people craving trustworthy sources of information.[23] As in all totalitarian states, a wide information gap divided the top leaders from the public. Senior officials enjoyed ample access to the international media and an extensive system of internal intelligence gathered by news organizations and other bureaucracies (called *neican* in Chinese). But the vast majority of the public was left to rely on rumors picked up at the teahouse and personal observations of their neighborhoods and workplaces. (In modern democracies, the information gap between officialdom and the public has disappeared almost entirely: U.S. government officials keep television sets on in their offices and learn about international events first from CNN, not from internal sources.)

MEDIA REFORM

Beginning in the early 1980s, the structure of Chinese media changed. Newspapers, magazines, and television stations received cuts in their government subsidies and were driven to enter the market and to earn revenue.

In 1979 they were permitted to sell advertising, and in 1983 they were allowed to retain the profits from the sale of ads. Because people were eager for information and businesses wanted to advertise their products, profits were good and the number of publications grew rapidly. As Qian Gang and David Bandurski note in chapter 2, the commercialization of the media accelerated after 2000 as the government sought to strengthen Chinese media organizations to withstand competition from foreign media companies.

By 2005, China published more than two thousand newspapers and nine thousand magazines.[24] In 2003, the CCP eliminated mandatory subscriptions to official newspapers and ended subsidies to all but a few such papers in every province. Even nationally circulated, official papers like *People's Daily*, *Guangming Daily*, and *Economics Daily* are now sold at retail stalls and compete for audiences. According to their editors, *Guangming Daily* sells itself as "a spiritual homeland for intellectuals"; *Economics Daily* markets its timely economic reports; and the *People's Daily* promotes its authoritativeness.[25]

About a dozen commercial newspapers with national circulations of over 1 million readers are printed in multiple locations throughout the country. The southern province of Guangdong is the headquarters of the cutting-edge commercial media, with three newspaper groups fiercely competing for audiences. Nanjing now has five newspapers competing for the evening readership. People buy the new tabloids and magazines on the newsstands and read them at home in the evening.

Though almost all of these commercial publications are part of media groups led by party or government newspapers, they look and sound completely different. In contrast to the stilted and formulaic language of official publications, the language of the commercial press is lively and colloquial. Because of this difference in style, people are more apt to believe that the content of commercial media is true. Daniela Stockmann's research shows that consumers seek out commercial publications because they consider them more credible than their counterparts from the official media. According to her research, even in Beijing, which has a particularly large proportion of government employees, only about 36 percent of residents read official papers such as the *People's Daily*; the rest read only semiofficial or commercialized papers.

Advertisers and many of the commercial media groups target young and middle-aged urbanites who are well-educated, affluent consumers. But publications also seek to differentiate themselves and appeal to specific audiences. The Guangdong-based publications use domestic muckraking to attract a business-oriented, cosmopolitan audience. Because they push the limits on domestic political reporting—their editors are fired and replaced frequently—they have built an audience of liberal-minded readers outside Guangdong Province. According to its editors, *Southern Weekend* (*Nanfang Zhoumo*), published by the *Nanfang Daily* group under the Guangdong Communist Party Committee, considered one of the most critical and politically influential commercial newspapers, has a larger news bureau and greater circulation in politically charged Beijing than it does in southern China.[26] The Communist Youth League's popular national newspaper, *China Youth Journal*, has been a commercial success because it appeals to China's yuppies, the style-conscious younger generation with money to spend. The national foreign affairs newspaper, *Global Times*, tries to attract the same demographic by its often sensational nationalistic reporting of international affairs, as I discuss in chapter 10.

Media based out of Shanghai, the journalistic capital of China before the communist victory in 1949, are comparatively "very dull and quiet," according to Chinese media critics. The cause they cite is that the city's government has been slow to relinquish control.[27] Shanghai audiences prefer *Southern Weekend*, *Global Times*, and Nanjing's *Yangtze Evening News* to Shanghai-based papers, and Hunan television to their local stations.[28]

Journalists now think of themselves as professionals instead of as agents of the government. Along with all the other changes referred to above, this role change began in the late 1970s. Chinese journalists started to travel, study abroad, and encounter "real" journalists. The crusading former editor in chief of the magazine *Caijing* (*Finance and Economy*) and author of chapter 3, Hu Shuli, recalls that before commercialization, "the news media were regarded as a government organization rather than a watchdog, and those who worked with news organizations sounded more like officials than professional journalists. [But] our teachers . . . encouraged us to pursue careers as professional journalists."[29] Media organizations now compete for the best young talent, and outstanding journalists have been able to bid up their salaries by changing jobs frequently. Newspapers and magazines are also recruiting and offering high salaries to bloggers who have attracted large followings. Yet most journalists still receive low base salaries and are paid by the article, which makes them susceptible to corruption. Corruption ranges from small transportation subsidies and "honoraria" provided to reporters for coverage of government and corporate news conferences to outright corporate bribery for positive reporting and extortion of corporations by journalists threatening to write damaging exposés (see chapter 3). Establishing professional journalistic ethics is as difficult in China's Wild West version of early capitalism as it was in other countries at a similar stage of development.

Some journalists also have crossed over to political advocacy. In one unprecedented collective act, the national *Economic Observer* and twelve regional newspapers in March 2010 published a sharply worded joint editorial calling on China's legislature, the National People's Congress, to abolish the system of household residential permits (*hukou*) that forces migrants from the countryside to live as second-class citizens in the cities.[30] The authorities banned dissemination and discussion of the editorial but only after it had received wide distribution. At the legislative session, government leaders proposed some reforms of the *hukou* system, but not its abolition as demanded by the editorial.

dissent

MEDIA FREEDOM AND GOVERNMENT CONTROL

All authoritarian governments face hard choices about how much effort and resources to invest in controlling various forms of media. In China, as in many other nondemocracies, television is the most tightly controlled. As Chinese television expert Miao Di explains in chapter 4, "because of television's great influence on the public today—it is the most important source of information for the majority of the population, reaching widely into rural as well as urban areas—it remains the most tightly controlled type of medium in China by propaganda departments at all administrative levels." All television stations are owned by national, provincial, municipal or county governments and used for propaganda purposes. Yet television producers must pay attention to ratings and audiences if they want to earn advertising revenue. As Miao Di puts it, "television today is like a double-gendered rooster: propaganda departments want it to crow while finance departments want it to lay eggs." The way most television producers reconcile these competing objectives is to "produce leisurely and 'harmless' entertainment programs," not hard news or commentary programs. Yet exceptions exist; Hunan television has found a niche with a lively nightly news show that eliminates the anchor and is reported directly by no-necktie journalists.

In the print realm, the government controls entry to the media market by requiring every publication (including news Web sites with original content) to have a license and by limiting the number of licenses. Only a handful of newspapers, magazines, and news Web sites are completely independent and privately financed. The rest may have some private financing but remain as part of media groups headed by an official publication and subordinate to a government or CCP entity that is responsible for the news content and appoints the chief editors. The chief editor of *Global Times*, appointed by the editors and CCP committee of *People's Daily*, acknowledged this in my interview with him: "If we veer too far away from the general direction of the upper level, I will get fired. I know that." However, there is a degree of variation. For example, magazines are somewhat more loosely controlled than newspapers, presumably because they appear less frequently and have smaller readerships. Additionally, newspapers focusing on economics and business appear to be allowed wider latitude in what they can safely report.

The publication that set a new standard for bold muckraking journalism is *Caijing (Finance and Economics)*, a privately financed independent biweekly business magazine with a relatively small, elite readership. In chapter 3, former *Caijing* editor in chief Hu Shuli explains that "the Chinese government's control of the economic news arena, both in terms of licensing and supervision, has been relatively loose when compared with control over other news . . . [so much so that] even in the aftermath of the Tiananmen Square event of 1989, economic news was little affected by censorship, while all other kinds of news were strictly monitored and controlled." Her analysis of the emergence of financial journalism in China recognizes the path-breaking role of private entrepreneurs and professional journalists, but also credits the "reform-minded economic officials" who appreciate the importance of a free flow of information for the effective functioning of a market economy. She notes that these economic officials didn't call out the CCP Propaganda Department even when *Caijing* broke an embarrassing scandal about the Bank of China's IPO in Hong Kong at the very time when the National People's Congress was holding its annual meeting; this is considered a politically sensitive period during which the propaganda authorities usually ban all bad news. Evan Osnos, in his *New Yorker* profile of Hu Shuli, observes that the differences among senior officials on media policy may protect *Caijing*; the magazine "had gone so far already that conservative branches of the government could no longer be sure which other officials supported it."[31]

In 2010, Hu Shuli and most of the staff of *Caijing* resigned in a conflict with the magazine's owners over editorial control and established Caixin Media, which publishes a weekly news magazine (*Century Weekly*), a monthly economic review (*China Reform*), and a Web site (Caing.com). Caixin is the first media organization in China to establish a Board of Trustees to safeguard its journalistic integrity. *Caijing*, its reputation damaged by the mass exodus of its journalists, is seeking to recoup by publishing exciting stories such as one that urged that Hubei governor Li Hongzhong be fired if he failed to apologize for ripping a journalist's tape recorder out of her hand when she challenged him at a press conference with a question he didn't like.[32] The heated competition between the two media groups is likely to drive them to venture beyond business journalism with taboo-breaking stories that test the tolerance of the government.

Although China's leaders have embraced the Internet as a necessary element of the information infrastructure for a modern economy, as the size of the online public has grown, they have invested more and more heavily in controlling online content and containing its powerful potential to mobilize political opposition. The Internet offers individuals the means to learn about fast-breaking events inside and outside China, to write and disseminate their own commentaries, and to coordinate collective action like petitions, boycotts, and protests. The concept of the Netizen (*wangmin*) is laden with political meaning in a system lacking other forms of democratic participation.[33] As Xiao Qiang, the UC Berkeley–based editor of *China Digital Times*, observes in chapter 9, "The role of the Internet as a communications tool is especially meaningful in China where citizens previously had little to no opportunity for unconstrained public self-expression or access to free and uncensored information. Furthermore, these newfound freedoms have developed in spite of stringent government efforts to control the medium."

From the standpoint of the CCP leaders, the Internet is the most potent media threat. Young and well-educated city dwellers, whose loyalty is crucial for the survival of CCP rule, flock to the Internet for information, including information from abroad.[34] That is why the CCP reacted so defensively to the Google showdown and firmly refuses to permit unfiltered searches. Additionally, the Internet's capability for many-to-many two-way communication facilitates the coordination of collective action around the common knowledge of online information. There is no way for CCP leaders to predict whether virtual activism will serve as a harmless outlet for venting or a means to mobilize antigovernment protests in the street.

Government controls include the "Great Firewall," which can block entire sites located abroad and inside China and ingenious technological methods to filter and inhibit searches for keywords considered subversive. But as Xiao Qiang notes in chapter 9, "the government's primary strategy is to hold Internet service providers and access providers responsible for the behavior of their customers, so business operators have little choice but to proactively censor content on their sites." In addition, human monitors are paid to manually censor content.

Ever since the Mao Zedong era, the methods used by CCP leaders to inculcate political loyalty and ideological conformity have reflected an acute awareness that peer groups have a more powerful impact on individual attitudes than authority figures. It is for this reason that every Chinese citizen was required to undergo regular criticism and self-criticism in small groups of classmates or coworkers. Today's propaganda officials are applying this insight to their management of the information environment created on the Internet. To augment its censorship methods and neutralize online critics, the CCP has introduced a system of paid Internet commentators called the Fifty-Cent Army (*wu mao dang*). Individuals are paid approximately fifty cents in Chinese currency for each anonymous message they post that endorses the government's position on controversial issues. Local propaganda and Youth League officials are particularly keen to adopt this technique.[35] These messages create the impression that the tide of social opinion supports the government, put social and psychological pressure to conform on people with critical views, and thereby presumably reduce the possibility of antigovernment collective action. The July 2009 regulation that bans news Web sites from conducting online polls on current events and requires Netizens to use their real names when posting reactions on these sites appears to have the same aim of disrupting antigovernment common knowledge from forming on the Internet.[36]

The large commercial news Web sites Sina.com, Sohu.com, and Netease.com are probably the second most widely used source of information in China after television, and the first place better-educated people go for their news. These sites have agreements with almost every publication in China (including some blogs) and many overseas news organizations that allow them to compile and reproduce their content and make it available to millions of readers. They are privately owned and listed on NASDAQ, but they are politically compliant, behaving more or less like arms of the government. To keep their privileged monopoly status, they cooperate closely with the State Council Information Office, which sends the managers of the

Web sites SMS text messages several times a day with "guidance" on which topics to avoid. The Information Office also provides a list of particularly independent publications that are not supposed to be featured on the front page. The news sites have opted to reduce their political risks by posting only hard news material that has first been published elsewhere in China. Although they produce original content about such topics as entertainment, sports, and technology, they never do so with respect to news events. Furthermore, with very rare exceptions, such as the 9/11 attacks, they never publish international media accounts of news events directly on the site.

Despite the CCP hovering over it, the Internet constitutes the most freewheeling media space in China because the speed and decentralized structure of online communication present an insuperable obstacle to the censors. In Xiao Qiang's words from chapter 9, "When one deals with the blogosphere and the whole Internet with its redundant connections, millions of overlapping clusters, self-organized communities, and new nodes growing in an explosive fashion, total control is nearly impossible." In the short time before a posting can be deleted by a monitor, Netizens circulate it far and wide so it becomes widely known. For example, speeches from foreign leaders, like President Obama's inaugural address, are carefully excerpted on television and in newspapers to cast China in the most positive light. Yet on the Internet you can find the full, unedited version if you are motivated to search for it. There is no longer any hope for authorities to prevent the possibly objectionable statements about China by politicians in Washington, Tokyo, or Taipei, or the cell phone videos and photographs of violent protests in Lhasa or Urumqi, from reaching and arousing reactions from the online public. Once news attracts attention on the Internet, the audience-seeking commercial media are likely to pick it up as well. Xiao Qiang argues that "the rise of online public opinion shows that the CCP and government can no longer maintain absolute control of the mass media and information," and that the result is a "power shift in Chinese society."

HOW ARE THE COMMERCIAL MEDIA AND INTERNET CHANGING CHINESE POLITICS?

Like all politicians, Chinese leaders are concerned first and foremost about their own survival. A rival leader could try to oust them. A mass protest movement could rise up and overthrow them, especially if a rival leader ches out beyond the inner circle to lead such a movement. If leaders lose support of the military, the combination of an elite split and an opposi-movement could defeat them. The trauma of 1989 came close to doing just that. Thousands of Chinese students demonstrated in Beijing's Tiananmen Square and over 130 other cities, and CCP leaders disagreed on how to handle the demonstrations. The CCP's rule might have ended had the military refused to obey leader Deng Xiaoping's order to use lethal force to disperse the demonstrators. In that same year, democracy activists brought down the Berlin Wall, and communist regimes in the Soviet Union and Eastern Europe began to crumble. No wonder that since 1989, China's leaders have worried that their own days in power are numbered.

Because commercial journalism was still in its infancy and the Internet had not yet been built, the mass media played a more minor role in the 1989 crisis than it has since then. During the crisis, students, frustrated by what they considered the biased slant of the official press, spread the word about their movement by giving interviews to the foreign press and sending faxes abroad. One market-oriented publication, the *World Economic Herald*, based in Shanghai, faced down Jiang Zemin, then the party secretary of the city, and published uncensored reports. The restive journalists at the *People's Daily* and other official papers, with the blessing of some liberal-minded officials in the Propaganda Department, reported freely on the student movement for a few days in May. The Communist Party leaders were almost as worried about the journalists' rebellion as they were about the students' one.[37] After the crackdown, party conservatives closed down several liberal newspapers including the *World Economic Herald* and blamed the crisis in part on the loosening controls over the press that had been introduced by former leaders Zhao Ziyang and Hu Yaobang.[38]

Since Tiananmen, Chinese leaders have paid close attention to the destabilizing potential of the media. The formula for political survival that they adopted, based on their 1989 experience, focuses on three key tasks:[39]

- Prevent large-scale social unrest
- Avoid public leadership splits
- Keep the military loyal to the CCP

The three dicta are interconnected: if the leadership group remains cohesive despite the competition that inevitably arises within it, then the CCP and the security police can keep social unrest from spreading out of control and the government will survive. Unless people receive some signal of permission from the top, protests will be suppressed or fizzle out before they grow politically threatening. But if the divisions among the top leaders come into the open as they did in 1989, people will take to the streets with little fear of punishment. Moreover, were the military leadership to split or abandon the CCP, the entire regime could collapse.

Though commercialization of the media and growth of the Internet have consequences across all three dimensions, today their effects are felt primarily in the efforts to prevent large-scale social unrest. As the chapters in this book describe, the media and Internet are changing the strategic interactions between leaders and the public as the leaders struggle to head off unrest and maintain popular support.

WATCHDOG JOURNALISM: HOW TO REACT WHEN THE DOG BARKS

As noted earlier, the politicians at the top of the CCP are of two minds about whether the media and Internet prevent or encourage large-scale social unrest. On the positive side, the media and Internet provide information on problems so that national leaders can address them before they cause crises. But on the negative side, the market-oriented media and Internet have the subversive effect of facilitating collective action that could turn against CCP rule.

The elite's extreme nervousness about potential protests makes them highly responsive when the media report on a problem. The pressure to react is much greater than it was in the prereform era when the elite relied entirely on confidential internal reporting within the bureaucracy to learn about problems on the ground. Once the media publicize an issue and the issue becomes common knowledge, then the government does not dare ignore it.

Chinese journalists take particular pride in exposés that actually lead to improved governance and changes in policy. One of the earliest and best examples was the reporting about the 2003 death in detention of Sun Zhigang, a young college graduate who had migrated to Guangdong from his native Hubei Province. Qian Gang and David Bandurski, as well as Benjamin Liebman, describe in chapters 2 and 7 how the initial newspaper story published by the *Southern Metropolis Daily*, a bold Guangdong commercial newspaper, circulated throughout the country on the major news Web sites and transformed Sun's death into a cause célèbre that sparked an emotional outpouring online. This emotional outpouring in turn inspired a group of law students to take the issue of the detention and repatriation of migrants directly to the National People's Congress. Only two months after the first article, Premier Wen Jiabao signed a State Council order abolishing the practice of detaining migrants who did not carry a special identification card and shipping them back to their homes.

Although such instances of actual change in policy are rare, public apologies by high-level officials in response to media criticism are becoming more common. In 2001, Premier Zhu Rongji became the first PRC leader to apologize to the public for a cover-up when he took responsibility for an explosion that killed forty-seven children and staff in a rural school where the students were manufacturing fireworks. Premier Zhu initially had endorsed the far-fetched explanation offered by the local officials of a deranged suicide bomber. But when, despite a blackout of the Chinese media, the accounts of Hong Kong and foreign journalists who had interviewed villagers by telephone spread in China over the Internet, Premier Zhu offered his apology in a televised press conference.[40]

Premier Wen Jiabao has followed the example of his predecessor. He apologized for the melamine-tainted milk and infant formula that killed six and sickened hundreds of thousands of babies. The massive food safety story was originally suppressed by propaganda authorities in the lead-up to the 2008 Olympics, but the scandal was broken by the local press in Gansu Province and the official Xinhua News Service following the games. Premier Wen also apologized for the crippling snowstorms in January 2008 that stranded millions of Chinese eager to get home for the Spring Festival break.

To deflect blame and show how responsive it is to media revelations of official negligence or malfeasance, the central government also has sacked the senior officials implicated in such scandals. The number of such high-profile firings or resignations has increased over the past decade with the growth of investigative journalism. Several good examples are described in this book.

Increasingly, officials at all levels are making a conspicuous show of their receptiveness to online public opinion. They publicize their chats with Netizens. Government agencies have opened up Web sites for citizens' petitions. Law enforcement officers have starting inviting Netizens to provide information for their criminal investigations. In one case, a creative local propaganda official who was a former Xinhua reporter invited a number of bloggers to join a commission investigating the suspicious death of a prisoner. The bloggers had ridiculed as implausible the police's explanation that the prisoner had walked into the cell wall during a blindman's bluff game among the prisoners; they thought police brutality must be the explanation. The debate died down after the commission released a report that said they knew too little to conclude what had happened and the provincial prosecutors announced the prisoner had not died during a game but had been beaten by another prisoner. The official proudly explained that he had defused the issue by showing that "public opinion on the Internet must be solved by means of the Internet."[41]

MONITORING LOCAL OFFICIALS

Every government needs information about how its officials are performing their jobs in order to effectively implement its policies. The top officials of China's thirty-three provinces are appointed by the CCP central leaders in Beijing. Yet the central leaders are continually frustrated by their inability to get regional officials to follow their orders. In a rapidly growing market economy, the old top-down bureaucratic methods of monitoring local officials are no longer working. Local officials benefit more by colluding with local businesses to promote economic growth by spending on big development projects than by providing such social goods as environmental protection, health care, education, and quality food and medicine that are mandated but not fully funded by the central government. Corruption at the local level is rampant. Yet the poor provision of social goods by corrupt local officials could heighten public resentment against the government and threaten CCP rule on the national level.

Theoretically, there are several ways that Beijing could resolve the dilemma of how to oversee the performance of local officials. It could allow citizens to elect their own local leaders. It also could permit independent NGOs to monitor the performance of local leaders. A fully autonomous court system in which prosecutors put corrupt officials on trial and citizens sue for the benefits being denied them also would help. But CCP leaders have been too afraid of losing control to undertake such fundamental institutional reforms. They have chosen instead to rely on the mass media to serve as a fire alarm to alert the center to problems at lower levels.[42] From their perspective, using the media looks like a less dangerous approach because they still license media outlets and appoint most of their top editors, thereby retaining some power to rein in errant outlets. Media revelations of local malfeasance also benefit the center by deflecting blame for problems away from themselves and onto local officials. The publicity appears to be working; surveys indicate that Chinese people are more critical of the performance of local officials than of central ones, in contrast to the pattern in American politics.

The center's interest in using the media to monitor local officials has been evident since the mid-1990s. CCTV, with the encouragement of the powerful propaganda czar Ding Guangen (see chapter 2), created a daily program called *Focus* (*Jiaodian Fantan*) to investigate issues at lower levels in 1994. Miao Di, in chapter 4, discusses *Focus* in some detail. The program was blessed with high-level political support, having been visited by three Chinese premiers and praised by China's cabinet, the State Council. The show attracted a wide viewership and strengthened the credibility of television news overall. However, because local officials intervened so frequently to block exposés of their misdeeds, the show now has become much less hard-hitting.

The central authorities tolerate greater press openness on the type of problems that, if left unreported and unsolved, might stir up serious popular dissatisfaction—in particular, problems with water and air pollution as well as food and medicine quality. Some national-level environmental officials have become adept at using media events such as, televised hearings on the environmental impact of important projects to mobilize public pressure on lower-level officials to comply with centrally adopted policies that are environmentally conscious. Veteran journalist Zhan Jiang describes the pattern in chapter 5, on environmental reporting: "as a general rule the center has an interest in receiving information that reduces the information gap between the center and localities regarding potentially volatile problems resulting from negligence by local officials." However, as he illustrates with the case of the Songhua River chemical spill once journalists pull the fire alarm and alert Beijing and the public to a crisis, then the center tries to reassert control over the media to cool off public emotions and convey an image of a competent government that is solving the problem.

Recently, the central official media have been given the green light to pull the alarm on abuses by local officials. For years, reports have been circulating in the foreign human rights community and the international press about provincial and municipal governments that detain local citizens who have come to Beijing to petition central officials about their grievances with local officials. They lock up the petitioners in illegal detention centers ("black jails") on the outskirts of Beijing, ostensibly for "legal education," and then ship them back home. In November 2009, the official magazine *Outlook* (*Liaowang*) broke the story of these illegal jails and the report appeared on the Xinhua Web site.[43]

Not surprisingly, local officials are wary of media watchdogs and do what they can to fence them out. As Tsinghua University journalism professor Li Xiguang has noted, "The central government, in the fight against the widespread corruption of the local government, encourages journalists to write exposes of the corruption. But the local governments are very much protective of themselves and of their power, so there is a conflict between the central government and the local government in dealing with journalists."[44] Censorship by provincial and local branches of the CCP Propaganda Department and the State Council Information Office is viewed by journalists as tighter than that at the national level. The essays in this book offer numerous examples of local governments' blackouts of critical news stories and the strategies journalists and activists use to evade them.

Ever since the 1990s, regional commercial newspapers have been doing investigative reporting of corruption and other abuses on the part of local officials, but only outside their own home provinces. This practice is called cross-regional reporting (*yidi jiandu*). Since all local newspapers are part of media groups belonging to the local government and CCP establishment, editors naturally are inhibited from biting the hand that feeds them. Exciting stories about the sins of other people's officials may be second best but are better than nothing. Reporters are willing to brave police harassment or violent attacks by paid thugs to get the goods on bad governance by officials in other places. Often they don't have to go to the scene to report the story. As Ben Liebman describes in chapter 7, journalists blocked by local bans from writing about local malfeasance can simply e-mail the information to colleagues from other regions who then write the exposé.

Complaints from provincial and municipal officials about nosy reporters pushed the CCP Propaganda Department to ban the practice of cross-regional reporting in 2004. Because the order was largely ignored, a year later provincial leaders raised the issue again, this time at the level of the Politburo.[45] Provincial leaders are a powerful group within the CCP, constituting the largest bloc in the Central Committee and one-quarter of the Politburo.

The interests of these leaders incline them to favor tighter restrictions on investigative journalism. As a result of their complaints, cross-regional reporting has been restricted to stories about officials at the county level or below. Only national-level media dare to publish exposés of provincial and municipal officials, and even then they usually wait until they get wind of an official investigation before reporting on the case.

Meanwhile, local officials are learning the art of spin; they hold press conferences and online chats with Netizens to present an appearance of openness and candor—for example, Chongqing Party Secretary Bo Xilai invited television cameras to broadcast live his negotiations with striking taxi drivers in 2009.

The expansion of Internet access and the growth of the Web also make it increasingly difficult for local officials to enforce media blackouts on sensitive issues. Several chapters in this book discuss the 2007 case of the Xiamen PX chemical plant, a project ultimately defeated by the mobilization of environmentally conscious public opinion that breached a local media blockade. As Xiao Qiang tells the story (chapter 9), the outcome resulted from the "gap in control between local authorities as well as between local and central authorities [that] can provide a space for Netizens to transmit information. . . . One of the most vocal advocates for the issue was the blogger Lian Yue, whose Weblog was not hosted within Fujian Province. Because officials outside Fujian, including the central government, did not share the local government's interest in censoring news about the PX plant, Lian Yue was able to continue his Weblog and even get coverage in newspapers published outside Fujian."

MEDIA CREDIBILITY AND GOVERNMENT TRANSPARENCY

Competition from the commercial media and the Web-based media has created what Qian Gang and David Bandurski call a credibility gap problem for the official media. In chapter 2, they compare the ways stories are covered in various kinds of newspapers, vividly illustrating that commercial newspapers' reporting is far more informative and reliable than that found in official newspapers. Readers are abandoning the official media, and their preference is heightened during crises that arouse their interest and motivate them to search for reliable information.

Daniela Stockmann, in chapter 8, provides new data about how people in China choose between different types of news sources. They use the official press to get information on the government's current policy position, but turn to the commercial media and the Internet for credible "real news." As she explains, it is "the perceived disassociation from the government that lends credibility to the nonofficial media." Stockmann happened to be doing a survey on media usage in Beijing in spring 2005 when student protests against Japan erupted. This serendipity gave her the rare opportunity to compare the way people use the media during normal times and during a crisis. What she discovered was that during a crisis, people have a particularly keen nose for where to find credible information. Even when the propaganda authorities ban reporting of protests and try to homogenize coverage in all types of media, people are more likely to abandon official sources and turn to the commercial press and the Internet than during normal times.

The severe acute respiratory syndrome (SARS) epidemic in China in 2003 is referred to by several authors as a turning point in the relations between the government, the media, and the public. By ordering the media to play down early reports of people falling ill with a mysterious disease, a cover-up that allowed the virus to spread and kill more people, Beijing deepened public skepticism about the reliability of the official media and of the government itself. More important, the cover-up taught the public to look to new sources for the true facts. The searing SARS experience also spurred the determination of journalists to meet people's need for accurate information during a crisis.

The flight from official sources creates a serious problem for Chinese leaders, who need to prevent panic and antigovernment reactions during crises. Leaders plausibly worry that a widespread environmental or food safety catastrophe that angers large numbers of people about the same issue at the same time could snowball into a revolt against the CCP.

Competition from the commercial media and the Web and the narrowing of the information gap between officials and the public forces the government to be more transparent to maintain its credibility. The State Council Information Office and Tsinghua University have trained hundreds of official spokespeople for central, provincial, and municipal government agencies to give press briefings. The central government launched an E-government initiative, and almost every government agency (including very sensitive ones like the Ministry of State Security) now posts information on its Web site.

The trend toward government transparency got a major boost from the Regulations on Open Government Information that went into effect in 2008. The regulations require officials to release information during disasters and emergencies and permit citizens to request the release of government information. An activist took advantage of the opening to request budgets from government agencies. When in October 2009 Guangzhou released departmental budgets and Shanghai refused to do so on the grounds that this information constituted state secrets, the media and online public went wild criticizing Shanghai's excuse.[46] Xinhua piled on by reprinting many of the critiques, including a hard-hitting advocacy of transparency by *China Youth*. "It is a worldwide custom for governments to have their budgets as open information to the public. This is also a common sense for democratic governance."[47] A Guangzhou newspaper had been the first to break the story, taking pleasure in highlighting how its hometown was showing up Shanghai.[48] A few days later, Shanghai succumbed to the tidal wave of censure and announced that it would release the budgetary information.

Another major move toward transparency is happening within China's Xinhua News Service. Traditionally the mouthpiece of the central CCP Propaganda Department, Xinhua has undergone a remarkable makeover and emerged as a more or less genuine news organization that competes avidly with the commercial media and has begun to earn the respect of the journalistic profession. The new Xinhua breaks important stories like the melamine-tainted baby formula scandal and, as of 2008, has a green light from the CCP to report mass protests. During the 2008 Sichuan earthquake, Xinhua reported casualty statistics minute by minute. Media reputations are hard to change, however. The public and the international media still doubt the accuracy of the accounting of the dead reported by Xinhua and the government. Activists like performance artist Ai Weiwei have shamed the CCP and dramatized the people's right to know by collecting and seeking to publish the names of children who died in the earthquake because of shoddy school construction. Huang Qi and Tan Zuoren, who published their investigations of the earthquake victims online, were convicted of revealing state secrets and subversion and sent to jail for long terms.

CCTV has been slower than Xinhua to get the message about credibility. Educated city dwellers are contemptuous of central television for its political docility and the poor quality of its programming. The official television organization made itself a laughingstock in February 2009 when its recently built skyscraper was destroyed in a massive fire ignited by the company's own Chinese New Year fireworks display. The CCTV evening news show buried the story of its own fire and headlined the fires occurring in Australia instead; in the meantime, cell phone photos and videos of the flaming building taken by people standing on the sidewalk were circulating all over the country. In the aftermath, the head of CCTV was sacked and a new team of executives brought in to remake the organization as a credible news source.

In chapter 7, Benjamin Liebman provides an interesting analysis of the way the Chinese courts are responding to the new media environment by what he calls a kind of "controlled transparency." To defend the integrity of the legal system from the pressures created by media frenzies and online lynch mobs, some legal reformers have called for the courts to provide more information about their cases. Yet by and large, judges have reacted by moving in the opposite direction. Particularly at the local level, "judges argue that controls on media coverage of the courts are necessary to prevent biased coverage that subverts courts' authority."

It took intervention by top leader Hu Jintao in June 2008 to lift the ban against media reporting of mass protests, a giant step toward transparency that many observers believed would never happen because the CCP would not want to send any signal that might encourage copycat protests. This breakthrough is a testament to the importance the central leaders place on maintaining the credibility of the CCP and the government for their own political survival.

The successful experiment with information transparency during the May 2008 Sichuan earthquake may have emboldened leaders to free up reporting of protests, too. On 20 June 2008 Hu paid a well-publicized visit to *People's Daily* to honor the newspaper on its sixtieth anniversary, chat online with Netizens, and give a speech that emphasized the importance of the government "taking the initiative" in shaping public opinion by allowing the state media like Xinhua, CCTV, and *People's Daily* to report breaking news: "We must perfect our system of news release, and improve our system for news reports on sudden-breaking public events, releasing authoritative information at the earliest moment, raising timeliness, increasing transparency, and firmly grasping the initiative in news propaganda work. In the struggle that followed the recent earthquake disaster, we quickly released information about the disaster and the relief effort . . . earning high praise from cadres and the people, and also earning the esteem of the international community."[49]

Just a week after Hu's speech, the first "mass incident," as the Chinese call protests, was reported in the official media. In Weng'an county, a remote region of Guizhou Province in China's southwest, tens of thousands of angry people demonstrated over the drowning death of a young woman. The police had called the death a suicide, but the relatives and friends of the victim claimed it actually was a rape-murder by well-connected local youths. The dramatic images of protesters burning the police station spread instantaneously across the Internet, and the story appeared shortly thereafter on the Xinhua News Service. A year later, when local protests over the suspicious death of a hotel waiter in Shishou City, Hubei Province, were not reported in the media for five days, a commentary in the online version of *People's Daily* drew the contrast with Weng'an. It quoted the Guizhou CCP secretary's statement, "Our commitment to information transparency was the most important reason for the swift settlement of the incident," and drew the conclusion that "information transparency helps enhance the government's credibility."[50]

LISTENING (TOO CLOSELY?) TO PUBLIC OPINION

China's insecure leaders pay close attention to the commercial media and the Internet and treat it as a reflection of what the public actually is thinking. Lacking elections or scientific polls about public attitudes to inform them about citizen views, Chinese politicians in the past had to rely on internal reports generated by their bureaucratic hierarchies. However, nowadays they can read citizens' views on the Internet in raw, unfiltered form. They also can follow trends in public opinion from articles in tabloid newspapers and magazines that sound far more genuine than the hackneyed accounts they used to read in the official press. All media, including Xinhua, pepper their stories with online quotes from Netizens as a way of enhancing their journalistic credibility. Of course the new practice of planting positive online commentary will make it harder for government officials to draw accurate inferences about public opinion from online opinion. Whether government officials and Internet readers will discount positive comments as false and give credence only to the critical ones remains unclear. Each time the government swamps the Internet with pro-government postings, as it did during the Google controversy, it might alienate more people than it wins over. The popular blogger Han Han notes that by packing chat rooms with paid pro-government commentary, the authorities discourage genuine _{Neat} paradox praise for the government, because no one wants to be thought of as a member of the Fifty-Cent Army.[51]

Chinese officials know full well that the public opinion expressed on the Internet is not representative of the population as a whole.[52] In China as elsewhere, the people who speak out on the Internet are those with extreme points of view. Individuals with more moderate views are less eager to publicize them. Posting one's opinions online carries some danger that one will be flagged by the CCP as a potential troublemaker, so people concerned about their own careers are cautious about making their views known. A 2009 article in the official media argued that it is a mistake to draw inferences about public opinion from the Internet: "online public opinion simply cannot be equated with the opinion of society. The online community cannot stand in for the public, and Internet society cannot replace public society. After all, those able to get online and express their opinion are still a special segment of the people."[53] Yet it may be logical for politicians in authoritarian countries to pay attention to the more extreme views articulated on the Internet. Democratic politicians rely on public opinion polls with scientifically selected representative samples because they need to know what the average voter thinks in order to win elections. But politicians in China do not worry about winning elections. Their survival depends instead on being attentive to the people who feel so strongly about an issue that they might come out on the streets to protest. The individuals who fulminate on the Internet are the ones more likely to take the greater risk of participating in, or organizing, mass protests. No wonder that, as Qian Gang and David Bandurski write in chapter 2, "despite the fact that the media remain formally part of the party-government apparatus, CCP leaders are beginning to treat the media and Internet as the voice of the public and respond to it accordingly."

Two of the essays in this book highlight the dangers when China's jittery politicians become excessively attentive to public opinion as they hear it through the media and the Internet. In chapter 10, I describe how nationalist public opinion blows back on the foreign policy process. It has become impossible for the Chinese government to shield the public from news about Japan, Taiwan, and the United States that might enflame nationalist passions. The media compete for audiences by publishing exciting stories that appeal to these passions. Based on the information they get from the commercial media and the Internet, Chinese foreign policymakers form the impression that nationalist views are intensifying and spreading. I explain that Chinese leaders' fear of a nationalist movement that unites various groups in opposition to a government perceived as too weak in the face of foreign pressure has historical resonance: "Mass movements that accused leaders of failing to defend the nation against foreign aggression brought down the Qing Dynasty in 1911 and the Republic of China in 1949. China's current leaders make foreign policy with a close eye to nationalist criticism of government foreign policy in the media and on the Internet because they are intent on avoiding a similar fate."

Chinese leaders' hyperresponsiveness to popular nationalism sometimes causes them to box themselves into a corner from which it is difficult to escape. After Japanese Prime Minister Junichiro Koizumi started paying annual visits to the controversial Yasukuni Shrine where Japanese World War II veterans, including some convicted war criminals, are memorialized, the media and Internet backlash forced China's leaders to freeze all high-level diplomatic contacts with Japan for five years. As I say, another risk of media blowback is that it can "send policy dangerously off track during a crisis when the leaders' perception of an outraged public may drive them to make public threats that they feel they cannot back down from without losing their own popular support." I cite as an example China's conflicts with Europe and the United States over Tibet and the Dalai Lama following the 2008 crisis in which the public erupted in anger after viewing photos and videos of violent attacks on Han Chinese in Lhasa.

Media stories about criminal justice cases, similar to stories about hot-button foreign policy issues, also arouse intense public interest and emotion. Criminal justice, like foreign policy, is a domain in which China's leaders are hyperresponsive, to the extent that they often allow popular emotions to swamp professional judgment in determining outcomes.

In recent years, China has been swept by a craze of Internet-based vigilantism called "human flesh search engine," whereby Netizens investigate and harass individuals, often officials, whom they believe are guilty of an illegal or immoral act, or have been caught in the act by means of a cell phone photograph or video. These online true crime dramas, which often involve exposing local cover-ups, captivate millions of people throughout the country; the stories jump from the Internet to television and print tabloids and back again, churning up a tidal wave of public pressure on the authorities.

According to Benjamin Liebman, in many cases "the media are an important check on official abuses, coming to the assistance of victims of injustice, or pressuring courts to act fairly." But in other cases, "media coverage encourages CCP officials to intervene in the courts, predetermining the outcome of cases and reaffirming CCP oversight of the judiciary." Chapter 7 provides a number of examples in which the commercial media and people on the Internet mobilize, as he puts it, "populist demands for justice—or vengeance," which drive CCP politicians to order judges to impose harsher sentences on defendants and then claim credit for being responsive to the public's calls for justice. Such political interventions not only have questionable effects for procedural justice but also subvert the establishment of an independent judiciary. The courts, in turn, retaliate against media critics by means of defamation suits. Liebman raises the possibility that the CCP may actually benefit from this institutional design in which the courts and the media compete with one another, and the CCP keeps both from becoming completely independent. That is why, he concludes, "commercialization of the Chinese media will not necessarily lead to media freedom, and why media coverage of the courts will not necessarily improve the fairness of the Chinese legal system."

MEDIA COVERAGE OF LEADERSHIP POLITICS

Changes in China's media also make it more difficult for China's leaders to prevent the public from knowing about any differences among them selves. The lesson they drew from Tiananmen—and of the chaotic Cultural Revolution (1966–1969)—was that CCP rule can unravel once people outside the Politburo learn about the splits among top politicians. But in such a radically transformed information environment, how can they keep elite politics secret?

The history of press commercialization in China and other countries shows that publications inevitably start to try to satisfy the demand of white-collar elites and the public at large for information about what is going on behind the curtain at the top reaches of power. As early as the mid-seventeenth century, a publication called the *Beijing Gazette* was publishing, despite the objections of the emperor, information about internal debates stolen from the desktops of senior officials or leaked by them.[54]

So far, the leaders of the CCP have been more successful than the emperor at hiding their internal differences from the public. In Mao's China, people had to read between the lines of the formulaic coverage of leaders' activities and rely on the active rumor mill to figure out who stood where, who was ascendant, and who was in decline among the CCP leadership.[55] Not much has changed on this front. Reporting on leadership politics or internal deliberations remains taboo. To preserve the facade of unanimity and prevent any leader from reaching beyond the inner circle to mobilize ordinary people, all information about discussions in government and CCP meetings is blacked out.

Leaks of internal deliberations are remarkably rare considering the competition that inevitably occurs within any political oligarchy like China's. This is even more striking considering the desire of the market-oriented media to scoop their rivals with exciting news. The media provide hardly any glimpses behind the curtain. A Chinese journalist told me in an interview, "Leaks about top-level decision making only go to the *New York Times* because people know the Chinese media can't publish such stories."

One modest step toward transparency is that it is now permissible to report the mere fact that the Politburo held a meeting and to mention a couple of the general topics discussed in the meeting. People also took note when Xinhua reported in June 2009 that the mayor of the important southern coastal city of Shenzhen had been fired for "serious disciplinary violations" (which usually means corruption), although it took five days of official silence before the report appeared.[56]

The journalists who have received the harshest punishments, including lengthy jail terms, are those accused of revealing state secrets by reporting leaks about machinations at the top. Zhao Yan, a Chinese journalist in the Beijing bureau of the *New York Times*, was imprisoned for three years because he was accused of obtaining information from anonymous sources that Jiang Zemin planned to retire from his post as head of the Central Military Commission in September 2004. (According to other Chinese journalists, although the *New York Times* reported the story, Zhao Yan actually had nothing to do with acquiring the information.) Shi Tao, a journalist who sent an e-mail abroad revealing the instructions from the Propaganda Department discussed at a meeting of his newspaper, was sent to jail for ten years.

Yet it is only a matter of time before leaks about elite politics will start to appear first on the Internet and eventually in other media as well. Chinese journalist Guo Yukuan of CCTV and the magazine *Nanfang Chuang*, in a speech at a media conference in China, paid tribute to famous leakers Mark Felt, the "Deep Throat" source of the Watergate affair, Daniel Ellsberg, who released the Pentagon Papers, and Doctor Wang Xueyuan, who revealed exorbitant medical treatments and falsified medical records in Harbin Hospital Number 2. "If we look around," he said, "almost every influential news report has the shadow of a deep throat behind the scene."[57] Hong Kong newspapers, just across the border, have relied on leaks and guesswork to report on Beijing leadership politics for decades. How long can it be before such stories begin to appear in China too? To entertain a hypothetical idea, think about how easy it would be nowadays for a leader to reach out to a constituency by posting a manifesto on the Internet or granting a candid interview to the media. Certainly, ambitious politicians have already become skillful in using the media to burnish their public image. During 2010, Chongqing CCP Secretary Bo Xilai gained valuable publicity by prosecuting for corruption and mafia ties a large number of very senior local officials. His decisive actions were widely applauded in online forums, raising speculation that he was campaigning for a Politburo Standing Committee slot in the 2012 succession.

THE MILITARY AND THE MEDIA

The People's Liberation Army (PLA) has been a key player in Chinese politics since before the founding of the People's Republic in 1949. Today, the PLA has become a formidable professional force with international reach. Nevertheless, China's leaders never forget that in a domestic crisis the military also is the ultimate guarantor of CCP rule. In chapter 6, Tai Ming Cheung describes how CCP leaders are managing to keep the military satisfied and loyal in the new media environment.

The PLA's official media, especially the flagship *Liberation Army Daily*, has been protected from the transformations affecting the civilian media and remains fundamentally unchanged. It continues to operate according to the principle of "propaganda first, profitability second," presenting a "sterilized image" of the PLA to its troops and to the public. The *Liberation Army Daily* enjoys a captive audience of the PLA's 2.5 million soldiers, having successfully resisted the government's effort to end mandatory subscriptions to all military units. The civilian authorities don't dare to use the media, civilian or military, as a watchdog to monitor the PLA the way they do over local governments. The military media, moreover, push back against proposals to strengthen civilian control by putting the PLA under the government, describing the idea as a plot by "Western hostile forces" to separate the PLA from the CCP.

Many Chinese outside the PLA, especially high school and college-age men, are fascinated by military affairs. This audience is being tapped by commercial magazines, many of which are published by firms in the defense industries. As Cheung observes, "By highlighting the technological advances of U.S., European, and other Asian militaries, these publications have helped to create public support for China's own military spending, which buttresses the lobbying of the defense industry." The double-digit annual increases in official military budgets over the past fifteen years have kept the PLA preoccupied with upgrading its capabilities and invested in the political status quo.

THE PEOPLE'S RIGHT TO KNOW

The chapters in this volume illustrate how the commercialization of the media and growth of the Internet have combined to drastically increase the information available to the Chinese people and narrow the information gap between the government and the public. Politicians have been scrambling to exploit the benefits of this new information environment while reducing the risks of it subverting CCP rule. Different groups within the government undoubtedly give different weights to the benefits and risks, with economic officials favoring greater openness, and CCP propaganda officials having a reflexive preference for control. As a result, China's media policies are an inconsistent amalgam of improved transparency and responsiveness on the one hand and huge investments in more effective censorship on the other. The big question is whether these policies are gaining the CCP greater support or generating resistance that could have revolutionary consequences in the future. The information explosion has raised people's expectations about how much information they are entitled to receive. Access to news about popular culture, science and technology, and sports through the world is wide open. The CCP itself, in its speeches and regulations like the one on open government information, has recognized the legitimate right of the public to obtain information. Why then should people be deprived of knowledge about events happening in their own city or in the nation's capital?

Censorship of newspapers, magazines, and television is largely invisible, but censorship over the Internet is obvious. The very visible hand of the censor is intended to intimidate users with the omnipresent authority of the CCP; cartoon figures pop up to remind users that the eyes of the party are watching what they read and write online. But when users see a piece of news or a critical viewpoint suddenly disappear, followed by a flood of pro-government postings, as occurred during the Google facedown, it reveals the weakness of the regime, not its strength; users know just what kinds of innocuous information the CCP is afraid to allow to become common knowledge.

In chapter 9, Xiao Qiang argues that resentment against censorship is brewing: "The government's pervasive and intrusive censorship system has generated resentment among Chinese Netizens, inspiring new forms of social resistance and demands for greater freedom of information and expression." Netizens ridicule the CCP censors through clever jokes and spoof videos. This covert resistance subverts the moral authority of the CCP. What's more, as such resistance becomes common knowledge it raises the likelihood of outright opposition in the future. A cover-up that leads to massive harm or a hardening of controls over the media or the Internet during a crisis might spark such opposition. The rallying cry of the next Chinese revolution could be "the people's right to know."

Notes

1. China had a genuinely free press for a few days in May 1989, during the Tiananmen demonstrations. See Andrew J. Nathan and Perry Link, *The Tiananmen Papers* (New York: Public Affairs, 2001). After the crackdown, party conservatives closed down several liberal newspapers—*Shijie Jingji Daobao* (*World Economic Herald*) in Shanghai and *Jingji Xue Zhoubao* (*Economics Weekly*) in Beijing. They also criticized former leaders Zhao Ziyang and Hu Yaobang for making the mistake of loosening control over the press. See Liu Xiaobo, "The Tragedy of Hu Yaobang and Zhao Ziyang," Chinese Newsnet.com, March 2005, www.chinesenewsnet.com/MainNews/Opinion/2005_2_1_19_11_58_68.html.

2. "Internet" refers to the network infrastructure, and "Web" refers to the World Wide Web, the major way of accessing information on the Internet.

3. China Internet Network Information Center, *25th Statistical Report on the Development of China's Internet*, January 2010, http://www.cnnic.net.cn/uploadfiles/pdf/2010/1/15/101600. pdf.

4. Freedom House, "Freedom of the Press 2009: Table of Global Press Freedom Rankings," http://www.freedomhouse.org/uploads/fop/2009/FreedomofthePress2009_tables.pdf (accessed 23 August 2009).

5. Freedom House, "Freedom on the Net: A Global Assessment of Internet and Digital Media," http://www.freedomhouse.org/uploads/specialreports/NetFreedom2009/FOTN_Charts&Graphs.pdf (accessed 23 August 2009).

6. On 12 January 2010, Google's official statement was posted on its blog, http://googleblog.blogspot.com/2010/01/new-approach-to-china.html.

7. Hillary Rodham Clinton, "Remarks on Internet Freedom," The Newseum, 21 January 2010, http://www.state.gov/secretary/rm/2010/01/135519.htm.

8. A *Nature* magazine survey of Chinese scientists found that over 92 percent used Google as their primary search engine. *Nature*, 24 February 2010, http://www.nature.com/nature/newspdf/google_china_survey.pdf.

9. For an example of the official Chinese counterattack, see Jiao Xiang, "Google, Don't Become a Tool of Hegemony," *People's Daily Online*, 27 January 2010, translated by the China Media Project, http://cmp.hku.hk/2010/02/03/4453/.

10. He Qinglian, *Media Control in China* (Human Rights in China, 2003).

11. Bruce Bueno DeMesquita and George W. Downs, "Development and Democracy," *Foreign Affairs*, September–October 2005.

12. Since 2009, Twitter, Facebook, and YouTube have been blocked to Chinese Netizens. Blocking is used when the Chinese engineers have not yet invented a method for filtering the material, such as online videos.

13. Michael Suk-Young Chwe, *Rational Ritual: Culture, Coordination, and Common Knowledge* (Princeton: Princeton University Press, 2001), p. 7.

14. Thomas Schelling, *The Strategy of Conflict*, 2nd ed. (Cambridge, MA: Harvard University Press, 1980), p. 144.

15. "The Microphone Era," *Renmin Ribao Online*, 24 June 2009, Open Source Center, CPP20090625710023.

16. Evgeny Morozov, "The Digital Dictatorship," *Wall Street Journal*, 20–21 February 2010.

17. Ithiel de Sola Pool, "Communication in Totalitarian Societies," in *Handbook of Communication*, ed. Ithiel de Sola Pool et al. (Chicago: Rand McNally, 1973), p. 462.

18. Ibid., p. 488.

19. Benjamin L. Liebman, "Watchdog or Demagogue? The Media in China's Legal System," *Columbia Law Review*, 105, no. 1, 2005, p. 17.

20. A Beijing taxi driver, when discussing the communist regime in North Korea in 2006, said that the situation there was identical to Mao's China: "The people are ignorant. They only know what their leader tells them. If he says that some other country is bad, then they really hate that country. They have no other way of getting information."

21. Pool, "Communication in Totalitarian Societies."

22. William E. Griffith, "Communist Esoteric Communications: Explication de Texte," in *Handbook of Communication*, ed. Ithiel de Sola Pool et al. (Chicago: Rand McNally, 1971), pp. 512–520.

23. Pool, "Communication in Totalitarian Societies," p. 463.

24. Wang Guoying, "Annual Report of Newspapers in China 2005," *People's Daily Online*, 5 August 2005, http://www.media.people.com.cn/GB/40710/40715/3595542.html; and Yu Guoming, "Summary of China Media Industry Annual Report 2004–2005," 30 June 2005, http://www.china.org.cn/chinese/zhuanti/chuanmei/903486.htm.

25. Xinhua News Service, 1 July 2004.

26. An article in *Southern Weekend* on the territorial dispute with Japan over the Diaoyutai Islands by military scholar Cheng Yawen, is a good example of the more pragmatic approach to foreign policy typically adopted by publications in southern China. Cheng Yawen, "Return of Diaoyu Islands Is a Long Way to Go, China Should Be Patient, " *Southern Weekend* (*Nanfang Zhoumo*), 24 February 2005.

27. Sitting at lunch one day with journalists from *Xinmin Evening News*, Shanghai's leading evening tabloid, and *Wen Hui Bao*, a national CCP paper based on Shanghai, I saw why. The *Wen Hui Bao* journalists said they knew their paper was dying and they hoped that it could convert to a commercially viable paper. Unfortunately, they didn't have a clue as to how to successfully commercialize. The *Xinmin Evening News* reporters said that whenever an issue was sensitive (*mingang*), the papers would just publish the Xinhua version of the story. They were proud that their paper had been first in Shanghai to report the news of the inadvertent American bombing of the Chinese Embassy in Belgrade, Yugoslavia, in 1999. Their paper "played the issue much cooler than the northern [Beijing] press."

28. *Ta Kung Pao* (Hong Kong), Internet version, 10 July 2003.

29. "Interview: International Editor of the Year Hu Shuli," *World Press Review*, 50, no. 10 (October 2003).

30. China Daily.com, 2 March 2010, http://www.chinadaily.com.cn/china/2010–03/02/content_9522102.htm. On protests by journalists, also see Jonathan Hassid, "China's Contentious Journalists: Reconceptualizing the Media," *Problems of Post-Communism*, 55, no. 4 (July–August 2008), pp. 52–61.

31. Evan Osnos, "The Forbidden Zone," *The New Yorker*, 20 July 2009, p. 55.

32. Li Weiao and Rao Zhi, "Hubei Governor Li Hongzhong Grabs Female Reporter's Recorder," *Caijing*, 8 March 2010, http://www.caijing.com.cn/2010-03-08/110391938.html (article removed, now redirects to Caijing homepage). Text of the article can be found at Legal News Net, http://www.fzkx.net/NewsExpress/hot/201003/20100309115535.html; Taihu Pearl Net 太湖明珠网, http://news.thmz.com/col36/2010/03/2010-03-10717266.html; Tianya Forum http://www.tianya.cn/publicforum/content/free/1/1828455.shtml (accessed 23 May 2010).

33. Some Netizen activists have actually proposed the formation of a Netizens political party. See John Kennedy, "China: Netizen Party Announced," http://advocacy.globalvoicesonline.org/2008/02/09/china-netizen-party-announced/.

34. Yongnian Zheng and Guoguang Wu, "Information Technology, Public Space, and Collective Action in China," *Comparative Political Studies*, 38, no. 5 (June 2005), pp. 507–536, presents 2002–2004 survey data indicating that by far the highest priority use of Chinese Internet users is to read news.

35. Chinese bloggers are the best source of reporting on the practice, which was introduced in 2004 in Hunan Province and has spread widely since then. See China Digital Times, "Chinese Bloggers on the History and Influence of the 'Fifty Cent Party,'" http://chinadigitaltimes.net/2008/05/chinese-bloggers-on-the-history-and-influence-of-the-fifty-cent-party/.

36. Reported in *Ta Kung Pao* (Hong Kong), 1 August 2009, http://www.dwnews.com/gb/MainNews/Forums/BackStage/2009_7_31_16_2_33_171.html (accessed 19 August 2009).

37. Andrew J. Nathan and Perry Link, *The Tiananmen Papers* (New York: Public Affairs, 2001).

38. Liu Xiaobo, "The Tragedy of Hu Yaobang and Zhao Ziyang," Chinese Newsnet.com, March 2005, www.chinesenewsnet.com/MainNews/Opinion/2005_2_1_19_11_58_68.html.

39. I make this argument in my book *China: Fragile Superpower* (New York: Oxford University Press, 2007).

40. "Premier Zhu Rongji Meets the Press," 15 March 2001, http://www.gov.cn/english/official/2005-07/26/content_17166.htm (accessed 21 May 2010).

41. *Financial Times*, 18 July 2009.

42. The concepts of "police patrols" and "fire alarms" as methods by which principals monitor agents was first suggested by Mathew McCubbins and Thomas Schwartz, "Congressional Oversight Overlooked: Police Patrols versus Fire Alarms," *American Journal of Political Science*, 1984, pp. 165–179.

43. The Xinhua article, http://news.xinhuanet.com/lianzheng/2009-11/24/content_12533816.htm (accessed 8 December 2009), is no longer on the Xinhua site. The original *Liaowang* article on the black jails can be found at http://club.kdnet.net/newbbs/dispbbs.asp?boardid=76&id=3129734 (accessed 22 May 2010), and articles about it can be found on the other main news portals http://news.163.com/09/1126/00/5PoNIHHooo0120GR.html; http://news.sina.com.cn/c/sd/2009-11-25/035019119578.shtml; http://news.sohu.com/20091125/n268443257.shtml (accessed 22 May 2010).

44. National Public Radio, *On the Media*, 17 March 2006.

45. Propaganda officials from seventeen provinces and metropolitan areas sent a joint petition to the CCP Central Committee in September 2005 demanding the ending of cross-regional media supervision. As a result the CCP General Office issued a directive halting it. Zhao Yuezhi, *Communication in China: Political Economy, Power and Conflict* (Lanham, MD: Rowman and Littlefield, 2008), pp. 43–44; Jingrong Tong and Colin Sparks, "Investigative Journalism in China Today," *Journalism Studies*, 10, no. 3 (2009), p. 341.

46. Searches on 31 October 2009 for "Shanghai Bureau of Finance claims that budgets are state secrets so cannot be publicized," on Baidu turned up 5,200 separate results and on Google turned up 62,200 results.

47. *Zhongguo Qingnian*, 27 October 2009, http://news.xinhuanet.com/comments/2009-10/27/content_12335534.htm (accessed 31 October 2009).

48. *Yangcheng Wanbao*, 24 October 2009, http://www.ycwb.com/ePaper/ycwb/html/2009-10/24/content_631236.htm (accessed 31 October 2009).

49. Quoted by David Bandurski, China Media Project, http://cmp.hku.hk/2008/06/25/1079/. Bandurski has labeled this new, more active approach to the CCP's control of the media Control 2.0. For a full translation of Hu's speech, see CPP20080621701001 Beijing *Renmin Ribao Online*, in Chinese, 21 June 2008.

50. Open Source Center, CPP20090625710023 Beijing *Renmin Ribao Online*, in Chinese, 24 June 2009, p. 5.

51. Translated by chinaSMACK, 9 February 2010, http://www.chinasmack.com/bloggers/han-han-fifty-cent-party-must-work overtime/?utm_source=twitter&utm_medium=shortlink&utm_campaign=shortlinks.

52. Shirk, *China: Fragile Superpower*, pp. 102–103.

53. *Jiefangjun Ribao* [*People's Liberation Army Daily*], 10 March 2009, Open Source Center CPP20090311710007.

54. Personal communication from the late Frederick Wakeman.

55. During the Cultural Revolution (1966–1976), the struggle between Mao and other top leaders came out into the open in official newspaper and magazine commentaries, and unofficial Red Guard publications appeared.

56. "Shenzen Mayor Removed from Post for 'Serious Disciplinary Violations,'" *Xinhua Net*, 11 June 2009, http://news.xinhuanet.com/english/2009–06/11/content_11526098.htm (accessed 20 August 2009).

57. See Guo Yukuan, "Paying Respect to Deep Throat," http://www.zonaeuropa.com/20060323_1.htm (accessed August 21, 2009).

2

China's Emerging Public Sphere: The Impact of Media Commercialization, Professionalism, and the Internet in an Era of Transition

Qian Gang and David Bandurski

I N CHINA THERE IS an old saying about Lord Ye, who professes to love dragons but runs for dear life when finally confronted with one. The parable is a fair characterization of the deep ambivalence that China's leaders now feel toward the increasingly freewheeling commercial and Internet media. Since the 1990s China's leaders have encouraged the commercialization of the country's media: in 1998, China's media industry earnings totaled RMB 126 billion (USD 16 billion),[1] and by 2005, that figure had nearly tripled to RMB 320 billion (USD 40.5 billion).[2] China also has actively supported the development of Internet infrastructure to keep stride with its global competitors, spending USD 138 billion in the five years to 30 June 2005, and it had 384 million Internet users by 31 December 2009, including 346 million broadband users.[3]

But the implications of these changes have also, like Lord Ye's dragon, caused alarm and consternation among leaders who strongly believe that controlling the public agenda is critical to maintaining social stability and the Chinese Communist Party's (CCP's) hold on power. While actively encouraging the media to operate on market principles instead of relying on government subsidies, the CCP resists a redefinition of the role of media, which it still regards first and foremost as promoters of the party's agenda. Since the massacre of demonstrators at Tiananmen Square in 1989, "guidance of public opinion," the most common euphemism for agenda control, has been the centerpiece of propaganda work.[4] Nevertheless, media commercialization, developing norms of journalistic professionalism, and the growth of new media are combining to erode the CCP's monopoly over the public agenda and to open a limited public sphere.

The resulting tension between control and commercialization has altered the relationship between the CCP and the media, prompting the CCP to adopt new control tactics to uphold its influence on news and propaganda. Despite the fact that the CCP continues to punish editors who step over the line and the media remain formally a part of the party-state apparatus, China's leaders are beginning to treat the media and Internet as the voice of the public and to respond to it accordingly. In other words, the CCP seeks a power-maximizing balance between censorship and propaganda on the one hand and responsiveness on the other. Journalists in turn are developing their own tactics to gain audiences and challenge censors.

This chapter proceeds as follows: the first section discusses the nature and history of the commercialization of Chinese print media, in particular newspapers. The second section goes on to raise the question of an emerging credibility gap between party and commercial papers. Evidence suggests that consumers view commercial newspapers as more credible than their party competitors. Third, we address the development of a professional journalistic ethos and the struggle between the journalistic community and the state over how that ethos is defined. The fourth part addresses the expansion of the Internet and the growth of Web-based media and their effects on news coverage. In the fifth section, the prior sections are brought together to argue that commercialization, emerging professionalism, and the growth of Web-based media are all shifting agenda-setting power from the party-state apparatus to the media. Last, we conclude with an assessment of the transitioning relationship between the media and the party-state apparatus.

GO FORTH AND COMMERCIALIZE

The process of media commercialization that brought the CCP to its present amalgam of control and change began in the 1980s but was accelerated by the intensification of economic reforms in the mid-1990s. As trade and foreign investment grew, and as China sought to enter the World Trade Organization, the prospect of competition from foreign media loomed. But because the CCP still regarded the media as promoters of party ideology and social guidance, change came more gradually than in the economic sector. Nevertheless, during the 1980s a few foreign media groups did in fact strike up joint ventures—in areas that were deemed politically safe, such as computers and fashion. International Data Group led with *China Computerworld* magazine, set up in 1980 in coordination with a business arm of China's IT industry regulator, the Ministry of Information Industry. In 1988 the Chinese-language edition of the fashion magazine *Elle* followed suit.

A much bolder attempt by an overseas media investor to gain a foothold in the Chinese market came in August 1992, when Hong Kong businessman Yu Pinhai signed a joint venture deal with Guangzhou's *Xiandai Renbao.* While the contract yielded complete editorial control to the Chinese partner, Yu's company exercised its influence through Lie Fu, who managed the operations side. He introduced editorial methods and compensation systems in line with the global newspaper industry, put a system of totally computerized copy flow in place, and employed modern management techniques. The highly competitive *Xiandai Renbao* caused concern among Guangzhou's three top newspapers, *Nanfang Daily, Yangcheng Evening News,* and *Guangzhou Daily.*[5] Although an important first for overseas participation in the highly sensitive area of news, Yu Pinhai's newspaper venture was nevertheless doomed. Guangdong leaders shut down *Xiandai Renbao* on 1 January 1995.

Although early foreign competitors found themselves unable to gain footholds in China's media market, the threat of competition mobilized the media to move toward self-sufficiency. The big picture was about China's place in what the CCP still regards as a global information struggle. In the CCP's view, media strengthening—asset restructuring, changes in modes of operation, and the creation of engaging media products to foster domestic competition—is necessary for China to "face competition by international media groups and face the global struggle for public opinion."[6] Domestic competition continues to be regarded as an urgent matter of national strength.

The strategic global dimension of media strengthening became much more apparent in 2009, with news of massive government investment to enhance the global presence of core party media, and China's organization of the ostensibly nongovernmental World Media Summit, which was financed by the CCP and held in the Great Hall of the People.[7]

In the mid-1990s, fresh media offerings sprang up all over China. Newspapers such as *Southern Weekend*, a commercial spin-off of Guangdong Province's official *Nanfang Daily*, and a myriad of metro newspapers (commercially oriented daily tabloids or broadsheets) spiced up official news with consumer-relevant lifestyle, entertainment, and sports coverage. Investigative news programs like China Central Television's *Focus* came into being, offering a fresh approach to news and analysis. Naturally, political support was an indispensable component of their initial success and continued operation. *Southern Weekend* was able to weather several political storms with officials in Beijing because it had support from provincial leaders in Guangdong. The television program *Focus*, which routinely shed light on such social and political problems as administrative corruption, was supported by the country's top propaganda official, Ding Guangen, who actually had a role in its creation.

Commercialization meant a radical reconfiguration of the relationships between media and audiences, the tight grip of the propaganda apparatus notwithstanding. No longer were readers purely targets of CCP messages. The era of choice had arrived. Initially, the changes went forward in much the same way as they had at large state-owned enterprises— through experimental ventures. Generally, this meant party media or government offices used an existing publishing license to launch a commercial media spin-off.[8]

The new commercial newspapers drew massive audiences. By mid-decade, Wuhan's *Chutian Metropolis Daily* had a circulation of over 1 million or approximately 12 percent of the city's population.[9] In the late 1990s, as more commercial newspapers came onto the market, their growth contrasted sharply with circulation declines for official party newspapers. While reliable figures are somewhat problematic in China because independent circulation audits are rare, we can get a fairly clear picture of the shift to commercial papers by looking at official figures for average daily print runs at party and commercial newspapers (figure 2.1). In the ten years from 1993 to 2003, *Beijing Daily*, the official mouthpiece of municipal leaders in the capital, went from an average daily print run of 523,000

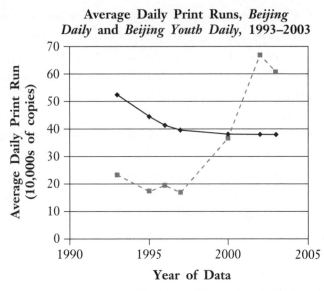

Average Daily Print Runs, *Beijing Daily* **and** *Beijing Youth Daily,* **1993–2003**

Year of Data

➤ *Beijing Daily*   ➤ *Beijing Youth Daily*

FIGURE 2.1.

copies to just 380,000 copies—a 27 percent drop. Over the same period, *Beijing Youth Daily*, a commercial newspaper published by the Beijing Communist Youth League, almost tripled its daily print run from 231,000 to 600,000.[10]

In southern China, Guangdong's official *Nanfang Daily* suffered a 14 percent drop in its average daily print run, from 876,000 copies per day in 1993 to 750,000 in 2003. However, the paper's commercial spin-off, *Southern Metropolis Daily*, which recorded a meager daily run of 41,000 in 1997, printed an astounding 1.4 million copies in 2003. The CCP's flagship newspaper, *People's Daily*, was no exception to the downward trend for party papers. In 1993, the newspaper had an estimated circulation of 2.78 million. Yet this figure had plummeted to 1.8 million only ten years later.[11]

Throughout the 1990s, the central government closed down or withdrew subsidies for local and regional publications to reduce the crowding out of central news media. Funding was maintained for key mouthpieces like *People's Daily* and the central Xinhua News Agency. Yet this tough love had the inadvertent effect of sending underfunded publications into the marketplace in search of their own commercial niches. This further stimulated media commercialization as the managers of many of these publications had to get creative to survive. The minor-league official newswire China News Service provides a good example: state funds to China News Service had been substantially reduced by the end of the 1990s, so in 1999 the news-wire capitalized on one of its licenses to launch *China Newsweekly*, a news-magazine that takes its cues from *Time* magazine and is now one of China's market leaders.[12]

But commercial ventures were not exclusive to media that had been cut loose from government subsidies. As media commercialization gripped the country, there was money to be made by everyone. Even *People's Daily*, the official organ of the CCP's Central Committee, jumped on the com-mercial bandwagon with the May 2001 launch of *Jinghua Times*, a metro newspaper sold at newsstands in Beijing. The newspaper, which offered thirty-two full-color pages at the time of launch and contained the usual range of consumer fare, expanded to forty-eight pages just nine months later.[13] *Jinghua Times* made China's annual top twenty list of most influen-tial commercial newspapers—based on such factors as circulation, adver-tising strength, and reader involvement—for the first time in 2006, and climbed to the number seventeen spot in 2007.[14] Once official publications have to compete for audiences, the style and substance of even these pub-lications change.

Despite the commercial evolution of China's media, however, the market remains highly regulated through the media licensing system. The CCP limits the number of licenses granted and the terms of the license may restrict the content of publications. For example, the weekly market-oriented magazine *Lifeweek* is barred from coverage of current affairs stories.[15] Asset allocation and investment, particularly foreign investment, are also rigorously controlled. Nevertheless, it is undeniable that the media now constitute an industry. The objective of propaganda officials is to bolster this industry under a regime of tight control.[16]

By the time President Hu Jintao came to power in 2002, the media com-mercialization process was already in high gear. The president's own media policy was, as expected, a marriage of commercialization and control. The policy, called the Three Closenesses (to reality, to people, and to life), urged journalists to make their reporting more relevant by moving away from dull regurgitations of official news releases.[17] The Three Closenesses was about creating more savvy, lively, and believable media products. The policy reit-erated the imperative of party control, or "guidance," but also underscored what had already become obvious—the media now had two masters, the party and the public.

THE CREDIBILITY GAP BETWEEN PARTY AND COMMERCIAL NEWS

One criticism of media commercialization in China has been that it leads to bottom-line thinking and sensationalism.[18] Numerous examples have been cited in support of this argument. In 2005, for example, editors at a leading commercial newspaper in China's western Sichuan Province were found to have convinced a young woman to donate her liver so they could publish a heart-wrenching front-page news story.[19] Commercial media need stories that sell. This imperative, combined with CCP news control, effectively encourages sensational yet politically innocuous content.

Yet commercialization has undoubtedly expanded content diversity. The variety of media offerings in China has mushroomed over the last decade, a fact patently obvious to anyone browsing newsstands, where a deluge of magazines, dailies, and tabloids beckons to passersby. Looking critically at major news stories and how they play out at the newsstand, one can also begin to recognize the interesting and important ways commercialization has begun to push the envelope and expand space for expression.

The most critical factor shaping the expanded content of news and media is the consumer, the person at the newsstand voting with his or her pocketbook. According to a study of newspaper readers in Beijing in 2004, nearly all respondents who said they read one newspaper (44 percent of the total) preferred commercial newspapers. Only those who habitually read two to three publications picked up party newspapers.[20] In a media environment increasingly driven by consumer choice, the news gap between party and commercial media is opening a corresponding divide in public trust and credibility, which has direct implications for the CCP's ability to guide and shape public opinion.

The source of the credibility gap is revealed by the way different types of outlets treat the same news story in China. When Beijing Vice-Mayor Liu Zhihua was stripped of his party rank in June 2006 on suspicion of corruption, propaganda officials issued a ban on independent reporting by Chinese newspapers. In other words, reporters were not to interview people related to the case, or other officials or experts. They were provided only limited information by Xinhua News Agency in the form of an official release, or *tonggao*. Officials regarded this as a highly sensitive corruption case since Liu Zhihua had been responsible for construction projects for the 2008 Beijing Olympic Games. If the scandal had bored deeper into the

CCP's ranks, it could have become a major international news story and stigmatized the games themselves. At the same time, Beijing's municipal leaders hoped to control damage so that the Liu Zhihua case did not implicate them. But on the other hand, this was a great story from a commercial and professional standpoint. How did party and commercial media handle it, and how did coverage differ from region to region?

On June 12, mention of the Liu Zhihua case did in fact appear in *People's Daily*, but the story was consigned to a tiny space on page 4, just above the weather report. The report made use of the official Xinhua release with a headline—"Standing Committee of Beijing Party Congress Opens 28th Conference"—that de-emphasized the real news that a top-level official had been removed for corruption at that meeting. Figure 2.2 shows page 4 of the June 12, 2006, edition of *People's Daily*.

As a central party newspaper, the managers of *People's Daily* did not necessarily seek to protect municipal officials in Beijing. Battles against local corruption are, after all, a regular feature of China's internal politics. But central officials certainly did not wish to taint the CCP as a whole or preparations for the 2008 Beijing Olympics by calling too much attention to the story.[21]

Turning to *Beijing Daily*, the official mouthpiece of Beijing's top leadership, we find that while coverage of the Liu Zhihua story was downplayed, it made the paper's front page. The item, again the content of the Xinhua release, was squeezed in at the bottom of the page. The lead stories, about attracting tourism to Beijing and new labor policies, emphasized the positive leadership of Beijing officials. In fact, the story directly above the Liu Zhihua item is a declaration of the need to fight corruption in the CCP's ranks. The point is to draw the public's attention away from the story and its implications for Beijing's leadership while maintaining some credibility by reporting the bare facts on the front page.[22] Unfortunately, *Beijing Daily* refused in May 2010 to provide or authorize the use of a high-resolution image of its 12 June 2006 front page, a reminder of the lingering sensitivity of a story of this nature in China's media environment.

Moving from party newspapers to commercial ones, the differences become conspicuous. *Jinghua Times*, as previously mentioned, a commercial spin-off of China's official *People's Daily*, had an interest in using the Liu Zhihua story to attract readers. With the ban on original reportage in force, *Jinghua Times* was forced to work with the same Xinhua material. The paper nonetheless differentiated itself by announcing the real news with a prominent headline at the top of page 1. The headline did not attempt

FIGURE 2.2. *People's Daily*, 12 June 2006. Liu Zhihua corruption story at bottom left, above weather map.

to obfuscate: "Beijing Vice-Mayor Liu Zhihua Removed from Office." A page jump referred readers to the inside of the newspaper, where they could discover the same story available to *People's Daily* readers.[23] If nothing more, the article's front-page placement sent a very different message about the relative significance of Liu Zhihua's removal from office.

The most startling differences in treatment appeared in commercial newspapers outside the nation's capital. Shanghai's *Oriental Morning Post*, a commercial spin-off of the official *Wen Hui Bao*, also placed the headline across the front page, directly beneath the banner.

However, in the *Oriental Morning Post*, readers were given more than just the Xinhua release.[24] Although the reporter did not directly violate the prohibition on reportage, the article includes more information on the case from an official government Web site: "According to the information made available to the public on the Beijing municipal government Website, 'Window on the Capital,' Liu Zhihua's 'job responsibilities' included: 'Assisting and presiding over [city] planning work, presiding over construction work, management of land and real-estate, sports [training, construction of sports facilities, etc.], building of light-rail and transportation.'"

The front-page article went on to mention the various municipal committees on which Liu Zhihua had served. All of this information could be used with relative safety because it had been publicly released on a government Web site. The information pointed unequivocally to Liu's central role in the Beijing government and suggested his relationship to key infrastructure projects and sports activities. While readers were left to put two and two together, the implications were clear. The story also highlighted the key role the Internet can play in helping reporters and editors act as professional journalists by expanding news stories. Variance in coverage of the Liu Zhihua case suggests that even in politically controversial cases where the CCP has a strong interest in monopolizing the message, media are finding ways to attract readers by adding their own voices. Nevertheless, stories like that of Liu Zhihua remain politically delicate. In May 2010, nearly four years after the original Liu Zhihua story, the *Oriental Morning Post* refused to provide or authorize the use of a high-resolution image of its 12 June front page, citing the sensitive nature of the story.

This gap in coverage between party and commercial publications has clear implications for media credibility and the CCP's exclusive power

FIGURE 2.3. *Jinghua Times*, 12 June 2006. Liu Zhihua corruption story in large bold headline text at the top of the page.

to set the public agenda. Readers are picking up commercial papers because they offer better entertainment and sports coverage. But it is also true that commercial papers have achieved a higher degree of credibility than their party counterparts, and this, in turn, has meant that public opinion is increasingly being shaped by commercial rather than party media.

This trend is particularly visible in the coverage of crisis events.[25] When a deadly gas explosion occurred in a coal mine in Henan Province in October 2004, the news was covered by both party and commercial newspapers. On October 22, the day after the explosion occurred, sixty or more miners were confirmed dead and more than eighty missing. China's top leaders, Hu Jintao and Wen Jiabao, issued a statement urging authorities to do their utmost to rescue miners trapped beneath the surface. Rescue crews were on the scene, as were survivors and family members of the dead and missing. On this occasion, reporting from the scene was permitted, and both party and commercial papers dealt with the same basic facts.

For the *People's Daily*, Hu Jintao and Wen Jiabao were the story. A headline on the newspaper's front page read: "Order from Hu Jintao, Wen Jiabao and Other Central Leaders: Spare No Effort in Rescuing Personnel Inside Mine in Gas Explosion at Henan Province's Zhengzhou Coal Electric [Group's] Daping Mine." The first line of the article mentioned that personnel had been "severely injured" in the "accident," but only in the last sentence was there mention of the number of dead and injured. All other details in the report dealt with the positive actions of top national and provincial leaders. The report on Daping also had to fight for space against a bigger news item about a meeting of the Politburo and its decision to hold "advanced education programs" for cadres.[26]

Virtually the same story made the front page of *Henan Daily*, the provincial party mouthpiece. The only difference was the addition of a photograph of a provincial party official on an inspection tour of Daping. The headline read "Hu Jintao, Wen Jiabao Place Great Importance on Accident at Daping Mine."[27] No number of dead or missing was given in the story, though these figures were supplied in another article below the first one. But the emphasis was again on the response by party officials, this time by Henan's top leadership.[28]

The official party newspapers obscured the human elements of the Daping story. Their portrayal of the tragedy read like a stage play starring only official actors. But readers who turned to *Beijing Youth Daily*, a newspaper

FIGURE 2.4. *People's Daily*, 22 October 2004. Daping Mine story at top right of page.

FIGURE 2.5. *Henan Daily*, 22 October 2004.

published by the Beijing chapter of the Communist Youth League and further toward the commercial end of the spectrum, found a very different account. This time the news about the Politburo meeting was crowded out, placed vertically along the left margin of the front page. A large photo directly in the center of the page showed rescue workers on the scene walking in single file, their faces blackened with soot. The headline was prominent: "Major Gas Explosion Occurs at Daping Mine."[29] Smaller subheads below announced the statement from Hu Jintao and Wen Jiabao and gave the most current numbers for dead and wounded, the same given in *Henan Daily*. The official news was still present, but the focus of the story pointed more directly to the human dimension of the explosion and its aftermath. It also avoided the word "accident" in the headline, which deflected responsibility from officials.

The most striking differences in coverage were revealed by newspapers such as *Southern Metropolis Daily* and the *Beijing News*, which are both leading tabloids and further along the commercial spectrum than *Beijing Youth*

FIGURE 2.6. *Beijing Youth Daily*, 22 October 2004.

Daily. On 22 October 2004, the front page of *Southern Metropolis Daily* was dominated by a large photograph of two rescue workers in Daping removing a victim in a body bag. The picture conveys the tragedy of Daping and shows readers a more personal aspect of rescue work. The headline, in a white font against a black background, is unmistakable: "Major Mine Disaster in Henan: 62 Dead 86 Missing."[30] The use of "disaster" rather than "accident," while it may seem a trifle to those in freer media environments, is a purposeful choice, guiding readers away from the focus on government action and leaving open the possibility of government responsibility for the losses. Furthermore, the Daping story did not have to share space with a story about the CCP's "advanced education program" for cadres.

Southern Metropolis Daily also provided a whole series of supplementary news reports, including vivid accounts from survivors at an on-site dormitory.

> "So many years and I've never come across anything as tragic as this," says 43-year-old Zhang Juyou. Hunan Province native Gao Wusong, who works in the same crew as Zhang Juyou, says he was even luckier because he felt uncomfortable that day and only worked until 9 before getting off. "I'd just eaten a little something in the dormitory when I heard a huge boom that shook the building."[31]

At the *Beijing News*, a commercial daily in the nation's capital, the focus was similarly on the relatives of disaster victims. The front-page headline read: "62 Die in Major Henan Mining Disaster." The photograph dominating the page was a close-up of a wallet-sized picture of a disaster victim resting in the palm of a relative's hand.

In provinces outside Henan, the differences in coverage between party and commercial newspapers were similarly conspicuous. Much like *People's Daily*, the official *Sichuan Daily* emphasized the actions of party leaders and referred to the disaster at Daping as an "accident."[32] In contrast, *Chengdu Commercial Daily*, a tabloid in the capital of Sichuan Province, localized its coverage, making it relevant to readers in Sichuan: "Some miners told our reporter there were Sichuanese among the dead and that their families had already been notified by the mine. Owing to the long journey, the relatives had not yet arrived. As to specifically how many Sichuanese miners there were, they could not say clearly, and the mine does not yet have specific numbers."[33]

The disparities between party and commercial coverage in such situations is evident to Chinese readers. After Typhoon Saomai slammed into

FIGURE 2.7. *Southern Metropolis Daily*, 22 October 2004.

the coast of Fujian Province on 10 August 2006, media outside the province reported higher numbers of dead and injured than did local party media. A war of words soon ensued between Fujian's top leader, Party Secretary Lu Zhangong, and outside media. "Some media, including reporters from outside the Province, wrote many false reports based on hearsay, and the news was stirred up on the web," Lu was quoted as saying in the official *Fujian Daily* on 19 August. "I worry," he continued, "about whether the cadres of Ningde [an area heavily affected by the storm] will make it through faced with social pressures like this, whether they can continue without interference and do what we need to do in serving the people." Lu's remarks were criticized by commercial media and even by reporters for China's official Xinhua News Agency.[34] A reader's letter printed in *Southern Metropolis Daily* on 22 August remarked that looking "only at one kind of report from major local media in Zhejiang and Fujian, you would certainly think that those now suffering most [from Saomai] are the cadres."[35]

The bottom line is that party media are becoming increasingly irrelevant to the average Chinese reader, with direct implications for the CCP's ability to "guide" opinion. In the 2006 *Report on Development of China's Media Industry*, Tsinghua University Professor Li Xiguang argued that the failure to reform "mainstream" newspapers in China, by which he meant party newspapers, would mean "a serious disjoint between the party and government agenda and the public agenda."

Since 2007, the CCP leadership has driven a shift in news and propaganda policy that may be seen as a response to these new challenges facing the official agenda-setting process in China. In January 2007, as the government publicised a new Internet-cleansing campaign under the auspices of a drive against indecent content, President Hu Jintao said during a session of the Politburo that the party should pursue not just a policy of "managing" the Internet but also a way of seeking to actively "use" it. As though to illustrate the policy itself, the official news release carrying President Hu's statement was pinned to the top of the news sections at all major privately owned Internet portals—several of them listed on the U.S. Nasdaq exchange—for nearly a full week.[36]

This more active approach to news and propaganda policy was launched more formally in June 2008, when President Hu Jintao paid a visit to the official *People's Daily* newspaper and to *People's Daily Online* and delivered the first major media-related speech of his tenure as leader. Hu talked about the need for state media in China to "actively set the agenda" for major breaking stories, and he talked about Internet media and the new generation of commercial metro newspapers as propaganda "resources" that needed to be better utilized by the party.[37] This policy change, though in development for several years, was in many ways a response to the international image crisis China suffered as a result of unrest in Tibet in March 2008, which was a watershed moment for the CCP on the rethinking of news and propaganda. In the CCP's post-game analysis, Tibet was regarded as a failure of media policy. By resorting to traditional censorship tactics, shutting off access to the region, and dragging its feet in releasing an official version of facts and events, the CCP created an information vacuum that international media nevertheless occupied aggressively. The agenda, therefore, had been yielded to others.[38]

The shift in the CCP's approach to agenda setting can also be glimpsed in the rapid rise of a new media buzzword, "public opinion channeling," which has augmented and seemingly overtaken the Jiang Zemin–era term "guidance of public opinion." Essentially, Hu Jintao has moved away from a sheer emphasis on classic controls—banning content, shutting down media, shutting up reports—to a combination approach that involves pushing the CCP's message out more actively through commercial media and Internet as well as official media. This shift, which journalists in China have referred to as "grabbing the megaphone," or *qiang la ba*, can be seen as a direct response on the part of the leadership to changes in the nature of agenda setting, both domestically and internationally, as a result of media commercialization and the rapid development of new communications technologies. At the China Media Project, we have coined the term Control 2.0 to refer to a whole range of more active news and propaganda policies that have been pushed under Hu Jintao's leadership.[39]

Despite attempts to close the gap, the "disjoint between the party and government agenda and the public agenda" Tsinghua University Professor Li Xiguang spoke about still exists.[40] The CCP's censorship mechanisms allow officials to shut out or contain certain news events, and "channeling" enables them to disseminate through commercial media and the Internet what the CCP likes to call "authoritative" information and agendas. But there are limits to what these mechanisms can accomplish in China's increasingly diverse and market-oriented media environment, and journalists continually seek to push open new spaces, both professionally and commercially.

PROFESSIONALISM IN THE ERA OF TRANSITION

In Chinese academic circles and the media industry, the concept of professionalism, or *zhuanye zhuyi*, has taken on greater importance in recent
years.[41] While there is often little agreement about what professionalism
entails, a number of trends point to the emergence of a professional journalism community. A sense of social mission among Chinese journalists has
emerged as party news ideology has faded. As early as the Tiananmen
crisis, journalists joined the protests and reported on them freely for several
days in May before the crackdown. Media consumers are also a factor, with
newer concepts like "serving the consumer" tied closely to the journalist's
sense of purpose.[42]

CCP leaders have moved to co-opt the notion of journalistic professionalism since it came into use in the 1990s, redefining it as responsibility to the
party and society.[43] The creation of a national Journalist Day (8 November)
in 2000 was meant to recognize journalism as a profession of relevance to
society—following holidays for the nursing and teaching professions.[44] But
when China's propaganda chief and other officials honored journalists with
speeches on the inaugural Journalist Day, the theme was respect for the
CCP's news workers.[45] The theme did not resonate with journalists. *Southern
Weekend* wrote in a special issue that the social function of the media was to
"show care for the weak, to give strength to the powerless," and that journalists should express their "social conscience" by revealing the truth to the
people.[46]

The roots of this sense of journalistic mission in fact go back beyond the
present era to what Zhang Yuren has called the origins of "liberal press
theory" in China.[47] Zhang traces Western journalistic ideologies in China
back to the late Qing Dynasty and independent newspapers like Wang
Tuo's *Universal Circulating Herald*, launched in Hong Kong in 1874.[48] The
CCP's press system, while in part incorporating the "enlightenment tradition," transformed the relationship between the state and the press, co-
opting independent intellectual elements in journalism.[49] Tracing lineages
in this enlightenment tradition is a fuzzy process, but generally included
are such Mao-era press figures as Deng Tuo, the first editor in chief of *People's Daily*, and Liu Binyan, China's most celebrated reporter.[50]

This tradition, voiced in *Southern Weekend*'s Journalist Day dissent of
November 2000, was also at work in one of China's biggest press freedom
stories of 2006, the CCP's shutdown of the *Freezing Point* supplement to

China Youth Daily, the official publication of the China Youth League. *China Youth Daily* had become a lively and highly profitable commercial newspaper with national circulation, and *Freezing Point* was home to some of China's most outspoken journalism for roughly a decade. It was shut down in January 2006 after receiving repeated criticisms from propaganda officials.[51] The shutdown was followed by a wave of criticism not only from international media but from the journalism and academic communities within China. On 2 February, thirteen officials, including former bosses for some of China's most influential media, circulated an open letter speaking out against the shutdown of *Freezing Point*.[52] The letter was directed at the country's top leaders but also circulated on an overseas Web site. It called for more freedom of speech and advised leaders to "demolish every method of news censorship."[53] The signers of the open letter personified China's enlightenment tradition as well as the political reform tradition of the 1980s, during which time such officials as former premier and CCP General Secretary Zhao Ziyang and former CCP General Secretary Hu Yaobang had been strong proponents of press freedom.

In mid-February, it was announced that *Freezing Point* would be allowed to relaunch without its editors, Li Datong and Lu Yuegang. Li Datong has stated many times since that an outcry from the journalist community, academics, and more liberal officials prompted China's top leaders to step in and interdict the order from the Propaganda Department. The response from the journalist community in China, Li said, underscored deep-seated resentments about China's propaganda regime and a growing resistance to the docile role defined for journalists by the CCP.[54]

The *Freezing Point* episode is, on the one hand, a case of CCP leaders employing strong-arm tactics to control the media and the maneuverings of the Propaganda Department and leftist elements within.[55] On the other hand, it underlines the limitations of such tactics in China's era of transition. Criticism of the government's action presents leaders with a dilemma. As Minxin Pei observed, Hu Jintao might have chosen to take action against those coming to *Freezing Point*'s defense, but would have risked looking "politically clumsy." Leniency, by contrast, might have further emboldened media that were already chomping at the bit.[56] The end result was a calculated compromise.

The *Freezing Point* case is only one, albeit dramatic, example of how journalists in China are resisting the actions of the propaganda regime and the CCP's monopolization of the truth. Similar actions are happening regularly, on a smaller scale, throughout the media. One Chinese editor says the relationship between the propaganda regime and the media "looks increasingly like a game of cat and mouse."[57] Given China's political climate, she says, it is naive for journalists to suppose they can slip through the bonds of state control, reporting hard news simply by improving the level of their professional techniques. Still, journalists are finding ways to take stories in their own directions and push the bounds of censorship.

Commercialization and new media alone cannot provide the impetus for working around the limitations imposed by China's media control regime, or for promoting concepts like the public's right to know. However, in the hands of professionals with a bold vision of what role the media should play in China, they are potentially powerful tools for changing the nature of agenda setting in China. This trend becomes even clearer when we look at recent changes brought on by the growth of the Internet in the country, which brings the reader—or rather media consumer—more directly into the picture.

A READ/WRITE CULTURE EMERGES IN CHINA

A substantial body of research and speculation in recent years has explored the impact of new media on the profession of journalism globally. Much of this discussion has centered on the role of technology and the Internet as democratizing forces, giving everyone with a computer (or mobile phone or device) access an opportunity to participate directly in public affairs.[58] Journalist and new media expert Dan Gillmor says that while traditional media have, for the last century and a half, been either "one-to-many" (books, newspapers, radio, and TV) or "one-to-one" (letters, telegraph, and telephone), the Internet is transforming how we communicate.[59] Gillmor writes: "The Internet, for the first time, gives us many-to-many and few-to-few communications. This has vast implications for the former audience and for the producers of news because the differences between the two are becoming harder to distinguish."[60]

China's paradox of control in change is apparent in the development of Internet-based new media. China has plowed substantial investment into the development of its Internet infrastructure, and consequently the country's online population has boomed. By the end of 2008, 35.2 percent of the online public said they had their own Weblogs or personal Web sites that they regularly update, a level of response indicating that users are doing more than just reading.[61] At the same time, China's government has made ambitious attempts to manage the Web, even building controls into the Web infrastructure itself, what has been called China's "Great Firewall."[62]

The apparent contradiction between the promise of the Chinese Internet and persisting controls has sometimes thrown observers for a loop. Alarming accounts of tightening censorship are joined by seemingly incommensurate stories about how the Internet is changing the country or eroding CCP control. In "Death by a Thousand Blogs," *New York Times* columnist Nicholas Kristof argued that Chinese leaders are "digging the Communist Party's grave, by giving the Chinese people broadband."[63]

While simplistic assumptions about the revolutionary or destabilizing role of the Internet do not hold, there is little question that the Web is a force of change in China. Hu Yong, a mainland Chinese expert on new media and author of *The Internet Is King*, argues that though the Internet has had an impact on expression in China, these changes cannot be understood purely through the prism of Western democratic desires:

> I do not deny that the Chinese government places strict controls on the Internet. . . . Nevertheless, Internet control in China and the flow of information present a picture far more nuanced than that criticized by Western media. Internet activists outside China see the Internet as equal to democracy. When China's Internet is unable to realize the democratic results they envision, these activists feel angry and cannot understand. All they can see are the negative factors of the Chinese Internet, and it becomes easy to overlook the ways in which the Internet has significantly expanded space for free expression.[64]

In the above passage, Hu Yong is critical of both Internet idealists and pessimists for failing to recognize the complexities of China's media environment. The media in China no longer compose a "monolithic bloc," he says. Chinese society has stratified and diversified. Moreover, commercialization has moved to accommodate the demands of increasingly heterogeneous media consumers. The Internet allows these consumers to become producers of content and participate directly in a new kind of public discourse through tools like Weblogs, bulletin boards, and online forums—what Gillmor refers to as the "read/write promise of the Web."[65] Hu Yong's glass-half-full argument is that participatory forms of new media are a "testing ground for public opinion" and a "sign of the development of a civil society in China. . . . More groups and individuals can participate in the process of handling social affairs, and ultimately policy decisions will be more fair."

The implications of the Internet for the continued exercise of control and agenda setting have not gone unnoticed by Chinese leaders. A 2005 study in the official *News Line* urged that "actively pursuing the patterns of Internet dissemination, finding efficient means of guiding online commentary, and promoting the emergence and broad dissemination of correct online opinion are necessary for Internet media to seize the high ground in the manufacturing of opinion."[66] The document shows China's propaganda regime trying to come to terms with the new challenges posed by a read/write culture. In January 2006, *Guangming Daily*, a party newspaper published by the Central Propaganda Department, published a short analysis concluding that Internet media were impacting agendas on major news issues: "Internet media can not only amplify the play and influence of major news but can weaken the influence of party media in setting the agenda."[67]

At the root of these changes is the decentralization of communications, which allows Internet users to "choose their own agendas."[68] As with media commercialization generally, readers, as consumers of news products, decide what news to read and which links to follow. They respond to news, post their own comments, and answer the comments of others via either the news sites themselves, bulletin board sites, or personal Weblogs. Participation of this kind generates an unprecedented degree of interaction not only among Internet users but also between the Internet and traditional media. As one scholar, writing in a provincial-level party journal, put it: "The Internet is open to anyone . . . and every Internet user can freely choose. They can also express themselves, issuing corrections or dissensions. The trend of agenda-setting toward the personal and the individual is clear. The receiver's role in the process of agenda-setting is now greater than it has ever been."[69]

News now routinely bubbles up through the Web and makes its way into print and broadcast media, a process *Beijing Youth Daily* has referred to as "comment posting culture."[70] In some cases, stories generated from Internet postings reemerge on major Web portals in China, where they generate more discussion and commentary. In other cases, stories in the print media, including local newspapers, reach broader national audiences via Web portals and chat rooms, where they prompt both further postings and further reporting from traditional media, and so on.

For example, on 19 August 2006, a student from one of China's elite educational institutions, Tsinghua University, posted on the school's bulletin board site digital snapshots he had taken of parents of incoming freshmen sleeping on the school's athletic field and in doorways because they had been unable to find, or could not afford, local hotel rooms. Two days later the story appeared in one of the city's leading commercial newspapers, the *Beijing News*.[71] It then became the focal point of fierce discussion on a number of issues, from whether the school or the parents were responsible for paying for accommodations, to whether education fee reforms were needed nationwide. Between 21 August and 13 September close to sixty news reports and editorials on the topic appeared in scores of media nationwide.

COMMERCIALIZATION, PROFESSIONALISM, AND THE INTERNET SET THE AGENDA

One of the earliest and best examples of the Internet, media commercialization, and professionalism interacting to set the agenda for public discourse is the government's response to the outpouring of public rage in 2003 that followed the news of the beating death in a police detention and repatriation center of Sun Zhigang, a young college graduate who had moved to Guangdong to find work.

The detention and repatriation system under which Sun Zhigang was detained had been in force since May 1982. Its purpose was to assist cities in managing the migration of peasants from the countryside. The fear was that uncontrolled migration would impact public safety in the cities and strain their resources. The detention and repatriation system required all migrants to register and purchase temporary residency cards. Police could ask to see identification and essentially detain migrants who were not carrying or had not yet obtained their temporary residency cards. These migrants were packed off to local repatriation centers where they were either bailed out by family members or shipped back to their native towns or provinces.

Beginning with a 25 April 2003 report in *Southern Metropolis Daily*, Sun Zhigang's story became national news.[72] The original news story by reporter Chen Feng was posted the same day on major Web portals, taking the story into homes and offices across the country. While the story originated in the print media, the Internet was crucial to disseminating these reports and prompting further discussion.

Sun Zhigang had been in Guangzhou just twenty days, according to Chen's report. Having previously worked as a professional designer in Shenzhen, he had been hired by a clothing company in Guangzhou. Chen Feng's report explored the reasons behind Sun's detention and death, raising doubts about police files on the case: "How is it that in the documents signed by Sun Zhigang [while he was in police detention] he was listed as 'having no means of support'? This is a question not yet answered, and Director Xie of the Civil Affairs Bureau is also puzzled by this: 'As a university student, he would have had a high intelligence quotient, so why would he say he had no job?'"[73]

In the days that followed the *Southern Metropolis Daily* report and its enthusiastic reception on the Web, commercial newspapers across China reran the story, including *China Youth Daily*, *China Economic Times*, *Southern Weekend*, *Yangcheng Evening News*, *Huashang Daily*, and *Chutian Metropolis Daily*.[74] Party newspapers initially avoided the story altogether. In the days immediately following Chen Feng's report, the focus remained on the Sun Zhigang case itself. People wanted to know who was responsible for Sun Zhigang's death and how justice could be attained. In subsequent weeks, though, the debate turned to institutional ramifications, namely how to ensure that the situation did not reoccur.

As the local news story of Sun Zhigang's death expanded into a national debate on overarching questions of social policy in China, the media featured the views of independent experts. On 15 May 2003, *Southern Weekend* ran an editorial by Deng Zibin, a legal scholar with the Chinese Academy of Social Sciences, called, "We Must Not Have a Second Sun Zhigang."[75] Relating the Sun Zhigang case to the months-long cover-up of the outbreak of severe acute respiratory syndrome (SARS), Deng Zinbin said: "The spread of diseases of the natural world terrifies us. But the injuries done by social diseases not only terrify us but also anger us. The latter, because it happens through choice, is the most odious of injuries."

Much like the disaster reports from commercial media, Deng Zibin's editorial emphasized the value of individual human beings:

"Thoroughly investigating [the case] and dealing severely with the killers" . . . represents the feelings of the vast majority of people. But a further wish of the people, we can guess, is making sure cases like Sun Zhigang's do not happen again. This comes down to the fundamental rights and interests of the people, and these rights and benefits are in "taking the value of people as the base and freedom as the core and transferring this into political principles and structural principles."

The public furor moved from appeals for justice for Sun Zhigang's killers to demands for institutional change so that the lives of other Chinese would be valued and protected.

Like the SARS epidemic, the Sun Zhigang case highlighted the growing role of both commercialization and professionalism in the Chinese media. Chen Yizhong, the editor at *Southern Metropolis Daily*, kept abreast of the story as it developed and told his reporters to finish before propaganda officials could catch wind of it, and to check their facts scrupulously.[76] Other commercial media followed up on the story, adding viewpoints from a broad cross-section of experts and academics.

Nevertheless, it was the Internet that allowed the real-time interaction between media, experts, and ordinary members of society. The *Southern Metropolis Daily* was not the first domestic media outlet to raise questions about China's detention and repatriation system. A September 2000 article in *Legal Daily* had pointed out numerous problems in the detention process and said the system had already "lost its legal foundation."[77] Another *Southern Metropolis Daily* report in October 2001 had told the story of a young woman taken into detention and later released to a stranger who extorted money from her relatives.[78] These stories had not brought the country any closer to reforming the system because they had reached only limited audiences. The number of Internet users had tripled in the two years between the two *Southern Weekend* stories. Thus, when news reports on the Sun Zhigang case were replayed on major Web portals in China, they reached a wider audience than the commercial newspapers with metropolitan circulations. The *Southern Weekend* editorial even appeared on sites such as people.com.cn, which is run by the central mouthpiece *People's Daily.*[79]

Right on the heels of Deng Zibin's editorial, news came that three bold law students from Peking University had appealed directly to China's National People's Congress (NPC), its national legislature, for repeal of the country's law on detention and repatriation. On 14 May, the students, Xu

Zhiyong, Yu Jiang, and Teng Biao, delivered their formal opinion on the law to the NPC.[80] Xu Zhiyong had learned about the Sun Zhigang case through Peking University's bulletin board site.

Communicating through the Internet and by phone, Xu Zhiyong, Yu Jiang, and Teng Biao strategized about how to bring the focus of public opinion around to the question of reforming the detention system. They first explored a possible civil case on the behalf of Chinese who had been detained, but later settled on the idea, raised by Yu Jiang, that as citizens under China's constitution they were entitled to submit a formal opinion to the NPC.[81] Yu Jiang worked out a draft of the opinion and e-mailed it to Teng Biao, who sent his version to Xu Zhiyong. Xu made his own changes and emailed these back to Teng Biao, who faxed it to a legal working committee within the NPC.

News of the action by the three law students spread quickly through domestic newspapers and Web sites after an initial report in *China Youth Daily* on 16 May.[82] The next step came as five legal experts, including He Weifang of Peking University, supported the efforts of the law students.[83] They advised the Standing Committee of the NPC to launch an investigation into the law's constitutionality.[84] Through June 2003, the tide of media coverage continued, with Sun Zhigang and the detention system becoming the focus of widespread debate in all corners of Chinese society. On 19 June, *Southern Weekend* ran another editorial, "Realizing Justice Even If the Sky Falls." The author, a professor at China University of Political Science and Law, wrote, "I believe that no matter what inconvenience the repeal of this system causes, the constitution must be upheld. The atmosphere of freedom cannot be polluted by the detention system!"[85]

The next day, the professor's wish came true. Chinese Premier Wen Jiabao signed State Council Order 381, abolishing the detention and repatriation system. As the State Council moved to repeal the detention system, propaganda officials were meeting behind closed doors to silence media they felt had been overly bold in reporting on the Sun Zhigang case and the SARS epidemic that spring.[86] Even as the media celebrated their crucial role in an important policy achievement, more than ten publications were censured, including *Caijing* magazine, *Lifeweekly*, an outspoken general affairs magazine, and *China Economic Times*, a newspaper published by the State Council's Development Research Center.[87] Problems with the authorities would harry *Southern Metropolis Daily* throughout the coming year, culminating in the arrest of its editor, Chen Yizhong, and two colleagues in March 2004.[88]

Nevertheless, the Sun Zhigang case dramatically demonstrates how the Internet can combine with commercialized media to drive the CCP's agenda and spark a rapid response from national leaders.

The power of the new media and China's emerging read/write culture was again showcased in 2007, when residents of the southern city of Xiamen opposed the building of a new chemical plant in the dense urban area. This time, technology provided more than just a broader platform for dissemination and discussion of professional news stories—it offered a means of circumventing control efforts once propaganda authorities decided to censor the story.

In February 2004, the municipal government of Xiamen approved the so-called Xiamen PX project, a large-scale chemical factory being built by Taiwanese businessman Chen Yu-hao, and in July 2005 an environmental impact assessment report was prepared. However, Xiamen residents were never consulted in this process.[89] The controversy began in November 2006 when Zhao Yufen, a local chemistry professor from Xiamen University and a delegate to the official advisory body, the Chinese People's Political Consultative Conference (CPPCC), wrote a letter to the city's top leader, CCP Secretary He Lifeng, expressing his concerns about the project.[90] The three-hundred-acre facility, located in a largely residential area across a narrow channel from downtown Xiamen, was gearing up to produce paraxylene (PX), a toxic chemical used as an industrial solvent.[91]

Xiamen officials were determined to go ahead with the project and Professor Zhao was urged to keep quiet. Instead, he wrote a letter to the two top leaders in Fujian Province, CCP Secretary Lu Zhangong and Governor Huang Xiaojing. The result was a 6 January 2007 meeting between top Xiamen officials and several academics, including Professor Zhao, who had concerns about the project.[92] Officials present, including He Lifeng, paid no heed to the experts' warning, emphasizing instead the importance of the project to the local economy.

In March 2007 Professor Zhao instigated the drafting of a petition against the project on the grounds that it posed a health danger to Xiamen residents.[93] The petition received signatures from delegates to the annual session of the CPPCC in March and drew some coverage in mainland newspapers as well as media in Taiwan and Hong Kong.[94]

On 11 March, Guangdong's *Southern Metropolis Daily* became the first newspaper to cover Zhao Yufen's petition.[95] In a page 5 story that also ran on the popular Web portal Sohu.com, the newspaper quoted Professor Zhao and more broadly criticized development projects undertaken by local officials in China without due consideration for the citizens.[96] The article provided key figures on the Xiamen PX project, including the number of residents living in the immediate vicinity (approximately 100,000), and it also reviewed past industrial accidents in China. Within a week, three newspapers, the *China Chemical Industry News, China Youth Daily*, and *China Business*, ran news features on the project that emphasized the issues raised by the CPPCC delegates.[97] As news of Professor Zhao Yufen's petition made the rounds in national commercial newspapers and on the Web, top CCP leaders in Xiamen suppressed local coverage of the story. According to a report published by China's *Oriental Outlook* magazine in May 2007, Xiamen Municipal Secretary He Lifeng held an urgent meeting in March at which he urged leaders to ignore the criticism and move ahead with the project as quickly as possible.[98]

As Xiamen media were prevented from reporting on opposition to the PX project, new technologies began showing their strength.[99] Xiamen-based freelance journalist Zhong Xiaoyong started following the PX story on his personal Weblog, written under the penname Lian Yue, in late March. A well-known columnist for several leading commercial newspapers, Zhong had formerly worked as an editor for *Southern Weekend* and *21st Century Economic Herald.*

Zhong first posted about the chemical plant on 18 March 2007. The post, which bore the suggestive title "Xiamen Commits Suicide," provided information on the decline of air quality in Xiamen during 2006 that was based on official statistics, and then ran in full the *China Business* report that was published on the same day.[100] Over the next few months, visits to Zhong's blog soared as the site became an important source of Xiamen PX-related information, particularly in Xiamen itself, where the content was pasted across local chat rooms.[101]

As he aggregated news stories on his blog, Zhong also wrote a number of critical editorials for major commercial newspapers outside his home province, including Hunan's *Xiaoxiang Morning Post* and Guangdong's *Southern Metropolis Daily.* Zhong's first editorial, "The Public Will Not Be Safe," published in the *Xiaoxiang Morning Post* on 22 March and concurrently on

Zhong's blog, contrasted the safety concerns with the propaganda put out by local CCP officials.[102] After a rundown of government documents in Fujian Province extolling the project's virtues, Zhong wrote sarcastically:

> Any cheerful city resident, seeing this news and then turning to the biblical chapter of Genesis, might suppose God was a bit lazy during those six days, that He didn't work hard enough and that the world He created was still missing something. My, how could Adam and Eve have lived happily in the Garden of Eden without a PX project of their own?

After listing the dangers posed by the plant, including figures from the original *China Business* story, Zhong wondered at how the opposition could be pushed aside nonchalantly, so that even a report to the national CPPCC brought no real action to protect the residents of Xiamen. "Even if there are voices of opposition at the national Chinese People's Political Consultative Conference, public safety can be sacrificed," he wrote. "When you think about it, how many of these dangerous projects must we have across the nation that cannot bear public criticism? All of us live in a public space marked by public danger."

Discussion of the Xiamen PX project continued through April and May 2007 as a handful of reports from such newspapers as *Southern Metropolis Daily* and *Information Daily* buzzed through cyberspace, augmented in real time by comments in chat rooms and on blogs.[103] Residents in Xiamen transmitted text messages in protest of the project on 27 May. The city leadership nevertheless persisted in their plans. On 28 May 2007, top municipal officials pushed their message about the project's safety through the *Xiamen Evening News*, a commercial paper under the official *Xiamen Daily* group.[104] The article bore the headline "Haicang PX Project Has Already Been Approved According to Nationally Recognized Legal Procedures and Is Under Construction."

On the morning of 29 May, the Xiamen government sent out a notice ordering all departments to work together to ensure the project went ahead smoothly.[105] But as municipal leaders were digging in, public opinion spiraled out of control in cyberspace. By 29 May newspapers outside Xiamen were reporting that short text messages of protest had been sent among more than 1 million people in Xiamen as well as mobile subscribers in other cities.[106] One of the messages, posted online by a Web user at Oeeee.com, read, "PX is paraxylene, a dangerous chemical and highly cancerous with a high rate of fetal malformation (in the words of Chinese Academy of Social Science Professor Zhao Yufen)." The text messages called on Xiamen residents to turn out in force on 1 June to publicly protest the Xiamen PX project.[107]

The turning point came late in the day on 29 May as Xiamen leaders met with top provincial leaders to discuss how to handle the public opposition.[108] The following day, Xiamen leaders called a press conference and announced they would "postpone" the project.[109] But the 30 May press conference did not slow the momentum building among Xiamen residents. Calls for a public show of opposition continued through the Internet and mobile text messages in the final days of May, despite attempts by the municipal branch of the Public Security Bureau to block the mobile network-based movement and to round up residents who issued calls for protest.[110] One Xiamen resident, Wu Jian, was taken into custody by police on 29 May after posting a call to "march" in a chat room on the popular Shenzhen-based Web portal QQ.com.[111] Despite the government's efforts, thousands of protesters took to the streets in peaceful protest on 1 and 2 June.[112]

Contravening the blanket ban by central propaganda officials on coverage of the protests in the domestic media, Xiamen residents used their mobile phones to transmit eyewitness accounts of the demonstrations across the country. Wen Yunchao, a Xiamen-based blogger, wrote, "The second police defense line has been dispersed. There is pushing and shoving. The police wall has broken down."[113]

In the wake of the protests, leaders in Xiamen finally set into motion a process of public consultation, which culminated in their December 2007 decision to relocate the chemical plant.[114] *People's Daily* lauded the new responsiveness of the Xiamen government in a 20 December editorial on page 5, praising it for "turning from a passive to an active posture in dealing with public challenges" and "creating new channels for communication" with citizens.[115] A few comments from Web users appeared on the same page. "As for the future of the Xiamen PX Project," wrote one, "I think that aside from considerations of economic benefit, more should be done to consider the well-being of the environment and public opinion."[116]

In the wake of the Xiamen PX protests, party leaders have fought to reclaim agenda-setting power from the new technologies and professional journalism. President Hu Jintao delivered a major media policy speech on

20 June 2008 that launched the drive for central party media to cover breaking news more aggressively in order to shut out the freewheeling commercial media. This strategy—Control 2.0, which party leaders call by the new buzzword "public opinion channeling"—marks the CCP's attempt to forestall the trends we have highlighted in this chapter.

Yet despite the CCP's efforts, media commercialization, journalistic professionalism, and the growth of new media continue to transform the ecology of agenda setting in China. For example, in August 2009, news of a mass lead poisoning case in Fengxiang, a village in Shaanxi Province, came to light after concerned villagers reached a local commercial paper, *Sanqin Metropolitan Daily*. Ten years ago, this story might very well have disappeared, escaping the notice of other media and eventually falling victim to local propaganda officials. But thanks to distribution by commercial news Web sites with much broader reach, the *Sanqin Metropolitan Daily* story rapidly became national news. The gap between party and commercial coverage was again decisive. *Sanqin Metropolitan Daily* is a commercial spin-off of the official *Shaanxi Daily*, which remained silent on the story even as it went national.

CONCLUSION

Much like the dragons of Lord Ye, the modern Chinese media evoke a deep ambivalence among CCP and government officials. The Internet and Web-based media have combined with commercialization of traditional media and a new professionalism among Chinese journalists to heighten pressure against the existing news control regime. True, the political impact of these trends may not look impressive in the face of prominent cases of CCP control like the shutdown of *Freezing Point* or the jailing of *Southern Metropolis Daily* editor Chen Yizhong. The present generation of Chinese leaders is weaker than the paramount leaders of the past: though they still exercise some control over the media, this control is challenged on a daily basis by professional journalists and online commentators. As former *Freezing Point* editor Li Datong said during a meeting in Hong Kong with top journalists from the mainland and Taiwan prior to his supplement's shutdown, he believed Chinese media professionals had now entered a "strategizing" phase (*boyi jieduan*) in which they could deal with leaders on their own terms.[117] "Before it wasn't possible to strategize," said Li. "Now do you think

I can't play a couple of chess moves against government authorities? We believe we now have the space [to do this]." Li further raised two possible strategies open to journalists. The first was to use professional techniques to publish articles that were outside the official agenda, or that "central party papers would never publish." The second, he said, was a strategy of "direct confrontation." *Freezing Point*, as an example of the latter, had resisted an official order to run a piece of traditional propaganda in its pages. Li Datong's flat refusal to bow to propaganda officials shows both the professional will to oppose the CCP's news agenda and the institutional possibility, under certain conditions, of resisting party pressure and maintaining journalistic autonomy.

The eventual shutdown of *Freezing Point* of course underscores the limitations of Li Datong's strategy of confrontation. The more common pattern is a calculated testing of boundaries wherein journalists seek to creatively circumvent official bans on reporting. But the more important point is that the nature of the game has changed. Chinese media are employing various strategies to advance their own agendas, uphold their professional principles and, of course, gain audiences. Journalists are becoming more skillful at setting the agenda for public discourse while striking a balance between political survival and their professional ideals.

Notes

1. Figure in "Copyright: The Core Value of the Media Industry," *Renmin Wang* (*People's Daily Online*), 19 August 2004, http://www.people.com.cn/GB/14677/22114/36721/36725/2723149.html.

2. Cui Baoguo, Lu Jinzhu, and Li Feng, "Transition and Renewal: An Overall Report on Development of the Media Industry in 2006," in Cui Baoguo (Ed.), *Report on Development of China's Media Industry, 2006* (Beijing: Social Sciences Academic Press, 2006), pp. 4–5.

3. Figures regarding public spending on Internet infrastructure were found in Hu Yong, "Blogs in China," China Media Project Case Study (on file at the Journalism and Media Studies Centre, University of Hong Kong), 4 August 2005, p. 2. Figures regarding numbers of Internet users were found in China Internet Network Information Center, *25th Statistical Report on the Development of China's Internet*, January 2010, http://www.cnnic.net.cn/uploadfiles/pdf/2010/1/15/101600.pdf.

4. In the aftermath of Tiananmen, there was a strong conviction among those who came to power that the events of 4 June had been precipitated by mishandling of media

policy. Zhao Ziyang, China's ousted premier, purportedly told China's propaganda ministers on 6 May to "open things up a bit." There was "little danger in increasing the openness of the news," he said. As a result, many newspapers had openly expressed support for demonstrators in Beijing, "leading events in the wrong direction." "A Record of Major Events," *China Comment*, no. 7, 1989, Internal Edition.

5. Zhao Shilong, *Diaocha Zhongguo: Xinwen Beihou de Gushi* [*Investigating China: Stories behind the News*] (Beijing: China Fangzheng Publishing House, 2004), p. 7.

6. "Finding the Right Foothold and Point of View for Planning for the Future," *Chinese Journalist*, December 2002, http://www.chinesejournalist.cn/.

7. Discussion of the CCP's global media ambitions can be found in Pascale Trouillard, "China Unveils Its Global Media Ambitions," AFP, 11 October 2009. Discussion of the CCP-sponsored World Media Summit can be found in Li Congjun, "Writing a New Chapter in the Development of Xinhua News Agency," *Chinese Journalist*, February 2009, http://www.chinesejournalist.cn/html/.

8. Hu, "Blogs in China."

9. Jin Liping, "Our Predicament and Our Way Forward" (case study, China Media Project, Journalism and Media Studies Centre, University of Hong Kong, Hong Kong, October 2005), p. 2.

10. Data compiled from *Zhongguo Xinwen Chuban Tongji Ziliao Huibian* (China Statistical Data Collection of Press and Publication) Volumes 1993–1997, published by the China Statistical Press (Beijing); Volumes 2000–2003, published by the China Labor and Social Services Press (Beijing).

11. Cheng Qinghua, *Giving Ear to Liang Heng: In Media, Literature and Politics* (Beijing: Xinhua Publishing House, 2004).

12. Jin, "Our Predicament and Our Way Forward," pp. 1–2.

13. Overview of *People's Daily* publication, *People's Daily Online*, http://www.people.com.cn/paper/jianjie/bzjj_01.htm.

14. Media Development Research Center of China's General Administration of Press and Publications, *China Newspaper Industry Competitiveness Monitoring Report, 2007*, 29 December 2007, http://baoye.net/ie_edit/uploadfile/20080113012255899.doc.

15. Jin, "Our Predicament and Our Way Forward," p. 2.

16. Qian Gang, "Guidance/Supervision/Reform/Freedom: Looking at Chinese Media Through the Media Buzzword," *Twenty-First Century Bi-Monthly*, June 2006, p. 6.

17. Ibid., p. 14.

18. This point is raised by Li Xiguang in "China's Blue Pencil," *On the Media*, WNYC New York Public Radio, 17 March 2006, http://www.onthemedia.org/transcripts/transcripts_031706_bluepencil.html.

19. David Bandurski, "China's Yellow Journalism," *Far Eastern Economic Review*, Vol. 169, no. 5, 2006, pp. 49–51.

20. Ibid., p. 102.

21. "Standing Committee of Beijing Party Congress Opens 28th Conference," *People's Daily*, 12 June 2006, p. 4(A).

22. Ibid.

23. "Beijing Vice-Mayor Liu Zhihua Removed from Office," *Jinghua Times*, 12 June 2006, p. 1(A).

24. "Beijing Vice-Mayor Liu Zhihua Removed from Office," *Oriental Morning Post*, 12 June 2006, p. 1(A).

25. Li, "Building Public Trust," p. 104.

26. "Politburo Holds Meeting: Decides to Launch Party-Wide Education Program to Preserve an Advanced Communist Party," *People's Daily*, 22 October 2004, p. 1(A).

27. "Hu Jintao, Wen Jiabao Place Great Importance on Accident at Daping Mine," *Henan Daily*, 22 October 2004, p. 1(A).

28. "Major Gas Explosion Occurs at Zhengzhou Mining Group's Daping Mine: Li Keqiang and Li Chengyu Travel at Night to the Scene to Lead Rescue Work," *Henan Daily*, 22 October 2004, p. 1(A).

29. "Major Gas Explosion Occurs at Daping Mine," *Beijing Youth Daily*, 22 October 2004, p. 1(A).

30. "Major Mine Disaster in Henan: 62 Dead 86 Missing," *Southern Metropolis Daily*, 22 October 2004, p. 1(A).

31. "A Pair of Fierce Roars Reverberate for Miles: Miners Fortunate Enough to Escape That Night Tell Their Stories," *Southern Metropolis Daily*, 22 October 2004, p. 6(A).

32. "Gas Explosion Accident Occurs at Henan's Daping Coalmine," *Sichuan Daily*, 22 October 2004.

33. "Sky-Shaking Coalmine Disaster Troubles Nation," *Chengdu Commercial Daily*, 22 October 2004, p. 1(A).

34. "War of Words Goes on between Xinhua News Agency and Fujian Province," *Ming Pao Daily*, 1 September 2006, p. 30(A).

35. Le Yi, "How to Report on a Disaster Scene a Typhoon Has Passed," *Southern Metropolis Daily*, 22 August 2006, p. 2(A).

36. David Bandurski, "Hu's News That Just Wouldn't Go Away: The Party Delivers Its Message Through China's Commercialized Media," China Media Project, 31 January 2007, http://cmp.hku.hk/2007/01/31/169/.

37. "Hu Jintao Speech During Inspection Work at *People's Daily*," *Renmin Wang* (*People's Daily Online*), 21 June 2008, http://politics.people.com.cn/GB/1024/7408514.html.

38. Bi Yantao, "The Tibet Incident and International Public Opinion Channeling," *Young Journalist*, May 2008, available at *Renmin Wang* (*People's Daily Online*), http://media.people.com.cn/GB/22114/42328/137046/8236193.html.

39. Qian Gang, "Central Party Media 'Grab the Megaphone,'" China Media Project, 21 August 2009, http://cmp.hku.hk/2009/08/21/1709/.

40. Li, "Building Public Trust," p. 104.

41. Lu Ye and Pan Zhongdang, "Imagining Professional Fame: Constructing Journalistic Professionalism in China's Social Transformation," *Mass Communication Research* (Taiwan), January 2002, pp. 17–59, http://www.jour.nccu.edu.tw/Mcr/0071/03.html.

42. Ibid.

43. Chen Lidan, "Talking about the Journalism Profession and Professionalism on Journalists Day," *Chinese Journalist*, November 2000, p. 11.

44. Ding Ximan, "Our Journalists: For New China's First Journalist's Day," *Chinese Journalist*, November 2000, p. 5.

45. Lu and Pan, "Imagining Professional Fame," pp. 17–59.

46. "Because We Are Journalists—Written on New China's First Journalists Day," *Southern Weekend*, 8 November 2000, special issue.

47. Zhang Yuren, *The Dangers and Adventures of Freedom: A History of the Idea of Liberal Journalism in China* (Kunming: Yunnan People's Publishing House, 2002).

48. Ibid., p. 74.

49. Lu and Pan, "Imagining Professional Fame," pp. 17–59.

50. Qian Gang, "The Death of a Newspaperman: I Too Have Criticized Deng Tuo," *Ming Pao Daily*, 16 May 2006.

51. David Bandurski and Lin Hui, "China's Shadow Censor Commissars," *Far Eastern Economic Review*, Vol. 169, no. 2, March 2006, p. 29.

52. Joseph Kahn, "Ex-Officials Protest Censorship by China," *International Herald Tribune*, 15 February 2006.

53. Jonathan Watts, "China's Old Guard Warns Censors of 'Social Disaster,'" *The Guardian*, 15 February 2006.

54. "Freezing Point Chief Editor Li Datong: Central Propaganda Department Provokes Major Trouble," *Ming Pao Daily*, 20 February 2006.

55. Bandurski and Lin, "China's Shadow Censor Commissars," p. 29.

56. Minxin Pei, "Media Control Gets More Tricky," *Straits Times*, 27 February 2006.

57. Jin, "Our Predicament and Our Way Forward," p. 4.

58. Dan Gillmor, *We the Media: Grassroots Journalism by the People, for the People* (Cambridge: O'Reilly Media, 2004), p. 29.

59. Ibid., p. 28.

60. Ibid., p. 26.

61. China Internet Network Information Center, *23rd Statistical Report on the Development of China's Internet*.

62. Charles Feng, "The Great Wall Is at My Door," *Twenty-First Century Bi-Monthly*, June 2006, p. 17.

63. Nicholas Kristof, "Death by a Thousand Blogs," *New York Times*, 24 May 2005, p. 21.

64. Hu, "Blogs in China," p. 2.

65. Gillmor, *We the Media*, p. 28.

66. Guo Chu and Xie Liang, "Seeking to Guide News-Related Commentary," *News Line*, 29 July 2005.

67. Zhang Shou, "Media Agenda-Setting under the Influence of the Internet," *Guangming Daily*, 12 January 2006, p. 10.

68. Qin Heng, "A Study of Interactivity in Agenda-Setting in Internet Dissemination," *Journal of the Party School of CPC Zhengzhou Municipal Committee*, no. 1, 2005, p. 67.

69. Ibid., p. 67.

70. "The Ups and Downs of 'Comment Posting Culture,'" *Beijing Youth Daily*, 6 August 2006.

71. "'Outdoor Dormitory at Tsinghua' a Warning Sign," *Beijing Youth Daily*, 22 August 2006.

72. Chen Feng, "The Death of Detainee Sun Zhigang," *Southern Metropolis Daily*, 25 April 2003.

73. Ibid.

74. Wang Kai, *China in Change: Media, Popular Will and Public Policy* (Shanghai: Fudan University Press, 2005), p. 20.

75. Deng Zibin, "We Must Not Have a Second Sun Zhigang," *Southern Weekend*, 15 May 2003.

76. Philip Pan, "In China, an Editor Triumphs, and Fails: Struggle between New Press Freedoms, Communist Party Evident by Jailing," *Washington Post*, 1 August 2004.

77. "Various Regions Rule Arbitrary Detention and Repatriation Urgently Needs Checking," *Legal Daily*, 1 September 2000.

78. "Six Questions We Have," *Southern Metropolis Daily*, 26 October 2001, p. 5(A).

79. Deng, "We Must Not Have a Second Sun Zhigang."

80. Du Juan, "So That the Tragedy of Sun Zhigang Never Happens Again," *Liaoning Daily*, 8 July 2003.

81. Ibid.

82. "Three Citizens Petition National People's Congress to Examine Constitutionality of Detention Law," *China News Service*, 16 May 2003.

83. "Man's Brutal Killers Receive Punishment in Guangzhou," *People's Daily Online*, 10 June 2003, http://english.peopledaily.com.cn/200306/10/print20030610_117933.html.

84. Du, "So That the Tragedy of Sun Zhigang."

85. He Bin, "Realizing Justice Even If the Sky Falls," *Southern Weekend*, 19 June 2003.

86. Kang Weiping, "Where Does the Danger Lie?" (case study, China Media Project, Journalism and Media Studies Centre, University of Hong Kong, Hong Kong, September 2004).

87. "Beijing Kills Issue of Caijing, Names More Than 10 Publications for Criticism," *Ming Pao Daily*, 25 June 2003, p. 21(A).

88. Pan, "Editor Triumphs, and Fails."

89. Zhu Hongjun, "Xiamen Abruptly Stops PX Project to Deal with a Public Crisis," *Southern Weekend*, 28 May 2007, http://www.nanfangdaily.com.cn/.

90. "Behind the CPPCC Petition: Experts and Officials Engage in Dialogue," *China Business News*, 18 April 2007, p. 6(A).

91. Edward Cody, "Text Messages Giving Voice to Chinese: Opponents of Chemical Factory Found Way Around Censors," *Washington Post*, 28 June 2007, http://www.washingtonpost.com/wp-dyn/content/article/2007/06/27/AR2007062702962.html.

92. "Behind the CPPCC Petition."

93. For more details about Professor Zhao, see Cody, "Text Messages Giving Voice"; for details about Professor Zhao's petition, see Zhu, "Xiamen Abruptly Stops PX Project."

94. Ibid.

95. "In an Effort to 'Be Inventive' Leaders Invent Short-Lived Projects," *Southern Metropolis Daily*, 11 March 2007, 5(A), http://news.sohu.com/20070311/n248644551.shtml.

96. Ibid.

97. "Multibillion Yuan Chemical Project in Xiamen Sparks Debate Over Safety and Danger," *China Business*, 19 March 2007.

98. "Xiamen City Announces Postponement of PX Project," *Southern Metropolis Daily*, 31 May 2007, http://www.nanfangdaily.com.cn/.

99. Cody, "Text Messages Giving Voice."

100. "Xiamen Commits Suicide," Lian Yue's Eighth Continent, 19 March 2007, http://www.lianyue.net/.

101. "Exemplary Lives: 10 Health Heroes for 2007," *Nandu Weekly*, 4 December 2007.

102. "The Public Will Not Be Safe," *Xiaoxiang Morning Post*, 22 March 2007.

103. "Zhao Yufen Just Wouldn't Give Up," *Information Daily*, 27 May 2007, p. 6. Online coverage of this article was made available on Netease (163.com) and then pasted from there onto the popular Tianya chat room at www.tianya.cn, http://1home.hainan.net/new/TianyaCity/Content.asp?idItem=323&idArticle=15985&page_num=1.

104. The use of this local commercial daily by Xiamen officials reminds us that commercial media remain a part of the official press structure and are subject to controls.

105. "Xiamen Decides to Stop the PX Project in Answer to Public Crisis," *Southern Weekend*, 5 June 2007.

106. "More Than One Million Xiamen Citizens Send Out the Same Short Message," *Shantou Tequ Wan Bao*, 29 May 2007, p. 10.

107. Cody, "Text Messages Giving Voice."

108. "Xiamen Decides to Stop the PX Project in Answer to Public Crisis."

109. "Xiamen Urgently Orders Halt to PX Project," *China Business News*, 1 June 2007, p. 4(A).

110. Cody, "Text Messages Giving Voice."

111. "The War of Xiamen Residents against the PX Project," *Southern Metropolis Daily*, 25 December 2007, p. 12(A).

112. Cody, "Text Messages Giving Voice."

113. Ibid.

114. "The War of Xiamen Residents against the PX Project."

115. Lu Xinning, "'Tigergate' Was Not the Only Case of Unexpected Turns," *People's Daily*, 20 December 2007, p. 5.

116. "Decision-Making Should Give More Consideration to the Opinions of the People," *People's Daily*, 20 December 2007, p. 5.

117. "Has the Age of Strategizing Arrived? A Dialogue in Lung Ying-tai's Home between Journalists from Both Sides of the Straits," *Ming Pao Daily*, 6 June 2006.

3

The Rise of the Business Media in China

Hu Shuli

A s THE ARTICLES IN this volume demonstrate, market reforms have led to significant changes in China's media industry. Among the most dramatic of these changes has been the growth of business journalism. Since 2000, the rapid expansion of capital markets in China has led to increased demand for financial news, which has, in turn, led to a boom in coverage and a highly competitive financial news market.

This chapter reveals what this market looks like, how it developed, and its journalistic strengths and weaknesses. Working from a social science perspective, I investigate the role the financial news plays in China's economy and society, and what broader trends it reflects in China's changing media industry.

COMPETING MEDIA

Financial news has become an increasingly prominent element among China's television, print, and Web-based media. Since 2001, national, regional, and local TV stations have launched special channels offering financial news, documentaries, and investigative journalism. The most dynamic changes, however, have affected business publications and their Web sites, as well as Internet news portals.

Financial coverage in China's print media includes three broad categories of newspapers and news magazines. In the first group are official papers—propaganda organs whose intended audience is party and government officials. This includes the *People's Daily* and *Economic Daily*. The second category consists of tabloid newspapers within the official system that in part bear responsibility for spreading propaganda, but also appeal to the general public to gain advertising revenue. These are primarily evening papers in cities. The third category consists of commercial publications, many geared toward business. Although most financial and business coverage appears in the commercial category, over the past decade an increasing number of pages in all types of publications have been devoted to economic and financial information.

Independent business magazines and newspapers started appearing in the late 1990s. *Caijing* pioneered this trend in 1998, and by the turn of the century a dozen other weekly newspapers and news magazines had followed suit. Examples include *21st Century Business Herald*, *Economic Observer*, *New Fortune Magazine*, and *Business Watch*. These publications combine emerging hallmarks of China's commercial media—coverage of cutting-edge issues and catchy layouts—while providing detailed and accurate financial information. The market further expanded with the arrival of propaganda-free, daily financial newspapers in 2004. This put official or semiofficial financial dailies such as *China Securities Journal, Shanghai Security Daily*, and *China Business* at a competitive disadvantage, forcing them to adjust to maintain readership.

In addition, China's news Web sites—attracting more than 100 million viewers daily—provide a useful platform for disseminating news to an information-hungry country. Operators of these sites have recognized the public's growing interest in securities markets and investing. China's main Web portals—www.sina.com, www.sohu.com, and www.netease.com—are publicly traded companies with stocks listed on the NASDAQ exchange. Each portal puts a high priority on offering as much news content as possible to attract a large volume of readers.[1] The portals have annual contracts with thousands of traditional media outlets for copyrighted material—contracts that let them edit news and headlines to fit their editorial views. These are prime news sources for educated, urban Chinese. Among the thousands of articles posted daily, financial news items are second only to general news in popularity.

Most sites are not allowed to gather news and could face copyright conflicts with traditional outlets. Yet they help information flow more freely. They've also increased the objectivity of reporting, as none espouse an ideological doctrine. In turn, many print publications have developed online versions. Some, such as *Caijing*'s Web site www.caijing.com, provide frequently updated, original online content (caijing.com publishes in both English and Chinese), while others simply repost printed material.

DRIVING FORCES

Approached from a demand perspective, the causes of the boom in China's financial news market are clear—the growth of capital markets has created significant bottom-up demand for timely and accurate financial news. More interesting is the supply-side perspective, where propaganda and media control remain important tools used by the Chinese Communist Party (CCP). Foreign observers attribute China's booming financial media to the government and the CCP's recognition of the need for capital market transparency. While in some ways this is true, there is more to the story.

Since the 1990s, government control of economic news in terms of licensing and supervision has been relatively loose compared with control over other types of news. The government has molded media policy to fit its overarching objective of economic development. Even after the 1989 Tiananmen Square incident, economic news was little affected by censorship while all other kinds of news were strictly controlled.

The securities markets that emerged in the early 1990s created a new dynamic for relations between CCP and financial news media. Securities markets shared the CCP's worries about information and communication, since news reports can fuel panics over economic developments. Information cascades can cause a financial recession or, worse still, an all-out crisis that could threaten regime stability. Consequently, it was no surprise that the growth of Chinese stock markets did not lead to a truly independent business media. And while negative general news reports remained taboo, negative securities market reports were permitted and regulated by the China Securities Regulatory Commission (CSRC), which helped with the pursuit of transparency.

The connection between financial news and regime stability was made clear by the role of the CSRC. Although the CSRC, as a financial regulator, does not have the same authority over the media as the CCP Propaganda Department, it uses a system known as designated information disclosure to control media coverage of the securities sector. Certain papers and magazines are designated by the CSRC as the only officially approved outlets through which listed companies can disclose information such as financial reports and official statements.[2]

During the 1990s, the system generated lucrative advertising revenues for selected outlets until at the end of the decade it weakened severely under the weight of popular demand for more thorough and transparent information about economic issues. Although formally still in place, it is less and less significant for actual reporting on corporations. The 1997–1998 East Asian financial crisis and financial reforms in the late 1990s created conditions for developing a more independent business media. The government's willingness to pursue greater market transparency and its efforts to list large, state-owned banks abroad forced more tolerance of critical business news reporting. At the same time, many reform-minded economic officials wanted to allow a freer press. These conditions combined to create a fertile environment for independent business journalism.

At first, gradual media deregulation created broad gray areas where opportunities for freer coverage existed uneasily beside potential risks—even traps. This gray area became more defined, and transparency was enhanced, as elite journalists worked to better professional standards and ambitious entrepreneurs flexed muscle. Together, these forces led to an upsurge in financial reporting, enhancing freedom and transparency in business reporting.

Development of China's professional media culture dates back several decades. Memories of the catastrophic Cultural Revolution (1966–1976) left the nation's journalists with a strong sense of the importance of independent thinking and professional standards. As a consequence, throughout the 1980s journalists developed a professional culture and sense of integrity. They also sought a political watchdog role. Among the most distinguished of these pioneer independent journalists was Liu Binyan of the *People's Daily*.

After the Tiananmen Square protests, many journalists at major official newspapers moved into business journalism. They started semiofficial, market-oriented newspapers but met challenges in pursuing independence, including cash-strapped editorial budgets. This, in turn, made clear the need for more substantial investment and better management.

At the same time, a new round of economic decentralization began in the early 1990s. Private foreign and domestic businesses stepped into the media market, cooperating with officials and journalists. While foreign companies eyed less risky areas, such as entertainment, many domestic companies chose a more daring route by focusing on business news. By the end of the 1990s, a new business model had emerged. Financing from Chinese entrepreneurs supported a crop of enthusiastic, independent journalists. Improved property rights and better corporate governance supported long-term investing in these media ventures. With the tacit approval of the government, the business media entered a new era of independence and development.

The model succeeded only because of rapid economic growth. Not coincidentally, business journals entered the market during an economic boom that was accompanied by a rising demand for business news and advertising. The print advertising market grew 116 percent between 2001 and 2004.[3] The business press received only about 5 percent of the advertising pie, but it was a huge slice—amounting to about USD 400 million.[4] Internet access has been another driver for growth by expanding the influence of business publications. It has also helped print outlets increase their information output and advertising options, while avoiding the headaches of dealing with China's postal system.

ECONOMIC REFORM ADVOCACY

While business journalism's boom led to greater demand for financial information, it also promoted a business environment conducive to the expansion of capital markets by educating the public. It helped potential investors become more aware of opportunities.

One example of this education role is the *China Business Times* (CBT), led by Ding Wang since the 1990s. CBT has a policy of "talking only business" and is devoid of political content.[5] But it is also an active advocate for economic reform. Based on personal connections as a former editor at the official *Economic Daily*, Ding made CBT a platform for the reform agenda, frequently publishing columns by economists and reform-minded officials while suggesting ways to advance market reform. CBT also introduced

Western-style reporting and layout to Chinese newspaper readers. Many national and local business newspapers have emulated CBT's format. The officially sponsored securities dailies—*China Securities News, Shanghai Securities News*, and *Securities Times*—adopted similar policies when they were launched and advocated capital market development. They adopted an "only stocks" policy, limiting their reporting to nonpolitical news on the securities markets. Other business papers also got on the bandwagon and extended news coverage from securities markets to other investment sectors. Together, these journals became advocates for developing capital markets. They also educated the public on various types of markets that many had perceived as complicated, technical, and even mysterious.

MARKET WATCHDOG

Another emerging trend in China since the late 1990s has been business journalism's role as a market watchdog. *Caijing* embodied this trend. *Caijing* was founded by a small group of journalists (including myself) in April 1998. We had a vision based on classic journalistic principles: editorial independence, reliable fact gathering, in-depth investigations, and thorough analysis. At that time, our investors agreed to the vision in principle and contributed sufficient capital to allow the magazine's business and editorial sides to operate separately.

Since the start, *Caijing* has conscientiously guarded the public's right to know. The first cover story, "Who Is Responsible for Qiong Minyuan described a real estate company whose stock trading was suspended for insider trading.[6] This was the first time a publicly traded stock had been suspended in China. Government securities supervisors did not want media exposure of this event, but *Caijing* broke the official silence. The story garnered a great deal of attention, stirred the financial community, and almost resulted in *Caijing* being banned.

Nonetheless, *Caijing* continued pushing the envelope. Two years later, a story titled "The Inside Story of Fund Management" sparked new furor.[7] Research by our reporters shed light on irregularities and rampant corruption in the financial industry, where ten management companies operated twenty-two funds backed by government affiliates. *Caijing* found fund managers were meeting in microphone-free saunas to secretly discuss portfolio manipulation.

Needless to say, people were enraged. After each firm attacked *Caijing* in the official media, the story became a watershed event as readers sided with *Caijing*. Prominent economist Wu Jinglian declared, "The stock markets cannot remain in darkness."[8] The CCP apparatus bent under pressure, and the new securities commission chairman, Zhou Xiaochuan (who today is Governor of the People's Bank of China), said the market should welcome media criticism.[9] Since then, journalists have been more willing to risk exposing price manipulations, profit falsification, and other forms of financial malfeasance.

A new stage in business journalism and capital markets began when several private business newspapers were launched in 2001, and CSRC declared the Year of Regulation, acknowledging the need to curb rampant stock manipulation.[10] This was not lip service; business media coverage that year had a palpable impact on government regulation. In August 2001, *Caijing* published "Ying Guang Xia Trap," a story that revealed how the nation's second-largest listed company had cheated investors and falsified profits by hundreds of millions of RMB.[11] Within ten hours of the story's publication and simultaneous posting on the Internet, authorities suspended trading of Ying Guang Xia shares. A CSRC probe found that profits had been inflated by RMB 700 million, and company officials went to jail. It was the first time Chinese courts sentenced company executives for giving false information.

Significantly, the probe was a direct result of investigative business journalism. Afterward, legislation was passed that allowed civil lawsuits for securities fraud, leading to China's first successful major class-action suit.[12] Ying Guang Xia shareholders won the case in 2004.[13] These developments led to many of the financial regulations governing China's stock market today. Furthermore, *Caijing*'s report had strong impact on other media outlets. CCTV, China's official national TV station, which had supported *Caijing*'s reporting in the fund management investigation, started a financial news channel in 2001. Independent newspapers also entered the market. As a consequence, the business media sector became more competitive, leading to substantial improvements in media transparency and professionalism. This relationship has become a virtuous circle: the new media exposure has changed business behavior in China so that it is now more transparent and accountable.

Proof that business media are affecting business accountability was apparent in the 2009 story of massive lending by state-owned banks. *Caijing* was investigating loans worth trillions of RMB that were issued by the government to encourage domestic investment and market liquidity and offset a global economic slump. *Caijing* obtained timely loan reports from the banks that confirmed what many had suspected—some of the borrowed money was being used for stock trades, fueling a bull market on Chinese stock exchanges. These reports would have been impossible without open, cooperative relations between bankers and reporters.

WIDER WATCHDOG

The business media go beyond financial reporting when issues are vitally important to readers. And the independent print sector has led the way. Sometimes identified as the "pan-financial press," these independent publications leverage their niche—finance—with maximum latitude, sometimes functioning as a watchdog in areas beyond the boundaries of business journalism. In 2002, for example, the weekly *21st Century Business Herald* exposed the unsolved bribery case of Lu Wanli, a former transportation director in Guizhou Province who fled to Fiji. The story forced government officials to dig deeper into the case and extradite Lu to face bribery charges involving USD 10 million. Other top provincial officials, including a former party secretary of Guizhou, were also charged in the case, and Lu was convicted and executed. *Caijing* later followed up with an investigation of corruption in Guizhou's road-building industry.

Independent business publications frequently pay attention to social issues in addition to covering securities markets, banks, and macroeconomic indicators. Negative news is no longer taboo. Big events, from natural disasters to environmental pollution, from embezzlement in state banks to corruption among top officials, are reported in detail by these independent publications. A remarkable example was coverage of severe acute respiratory syndrome (SARS) in 2003 and avian flu in 2005 by the independent media. Both events were first and primarily reported by business publications, which is indicative of the transition and perhaps the future direction of Chinese media in general.

When the SARS epidemic first erupted in Guangdong Province, it was reported by the regional press. Early reports caught *Caijing* off guard. But the magazine's journalists sensed the importance of a coming health crisis and felt obliged to follow the story. With the 20 February 2003 article, "Guangdong Disease Crashing against the National Disease Control

System," *Caijing* warned the nation about the impending disaster. It told the story of SARS in Guangdong and the weaknesses of the nation's disease control system. Between March and early April, as SARS spread nationwide, few domestic media outlets considered it a disaster; most ignored it. Meanwhile, *Caijing* reported SARS from all angles and dispatched reporters to Beijing hospitals, research labs, and government agencies, who together dug up enough data for a major story that ran on 20 April.

After initially banning coverage, the government finally agreed to transparency on the SARS issue after the April *Caijing* story. *Caijing* continued its in-depth investigation of the epidemic. In particular, journalists were concerned that migrant workers were among those most at risk from the epidemic. So another series of stories in early May—titled "SARS Spreading Westward"—looked at public health systems in areas such as the provinces of Shanxi, Sichuan, and Gansu.[14] Intense reader interest prompted *Caijing* to create a special task force of journalists and editors and to publish four special weekly editions focusing on the epidemic.[15] Other business outlets such as *21st Century Business Herald* and *Economic Observer* also followed the disaster. In late April, the *Observer* devoted its entire opinion section to a discussion on the SARS crisis and its deeper causes.[16] The 1 May 2003 issue of the *Herald* published a thirty-page SARS special edition.

Business media were also the first and most thorough in covering avian flu, or H5N1, in 2005. *Caijing* was the first to report the initial suspected human case in China. Two weeks later, the Chinese government confirmed the results. *Caijing*'s stories, such as "A Second and Deadlier SARS?" exposed weaknesses in control of the virus.[17] It was one of China's few objective reports on the epidemic, though publications including *21st Century Business Herald* and *China Business Daily* also reported on the avian flu issue.

In recent years, business journalists have excelled at environmental reporting as well. *Caijing* reporters have traveled along most of the nation's major rivers to document pollution's devastating effects, investigated environmental disasters ranging from a chemical plant explosion to a deadly landslide at a mine tailings site, and interviewed villagers as well as hydrologists with critical comments about the Three Gorges Dam project on the Yangtze River. Environmental stories with and without clear business angles have been fair game for *Caijing* and other members of the pan-financial press.

People often ask how *Caijing* and other independent media avoid the risks of reporting negative news. In fact, it is not so risky. Our judgments are based on cost-benefit analyses: we calculate an issue's importance and then weigh it against the risks of reporting. If the issue seems worthy of a fight, we report. We take risks because important news can have a significant impact on society. The publication of such stories presents the government with a fait accompli that forces them to address the issues. If facts corroborate the story, it is difficult for the government to criticize reporters and editors.

PERSISTENT CHALLENGES

Thanks to a steep learning curve, China's business media have established themselves as forces for social transformation. But serious challenges remain, along with major concerns regarding pressure and interference from the government. While censorship does not play the role it once did, it still affects the manner in which news is reported.

Other obstacles are tied to limited information access. Generally, financial news on securities markets or listed corporations is readily available. But for investigative business-related or official corruption cases, journalists need much more information and run into roadblocks almost every step of the way. Access to court records, police reports, and other government documents is severely limited. In addition, many government officials will not talk to journalists; they often refuse interviews without reason. This hampers reporting and increases the likelihood of inaccurate reporting.

In May 2008, new regulations for government information disclosure took effect. This was a positive move but, not surprisingly, the legislation was exceedingly difficult to craft.[18] The Chinese Academy of Social Sciences started preliminary research on the matter as early as 1999. Even though advocates sought only an administrative regulation with limited power, the legislation was sidelined until the State Council made it a priority in 2006.

In China, press freedom is limited: there is no legal protection for journalists and any journalist can easily be sued for defamation. Moreover, journalists face pressures not only from the government but also from private vested interests and corrupt officials. Through 2007, *Caijing* lost two of four legal cases brought against it. The lack of legal protection for the media seriously deters independent reporting. One study showed that 70 percent of China's media outlets have lost defamation cases, most involving public figures or entities. Moreover, courts are often biased toward hometown officials and business owners and tend to rule against journalists who have published exposés about them.

China's business media also face commercial challenges. They are among the most competitive sectors in the media industry, so a desire for quick money can lead to professional compromises in the newsroom that result in poor quality and inaccurate reporting. Irresponsible journalism is often explained away as a reaction to the rigid ideological training journalists received in the past. Yet it is also because sensational business news has become a hot commodity, leading to inaccuracy as well as media manipulation.

Indeed, commercial pressure has exposed the media to corruption. Besides conventional reporter bribery—payments for travel and news coverage, or even cash packages at press conferences—unprofessional behavior has been rising in the business media. The most egregious are incidents of reporters who blackmail company officials by threatening to publish negative stories.

Competition is a positive factor for an industry if market mechanisms work properly. The best survive and the worst fold. This progression will eventually make journalistic quality and professional integrity top priorities for the business media. But we cannot be completely optimistic under the present institutional arrangements in China, where the media are still subject to a difficult licensing regime. Although thousands of licenses have been issued, new ones are difficult to obtain. Such entry barriers inevitably lead to exit disincentives. Even for an unprofitable magazine or newspaper, a license is a valuable asset. Therefore bankruptcy, mergers, and acquisitions rarely occur, fostering inefficiency and twisted institutional arrangements.

Thus, today's business media landscape is complicated. A past problem was that too few dared to publish something "sharp," that is, politically sensitive news or opinion; but it might be said that today too many write what "looks sharp." In the past, there was a lack of information; the problem now is the lack of credible and accurate information. Today's readers have to be critical and careful when choosing what to read and believe. Overall, China's business media need to improve credibility.

Some publications are working to address these challenges through training and awards programs. *Caijing*'s fellowship program at Peking

University offers the nation's best business journalists a chance to study economics and journalism for three months. And every year, the independent publication *Southern Weekend* invites scholars and professionals to judge its best reports for special awards.

RESPECT FOR INDEPENDENTS

There is reason to be optimistic about what lies ahead for the business media and media as a whole in China. Determined efforts by Chinese journalists to bring greater openness to the markets and society are heartening. And despite some chaos and disappointment, these efforts have laid foundations for a better future for a free press and democracy.

The efforts of journalists have already helped change business behavior in China, especially in corporate and financial arenas. Ten years ago, a negative story about a company might have merely infuriated its top executives, prompting them to seek revenge. Today, these executives may feel embarrassed or angry, but they hesitate to openly condemn the media.

In March 2006, for example, *Caijing* exposed an RMB 200 million loss at the state-owned Bank of China, just as the bank was preparing an initial public offering for the Hong Kong stock exchange. Furthermore, the exposé coincided with an annual politically sensitive meeting of the National People's Congress. Bank officials and supervisors were embarrassed but, significantly, they all tried to respond to reporters rather than criticize *Caijing.* Just as significantly, no one complained to propaganda officials or urged government authorities to punish the media. It was a clear sign of progress.

As a sector, independent business media are also financially successful, offering hope for professional journalism in China. Despite continuing challenges from official competitors, several publications have succeeded in the marketplace. As of this writing, *Caijing* and a couple of other new independent publications have been profitable for several years. The business media's share of the advertising market has held steady for years at around 4 percent, but actual revenues have doubled. The market likes the independents.

China's business media have a promising future as the watchdog of business, financial markets, and society. Business news providers are the vanguard of what promises to be a larger movement toward independent, transparent journalism. The public is now more accepting of the kind of journalism pioneered in China by *Caijing* and other independent publications. As a result, demand will grow for journalism of high caliber. And the public will insist on its right to know what is really happening to the markets, their communities, and their government.

Since writing this chapter, Hu Shuli has resigned from her position as editor of *Caijing*, along with 140 out of 180 newsroom staff, due to conflicts with the publishers over the magazine's development. Hu Shuli and her team have established Caixin Media, which publishes the magazines *Century Weekly* and *China Reform*, operates a news website (www.caing.com) in both Chinese and English, and broadcasts a daily TV show. For the first time in the media industry, Caixin has established an independent Board of Trustees charged with setting editorial principles and appointing the editor in chief.

Notes

1. Sina.com has more than 280 million registered users worldwide, over 900 million daily page views, and is the most recognized Internet brand name in China and among Chinese communities globally; http://corp.sina.com.cn/eng/sina_index_eng.htm. Sohu. com has over 100 million registered users and 700 million daily page views; http://corp. sohu.com/indexcn.shtml. Average daily page views for NetEase in the month ending on 31 December 2008 exceeded 640 million; http://corp.163.com/eng/about/overview.html.

2. The term "designated information disclosure" (*zhiding xinxi pilu*) is used by the CSRC in official correspondence. Furthermore, the CSRC designated eight publications as official outlets for listed companies to disclose information: *China Securities Journal, Shanghai Securities News, Securities Times, Financial News, Securities Daily, China Reform News, China Daily*, and *Capital Week*.

3. Hui Cong D&B Market Research, *Analysis on Advertising of China's Financial Publications* (2005).

4. Ibid.

5. The quotation originates from Ding Wang, founder of *China Business Times*.

6. "Who Is Responsible for Qiong Minyuan *Caijing*, no. 1 (1 April 1998).

7. "The Inside Story of Fund Management," *Caijing*, no. 31 (5 October 2000).

8. The quotation from Wu Jinglian is taken from an interview conducted by an economic affairs television program broadcast by China Central Television, *30-Minute Economic Update*, China Central Television (Beijing: CCTV, 29 October 2000).

9. Zhou Xiaochuan, speech, China Listed Companies Exhibition, Shanghai (2 December 2000).

10. Seen from reports released at the National Meeting on Securities and Futures Regulation, Beijing (15 January 2001).

11. "Ying Guang Xia Trap," *Caijing,* no. 42 (5 August 2001).

12. The Supreme People's Court of PRC, *Announcement on Civil Lawsuits Triggered by False Statement in Securities Market* (15 January 2002).

13. The sentence was passed by Yinchuan Intermediate People's Court in September 2003.

14. "SARS Spreading Westward," *Caijing,* no. 83 (5 May 2003).

15. "Affected Hospital," "Migrant Workers Peril," and "The International and Domestic Affected Areas" are reports from four special weekly issues on SARS published by *Caijing* in May 2003.

16. This refers to the series of articles under the headline "Let Us Commit Ourselves Together," *Economic Observer* (26 April 2003).

17. "Avian Flu: A Second and Deadlier SARS?" *Caijing,* no. 144 (17 October 2005).

18. State Council of the People's Republic of China, *Regulations of the People's Republic of China on Open Government Information* (5 April 2007), effective 1 May 2008.

4

Between Propaganda and Commercials: Chinese Television Today

Miao Di

O N 1 MAY 1958, Beijing Television Station (the precursor of China Central Television, CCTV) made its first trial broadcast. This broadcast marked the birth of the Chinese television broadcast industry. The initial mission of China's television broadcast industry was "to take the responsibility to publicize policy, disseminate knowledge, and enrich people's life by taking advantage of its own strength."[1] In other words, the industry's key purpose was publicizing and disseminating government and Chinese Communist Party (CCP) propaganda.

Even today, an important goal of the national television industry remains to publicize and disseminate political propaganda—a fact reflected in the structure of China's television stations. Beginning in the 1970s, all provinces, as well as some cities and counties, began to set up their own television stations. By the end of 2007, there were 287 television stations in China, a nine-fold increase from 1978.[2] Except for some educational television stations, most are currently classified according to their corresponding administrative level within the Chinese state. Television stations are classified as follows:

- National: CCTV with sixteen channels, including English, Spanish, and French channels
- Provincial: Thirty-one provincial television stations, one in each province, with approximately two hundred channels in total
- Municipal
- County: The central government stopped supporting the creation of new county television stations at the end of the last century, although existing stations are allowed to broadcast their programs as usual.[3]

Thus the Chinese television system closely parallels the administrative apparatus of the government and CCP and ensures that different levels of government have their own propaganda channels.

In theory, all Chinese television stations are operated as part of regional networks. However, to ensure the diversity of regional networks and greater local ownership, television stations at municipal and higher administrative levels commonly broadcast on three to ten separate channels, in effect forming a multichannel system that allows for more localized operation and programming. At present there are 2,262 broadcast channels in China, more than in any other country in the world.[4]

At the end of the 1970s, every Chinese television station was still state controlled and operated. For example, CCTV was only one department of the larger Broadcasting Bureau of the Central Committee of the CCP, internally known as the Television Department. In its earliest days, CCTV did not have its own financial department; finances were instead controlled by the Broadcasting Bureau with all expenses met by the central government. Similarly, local television stations were fully supported by local governments. As a consequence, there was no need to allocate broadcast time for television commercials, and there was no real commercial television.[5]

COMMERCIALIZATION: PRESSURE TO COMPETE

But as China's television broadcast industry began to grow rapidly in the post-Mao era, the high costs of underwriting broadcasters became more apparent to provincial and local governments. Rising operating costs were becoming a burden to government budgets, and it became increasingly impractical to rely solely on central government subsidies to fund China's television stations.

The first set of reform measures to address this problem appeared in 1979. One of these was a fiscal reform initiated by the central government. The Ministry of Finance (MOF) adopted the "budget allocation method" with regard to specific public institutions, a new program meant to encourage them to both increase revenue and reduce expenses. CCTV along with some provincial television stations were the pilot institutions of this program. They began to change the conventional rules of relying on fiscal allocations and made their best effort to become commercially self-sustainable units. Although this policy did not initially attract much attention, it laid the groundwork for the development of China's commercial television industry.

Introduction of Advertising

The transition to a commercial television environment opened the door to new and creative sources of revenue and profit seeking. For example, one of CCTV's first innovations was to set up the China Television Service Company, which facilitated cooperation with overseas companies in producing programs and bringing foreign money into CCTV's coffers.

Of course, the most obvious way to make a profit, especially given the networks' powerful grip on the television market, was to broadcast advertisements during programs. Yet despite its control of the airwaves and a lack of legal restrictions preventing the broadcast of television commercials, CCTV initially faced constraints in this regard. At the time, it seemed clear that television stations at all levels should not broadcast commercials, so as to protect viewers and programming from commercial or cultural contamination.

Nonetheless, in 1979, only three years after the conclusion of the Cultural Revolution decade and at a very difficult time for all of China's industries, the first television commercial was broadcast. Shanghai residents were the first group to profit from television commercials. They suggested that television stations should not "beg with a golden bowl" anymore, and on 25 January 1979, Shanghai Television submitted an advertising business plan to the authorities, which was approved that very night. According to the authorities, the plan conformed to the principle that "all public undertakings should create opportunities to increase revenue."[6] At 3:05 P.M.,

28 January, Chinese New Year's Day, the first commercial was broadcast in Shanghai. It advertised a product called Shen Gui Tonic Wine and lasted for ninety seconds.

This event marked a new era in the history of the Chinese television industry. Gradually, commercials emerged in the programs broadcast at all administrative levels across China. As the number of commercials increased, the purity of the national television organization was somewhat affected, but revenue and funding increased rapidly, as did the development of the television industry itself.

In the 1980s, advertising profits continuously increased until they became the main source of income for television stations. In 1990, CCTV proposed a "budget and responsibility system" to the State Administration of Radio, Film, and Television (SARFT) and the MOF. At the time, the annual revenue from commercial advertising for CCTV was USD 21 million (100 million RMB) and government subsidies were USD 9 million (45 million RMB), making commercial advertising revenue worth more than twice as much as the subsidies.[7]

During the next decade, the Chinese advertising market expanded dramatically. CCTV's revenues from advertising grew from USD 21 million (100 million RMB) at the beginning of the 1990s to more than USD 605 million (5 billion RMB) in 2001.

As central and local television stations began to turn a profit and no longer relied on government subsidies, they were required to remit a portion of their revenues to the government. The amount of these remittances was substantially more than the subsidies that the government provided. The television industry was thus transformed from a net revenue-consuming to a net revenue-producing enterprise.

Take CCTV as an example: the government subsidies it received in 2001 were on the order of USD 1 million (8.27 million RMB), less than one-fifth of what they were ten years earlier. But its advertising revenue was USD 626 million (5.18 billion RMB), which was more than six hundred times as much as its government subsidies.[8] In 2004, the total advertising revenue of Chinese television was USD 3.74 billion (30.9 billion RMB), of which about USD 967 million (8 billion RMB) was earned by CCTV alone and another USD 1.89 billion (15.6 billion RMB) was earned by the provincial television stations. It is estimated that advertising accounts for more than 90 percent of the total revenue of the Chinese television broadcast industry.[9]

Because advertising has become the primary source of revenue for Chinese television, the industry attaches great importance to attracting viewers and winning the contest for viewership ratings. This has led television stations, and even channels and programs within the same station, to adopt new strategies to gain higher ratings in an atmosphere of ferocious competition.

Part of this fierce competition manifests itself in the struggle by local television stations to gain first or exclusive rights to broadcast popular television dramas. Tactics used to gain such an advantage sometimes involve violation of the rules. For example, at the end of 2005, Zhejiang, Anhui, Yunnan, and Shandong satellite TV stations bought nationwide broadcasting rights to *If God Has Affections* (*Tian Ruo You Qing*), a highly anticipated television drama. By contract, these stations were not supposed to broadcast the drama until the Chinese New Year of 2006 to allow local television stations to broadcast the program first. However, seeking to capitalize profits by being first to broadcast the show by satellite throughout the country, these stations ignored the contract and aired it at the end of 2005. As a consequence, the television stations with local broadcast rights suffered heavy losses.[10]

This case illustrates the still nascent institutionalization of broadcast rules and regulations in China. Due to the lack of consolidated legal rules, as well as conflicts of interest among national propaganda organizations, this situation and others like it tend to be settled through mediation alone with minimal compensation to the losers. Consequently such violations are frequent.

Additionally, television broadcasters all feel ratings-related pressures. In recent years CCTV and local stations have all phased out programs with low ratings, even canceling shows with long histories or educational value. For example, *Reading Time*, a talk show on book reviews, was originally launched in 1996 on CCTV 1, the most viewed television channel in China. Later, it was moved to CCTV 10, a science, technology, and education channel, due to its low ratings. In 2004 it was finally phased out because the ratings were judged too low and the broadcast time too valuable. Programs similar to *Reading Time* that air on local stations are also doomed.[11]

Chinese television since the 1990s has made a conscious effort to win broader audiences by introducing new genres from Taiwan, Japan, Europe, and America. This new wave of programming includes more entertainment features that appeal to the public. When compared to shows such as *Reading Time*, the content of these programs might be considered vulgar, but it is also true that today's programs are more entertaining than before.

PROPAGANDA: PRESSURE TO CONFORM

However, the commercialization of China's media is not a one-sided story—the function of Chinese television as a propaganda tool has yet to change. No matter how fierce competition is, Chinese television stations are not solely for-profit organizations. They are still organs of the party-state apparatus. In fact, because of television's great influence—it is the most important source of information for the majority of the population, reaching widely into rural as well as urban areas—it remains the most tightly controlled type of media in China. Propaganda departments at all administrative levels ensure that sensitive news or "vulgar" content, which may be published in books or newspapers (albeit with certain risks), absolutely cannot be broadcast on television.

Take the issue of homosexuality, for example. Many Web sites discuss homosexuality and some professionals have also published books on the topic without repercussions.[12] However, when *Having Good Talks* (*You Hua Hao Shuo*)—a talk show of Hunan Satellite TV—discussed this topic during regular programming, it was ordered to shut down permanently.

China's leaders are undoubtedly concerned with the fact that the majority of China's television viewers are less educated and have lower incomes than newspaper readers and Internet users. Their primary information source is television, as was confirmed by a 2006 survey that found that more people from poor areas rely on television for getting information than any other media source.[13] This is important because China's leaders firmly believe that maintenance of a "harmonious society"—and CCP sovereignty—depends in large part on preventing dissension and unrest among this demographic. Since this critical group mainly relies upon television for information, the CCP feels that is essential to retain tight control over the messages, propaganda, and culture that television programming promotes.

Government control in the age of commercial television means first that television stations must universally follow the government's propaganda guidelines.

Every time the CCP launches a propaganda campaign, all television stations are required to participate fully. For example, in early 2006, Hu Jintao, General Secretary of the CCP, proposed a moral code for Chinese citizens called the Eight Honors and Eight Shames, which was then was promoted everywhere on television, including news programs, talk shows, and entertainment programs. The campaign went so far as to include the contestants in *Super Girl*, an entertainment reality show on Hunan TV, who, without exception, sang the "Eight Honors and Eight Shames Song" in the show's finale.

To cite another example, 1 October 2009 marked the sixtieth anniversary of the founding of the People's Republic of China. As early as that April, television stations of all levels started to set up their propaganda plans. From the beginning of August to the end of September, they primarily broadcast programs featuring the accomplishments of New China and celebration activities. During the eight-day national holiday in October, programming was dominated by news reports about people's celebrations all around the country, TV dramas about the revolutionary days that were produced especially for the anniversary celebration, and a variety of retrospective programs, summarizing every aspect of social development. Even entertainment programs participated in this propaganda campaign.

As a general rule, every station voluntarily meets the national propaganda needs of the central government at various special dates, including the annual meetings of the National People's Congress and the People's Consultative Conference, National Day, and Chinese New Year. On these dates, stations carry programs complimenting the development, social advancement, national stability, and unity of today's China, and they restrict television dramas or news coverage with "negative" content.

In addition, when reporting about very important events, such as natural disasters, social incidents, diplomatic events, and so on, Chinese television stations at different levels must follow the government's propaganda guidelines. Therefore, the television audience never sees conflicting or different attitudes toward such major events.

As these examples indicate, government control over television media has both negative and positive aspects; negative in terms of censoring content deemed vulgar or dangerous, and positive in terms of active guidance of television content.

Guidance comes in the form of the Propaganda Ministry and SARFT documents and instructions, to which all television stations must adhere. For example, a paper issued by the SARFT in 2006 included these injunctions: "Make sure not to import too many foreign movies and TV programs, so that the market of domestic counterparts is prosperous. CCTV and each provincial TV station should only broadcast TV dramas reflecting the bright side of society in the prime time, and those must be of good quality."[14] From a censorship standpoint, inappropriate content is restricted. In 2004 SARFT banned crime dramas during prime time, a move intended to protect young audiences from being negatively affected by the shows' content. Crime dramas that were already made had to be rescheduled to air during late evenings.[15]

In the same year, the Shanghai Administration of Radio, Film, and Television decided that female television anchors should not be allowed to wear provocative outfits. Specifically, they were not allowed to show their belly buttons, and the hems of their skirts could not be higher than 15 cm above their knees. In addition to these broader moral prohibitions, all news content is subject to censorship requirements promulgated by the Central Propaganda Department. For just one example, the 2005 death of Zhao Ziyang, the former party leader who was ousted after the 1989 Tiananmen Square protest, received no coverage on Chinese television stations.

Tools of Government Control

The government has created two types of examination systems to censor the content of television programs. Television dramas and some key shows are subject to the *ex ante* examination system known as Category I. Under Category I, authorities on the administrative level at which a program is to be broadcast examine programs prior to broadcast. While some shows may be banned entirely, the authorities require the majority of programs to be modified. This examination can be very rigorous and can require modifying even tiny details of the program.

One example is *A Chinese Restaurant*, a sitcom produced by the famous Ying Da. Based on the lives of Chinese Americans, the show was finished by Ying Da in early 1999. At the beginning of the Category I examination, the

Beijing Administration of Radio, Film and Television regarded the show as excellent.

However, the U.S. bombing of the Chinese embassy in Belgrade on 7 May 1999 occurred just before the show's initial broadcast. In the aftermath of the bombing, Chinese opinion toward the United States turned very negative. The examiners now thought that particular conversations in the sitcom that discussed the United States as a developed country sounded inappropriate and would be negatively received by Chinese audiences. They therefore ordered that the contents be edited at the last minute. When the sitcom was finally broadcast on 30 June—more than a month after its originally scheduled air date—each episode was cut short by approximately five minutes. Perhaps not surprisingly, the sitcom was weakly received, generating poor reviews and ratings.[16]

Another example is CCTV's Chinese New Year Gala Show. This program is very popular in China, capturing an average of 60 percent of the viewing audience. Although it is an entertainment variety show, it has great influence on the Chinese population and authorities pay close attention to even minor details. Six months before airing, the authorities begin screening it for inappropriate or indecent content. During this rigorous examination, any political satire in the *xiangsheng* (a form of comedy dialogue called cross-talk) and the mini comedies that make up much of the show are removed. As a result, the program as a whole has been considered very boring in recent years. Though it has received harsh criticism from the audience several years in a row, the program bears the heavy weight of unifying and harmonizing the Chinese people, and allowing censorship is the only way for it to continue.

The second system of examination that the government uses to censor content involves an *ex post* review. In this case, authorities watch the programs when broadcast and keep a record of content and public reviews. "Problematic" series that stray too much from acceptable content may receive warnings or even be terminated after broadcast.

Having Good Talks, launched by Hunan Satellite TV in 1999 as mentioned above, is one example of the *ex post* censorship system. Because of the bold topics it covered and its open discussion style, the show had great influence on viewers and became one of the most popular shows on Hunan Satellite TV. However, because the show covered sensitive topics, it was continually warned by the authorities and the producer routinely had to write letters of apology for the show's "mistakes." One of these mistakes was an episode that depicted the lives of retired government officials.[17] Having already aired several such episodes that were condemned as "crossing the line," the show was finally terminated after an episode on Chinese homosexuals. The staff and the production team were then transferred to other sections of the station.

The story of *Having Good Talks* is not an uncommon one: programs frequently receive a "red card" for breaking government regulations, and producers may be demoted or even fired as a result. At the same time, producers often find it difficult to make informed decisions about program content since what is and is not permissible often is not explicitly defined and is in constant flux. Difficult content decisions depend on the producer's experience and political sensibility. As a rule, television producers tend to be conservative and cautious about content regarding social injustice and politics. Indeed, they are not nearly as aggressive as their print counterparts.

As the saying goes, television today is like a double-gendered rooster: propaganda departments want it to crow while finance departments want it to lay eggs. Chinese television producers must meet the censorship and propaganda demands of the government while at the same time they need to win over viewers and generate profits. This dilemma has important implications for the nature of television. Under the often conflicting pressures of propaganda and ratings, Chinese television stations—especially those local stations in fiercely competitive markets—would rather produce "harmless" entertainment programs than make serious programs on politics or social issues.[18] The following examples explain the current situation of Chinese television stations.

The Case of "Super Girl"

In June 2004, the most successful Chinese television program was *Super Girl* (*Chaoji Nusheng*), a knock-off of *American Idol* produced by Hunan TV. Like its American counterpart, *Super Girl* chose finalists by screening candidates located all over the country, and audiences voted for the winners via cell phone text messaging. Due to the extensive screening process, entertaining content, and audience participation, *Super Girl* became very popular nationwide, with an audience of over 400 million viewers. The nationwide rating was over 10 percent during the finals, and total revenue from cellular text messages reached RMB 15 million. The program sponsor, Mengniu Yogurt, also achieved outstanding sales records.[19]

But this widely popular and purely entertainment-oriented program had nothing to do with CCP ideology, a fact that attracted reaction from authorities. In July 2005, CCTV held a seminar on "the vulgar inclination of entertainment programs." Some famous anchors of CCTV and other television professionals participated and gave speeches. At least one participant, some say a high official of SARFT who suggested holding the seminar, criticized *Super Girl*. The seminar also featured criticism of vulgarity in several programs on CCTV, whether mentioning *Super Girl* or not.[20]

Contrary to expectations, after news of the seminar spread the public paid even more attention to *Super Girl*. Many remarks on the Internet and in newspapers and magazines strongly defended the show;[21] people who had not previously heard of the show began to watch. Contrary to the hopes of the authorities, criticism of *Super Girl* seemed to promote rather than deter viewership.

Among the reasons that SARFT disliked *Super Girl* was that it focused solely on entertainment, and that candidates were harshly criticized and even humiliated by judges. As late as 2006, Liu Zhongde, a former Minister of Culture, publicly condemned *Super Girl* as a vulgar program that contaminated an elegant art genre.[22] Another reason SARFT tried to oust *Super Girl* was competition between Hunan TV and CCTV. CCTV, as a central government-owned unit, has to remit a share of its profits to its regulatory organ, SARFT. According to statistics from the National Auditing Bureau, CCTV gave USD 48.3 million (400 million RMB) to SARFT in 2005.[23] This means that SARFT has a proprietary interest in CCTV's revenue. It is not difficult to understand how a successful show like *Super Girl* produced by a rival broadcaster incurred criticism from SARFT. Underlining this relationship, *Dream in China*, a similar show produced by CCTV, won encouragement and support from SARFT.

The case of *Super Girl* also illustrates the growing influence of consumer voices in China. With audiences supporting *Super Girl*, criticism from official media became progressively weaker since such reports might elicit animosity from audiences.

At the same time, however, the case also illustrates the limits of consumer sovereignty in China. Reacting to official criticism, the production team of *Super Girl* made a number of adjustments—to costumes, stage design, the host's style, and the lists of songs—in order to emulate the style of CCTV programs. During the final episode of 2005, the contestants dressed in relatively modest outfits and sang traditional patriotic songs like

I Love China and folk songs like *Clouds Chasing the Moon*. Famous artists were invited to the show and gave positive reviews. It seemed everything was in harmony. Xinhua News Agency reported that *Super Girl*'s finale ended in applause and cheers: "*Super Girl*, with its revolutionary image, serves as a wind direction indicator for the development of domestic entertainment TV programs."[24] In the annual analysis of Chinese television programs and films published by SARFT, *Super Girl* was described as "in the leading place of the reality TV shows in China."

Because of *Super Girl*'s success, the national viewership share of Hunan TV increased 60 percent in 2005 and the station ranked first among all provincial television stations, owning 3.4 percent market share, which is far more than the runner-up, Anhui TV Station (1.3 percent).[25] The top three finalists of the 2005 *Super Girl* all became overnight stars with millions of fans. In the wake of *Super Girl*'s success, CCTV and local television stations decided to produce various reality television programs. At the same time, SARFT issued regulations on all *Super Girl*–inspired programs, including restrictions on the primary screenings of national competitions, the rule that contestants must be over eighteen years old, and the guideline that comments made by the judges should not embarrass the contestants.[26] The last season of *Super Girl* was in 2006.

TELEVISION TABLOID NEWS: ENTERTAINMENT VERSUS NEWS CONTENT

Nonetheless, entertainment programming in China enjoys a relatively free environment compared to news programming. As national enthusiasm for entertainment-oriented programs and competition for ratings grew, news programs began to adapt to market competition. However, local television stations have always lacked reporting resources. Their newscasts mainly cover local officials' activities and achievements. Viewers therefore regard these reports as boring "conference news" or "journals of leaders' activities."

In the late 1990s, local stations occasionally began to report interesting life stories or even civil conflicts that were already widely reported. Some good examples include *Yuanyuan's Talk* of Beijing TV and *Evening News* of Hunan TV. These programs innovated by replacing the commonly known Xinhua style, where anchors read prepared text word for word, with a more natural and amicable "storytelling" style. This kind of tabloid-like television news program became very popular among viewers, especially the less educated demographic.

Just in Nanjing

A leader in this trend is the program *Just in Nanjing* (*Nanjing Lingjuli*), started on Jiangsu provincial TV's Metropolitan Channel in 2002. The program broadcasts live from the studio from 6:50 to 7:50 P.M. every night under the slogan "Just in Nanjing, we are right beside you." The anchor is a bald man named Meng Fei, who has a humorous style and speaks Mandarin mixed with some Nanjing dialect. The show mainly covers what's happening in the streets of Nanjing each day and its journalistic judgment is summarized as "people's content, people's trends, and people's perspectives." Viewers are welcome to submit digital footage for broadcast in the program. Interaction between viewers and the studio is encouraged.

One episode of the hour-long program began with clips of a naked drunken person on a street, which was followed by footage of an incident where two women wrestled with each other after having some trivial argument. The two women and bystanders were then interviewed on the program. Later on, a traffic accident was shown, followed by tips from the anchor on driving safely. The program also covered such general news as incidents of water leakage, blackouts, housing break-ins, unreasonable fines from authorities, or customers' complaints over counterfeit or junk products. In the past, local official media ignored these sorts of problems.

From 1999 to 2001, the average rating for the station's 6:50–7:50 P.M. time slot was only approximately 1.5 percent. Ratings rose considerably after the launch of *Just in Nanjing* to 9.2 percent between January and April 2003. These ratings account for 30.6 percent of all tuned-in viewers. *Just in Nanjing* itself became the most viewed television program in Nanjing, creating astonishing profits for Jiangsu TV. In 2004, advertising revenue from the show was over USD 13.14 (108.8 million RMB). To compare, the 2001 advertising revenue of the entire Jiangsu TV Metropolitan Channel was only USD3.38 (28 million RMB).[27]

The success of *Just in Nanjing* had a huge impact on local television programming throughout the country. In Nanjing alone there are eight imitation programs broadcasting between 6:30 and 8:30 P.M. At present, every local television station in China has at least one so-called citizens' news program. Some of these soft news programs are even more successful than *Just in*

Nanjing. Hangzhou TV's West Lake Pearl Channel created a local news program called *News Talk by Ar Liu Tou.* As is increasingly typical in local soft-news shows, the anchor speaks in the Hangzhou dialect instead of Mandarin. The program was hugely popular in Hangzhou, with ratings as high as 11–12 percent soon after its launch.[28] The audiences for such soft news programs consist largely of women and lower income and education groups.

Citizen News

Programs like *Just in Nanjing* appeal to the public's taste for popular entertainment. But they also reflect the CCP's growing sophistication about the need to improve the persuasiveness of propaganda by making it more realistic. *Just in Nanjing* arrived at the same time as the CCP announced a new propaganda policy. In 2003, CCP General Secretary Hu Jintao announced a doctrine called "three closenesses." This doctrine holds that news reporting and propaganda must be "close to reality, close to livelihood, and close to people." In April 2003, the CCP published "Ideas on Further Improving News Reporting about Conferences and Leaders' Activities," which suggests decreasing the amount of coverage on leaders' activities.[29]

The success of *Just in Nanjing* is therefore not purely a matter of content, but also a matter of timing. The producers of the program acted at the opportune political moment to introduce the concept of citizen news, claiming that it was entirely compatible with the ideas of the CCP.[30] Media researchers and SARFT are in broad agreement that innovations such as citizen news and telling people's stories are in line with the CCP's new propaganda approach.[31] Accordingly, citizen news quickly entered the mainstream as a permissible type of news reporting for local Chinese television stations.

While some communications researchers feel that citizen news helps reinforce the credibility of television news reporting, many believe that it is in fact nothing more than tabloid news on television.[32] Critics assert that it is driven by the lowest common denominator and "vulgar sensationalism." They point out that this kind of program is full of trivial content, such as family disputes, neighbors' arguments, and cases of vandalism and cheating. A further criticism is that truly newsworthy incidents are rarely covered.

Due to the trend of vulgar sensationalism, bloody footage is often shown on *Just in Nanjing.* According to statistics compiled by one researcher, of every twenty pieces of news in each day's program, at least half disclosed unseemly personal details in a "natural way." In one episode, a person brought a television reporter to the site where a couple would be caught having an extramarital affair.[33]

Despite the lack of attention to significant political news and social injustice, citizen news programs do offer the general public a view of real life as well as an opportunity for speaking out. Through such soft news programs, mainstream propaganda and commercial culture are combining to create an atmosphere of caring about people's livelihood and are nurturing a harmonious society. As a result, the censors seem to be tolerant of such programs. By the same token, some audiences have gradually become dissatisfied with such comparatively shallow news coverage and disheartened by their inability to find any serious news reporting on local television.[34]

OFFICIAL TELEVISION NEWS

The opposite of tabloid television news is the official news as represented by *CCTV News* (*Xinwen Lianbo*). *CCTV News* was launched on 1 July 1976, with the original name *CCTV National News* (*Quanguo Dianshi Xinwen Lianbo*), and renamed on New Year's Day 1978. At present, it broadcasts at 7:00 P.M. on CCTV 1. All local television stations are required to broadcast *CCTV News* on their main channels simultaneously. For example, cable television users in the Beijing area receive about fifty channels, but more than thirty of them broadcast *CCTV News* from 7:00 to 7:30 every night. This is one of the main reasons that *CCTV News*'s ratings are consistently high.[35]

The central monopoly on national news coverage is well established. During the Cultural Revolution, the only news resource for the general public was the official media. National news was primarily reported on China National Radio nightly at 8:00 P.M. and many people regularly listened to this program. On 1 September 1982, the central government declared that important news should be released first on *CCTV News* at 7:00 P.M.,[36] a rule that continues today.

With the growing popularity and availability of television sets, more people pay close attention to *CCTV News*. A survey conducted by professor Zhang Tongdao in 1998 showed that only 8.8 percent of interviewees said that they almost never watched *CCTV News*; 30.5 percent watched at least three times per week; 30.7 percent watched at least four or five times per week; and 25.7 percent watched six to seven times per week.[37]

Toeing the CCP Line—Affects on Content

As the primary television propaganda machine, *CCTV News* has always adhered to the principle of publicizing the policies of the CCP and government. Its reports focus on the activities of Chinese leaders and political conferences. They are full of meaningless content and presented in an inflexible style. Information of real interest to most viewers is very rare on *CCTV News.*

Professor Zhou Xiaopu of Renmin University in Beijing studied news coverage of *CCTV News* for one week in November 1999 and one week in November 2000. She found that so-called political news coverage accounted for 52.3 percent of the program. It mostly involved CCP leaders' activities, propaganda campaigns, and political announcements. International news coverage accounted for only 7.3 percent and was placed at the end of the program. In addition, studies have shown that, on average, events are reported on *CCTV News* two days after they actually happen.[38]

Another researcher conducted a study that calculated the frequency of some phrases used in *CCTV News* during one month in 2003. The following tallies reflect the focus on ideological slogans and positive reports:

- "Three represents" was repeated a total of 39,873 times[39]
- "Further studying," 30,799 times
- "Thoroughly understand," 30,087 times
- "Speech on July 1," 29,812 times
- "Crossing era," 23,433 times
- "Grand," 20,134 times
- "Wise," 20,122 times
- "Studied the speech and followed with actions," 8,903 times
- "Harvest," 3,421 times
- "Increase," 3,299 times
- "Out of poverty," 2,982 times
- "Happily," 2,568 times
- "A complete change," 2,447 times
- "Increased since last year," 2,344 times
- "Rise to," 2,157 times

Phrases of import to the public—including "unemployment," "burden on farmers," "students in poverty," "minimum welfare," and so on—were never mentioned.[40]

A snippet from a popular sarcastic poem on the Internet that goes by the name "Dictionary of *CCTV News*" reflects the public's contempt for *CCTV News*:

> All conferences solemnly started and ended with glory;
> All speeches are important, and the applause is warm;
> All the work is finished with success and all the achievements are
>   tremendous;
> All the effort is thorough and efficiency is remarkable; . . .[41]

As the most important disseminator of CCP propaganda, *CCTV News* receives the most rigorous examination from the authorities. At 5:30 P.M. each day, the director and deputy director of CCTV decide what stories are to be broadcast that evening. In the case of particularly significant news, the CCP's Central Committee Secretariat Office makes the decision. This system may explain why *CCTV News* is often slow in reporting important events.[42] The directors and producers of *CCTV News* would rather closely adhere to the principles issued by the Propaganda Department than risk broadcasting the "wrong" reports. This policy has of course hurt CCTV's credibility among audiences, as the following examples illustrate.

CCTV and Reporting of the 2003 SARS Outbreak and September 11 Attacks

At the beginning of 2003, severe acute respiratory syndrome (SARS) began to spread in southern China, causing significant panic among the public. However, *CCTV News* made no mention of this epidemic until an 18 February program in which *CCTV News* claimed that the pathogen behind the epidemic in Guangdong was the bacteria chlamydia. This information was reported despite disagreement from medical experts in Guangdong that was published in local newspapers. The rapid spread of SARS throughout the country was later partially attributed to this incorrect reporting. The authority and influence of *CCTV News* meant that some public health departments and medical institutions were less vigilant then they should have been in combating the spread of SARS.[43]

After the attacks of 11 September 2001, the CCTV News Center realized the importance of the event and immediately submitted a report to the authorities inquiring how they should handle the coverage. However, because there was no prompt feedback or explicit instructions from the regulators, it was not until three hours after the first plane hit the World Trade Center that CCTV 1 gave a report—a little more than one minute in length—on *Midnight News*. Many viewers had already received information on the attack through the Internet or by watching Phoenix Satellite TV (a television station based in Hong Kong that is permitted to broadcast in some parts of the mainland). Even during *CCTV News* the following day, coverage of the event was very brief and placed at the end of the program.

In contrast, Shanghai Satellite TV, Chongqing Satellite TV, and several other local television stations reported in a timely manner on September 11 by using footage from Phoenix Satellite TV. Interestingly, while these television stations received criticism from SARFT, they faced no substantial punishment. The prestige of CCTV was damaged by its noncoverage of this event. Despite backing from the central government and longtime viewer loyalty, *CCTV News* has gradually lost many of its viewers.[44] Today, the majority of *CCTV*'s viewers are middle-aged and senior citizens as well as Chinese officials at all levels.

To improve the network's ratings and attract a younger audience, producers of *CCTV News* have tried to change the show's rigid way of news reading. But such changes have not yet had any substantial impact, and the station's main function as a propaganda machine remains unchanged. The low opinion of CCTV among young people was put into high relief when part of the new CCTV building complex burned in a spectacular fire caused by the staff New Year fireworks display on 9 February 2009. Photos and videos of the fire were immediately posted online, but CCTV itself hardly mentioned it at all on its news report, instead leading with a story about the wildfires in Australia. CCTV was subsequently fiercely ridiculed by Internet public opinion.

CHINESE TELEVISION AS A WATCHDOG

Chinese television has not traditionally fulfilled the role of social and political watchdog. Yet with the deepening of economic reform in China, this situation is changing.

The first television report of the so-called negative side of society ran in September 1979, when *CCTV News* broadcast a story about an event that had happened a few months prior: On 1 May, the Labor Day holiday in China, a journalist had shot footage of more than a dozen official sedans in the parking lot of the Wang Fujing department store. Since almost no Chinese citizens possessed cars of their own at that time, the reporter challenged, "I don't think people parked at Wang Fujing are driving to work on the holiday!"

Though it took officials a few months to review and approve this piece, the belated report still had strong repercussions. CCTV received more than one thousand feedback letters from viewers. In perhaps the first investigative follow-up by a television journalist, Zhang Changming, who reported the story, later went back to the same parking lot and found no cars there.[45]

On 1 April 1994, another step forward came when the program *Focus* (*Jiaodian Fantan*), produced by the News Commentary Department of CCTV, began broadcasting from 7:38 to 7:50 P.M. every night on CCTV 1. This program immediately aroused the public's interest. Its slogan was "reporting current affairs, analyzing news background, investigating hot issues of society, commenting on topics of public interest." As the first program of its kind, *Focus* successfully disclosed the truth about many social problems, such as mandatory fund-raising, business fraud, baby abandonment, homeless children—and even boldly exposed some government officials' wrongdoing and corruption.[46] These reports greatly increased the perceived reliability of television news reporting as a whole. From its inception, many government departments paid great attention to the program and even began working to solve the problems it disclosed. In 1995, *Focus* broadcast a special report called "Illegal Tree-Cutting Has Endangered Rail Lines," about illegal cutting and damage to forests in northern China. The State Council openly praised this show by saying "it is a good report." Later, the Chinese government enacted a national forest preservation policy.

At the end of the same year, a report named "How Did the Reserved Grains Disappear?" aired on *Focus*. The report described how illegally closed barns caused the loss of 850 tons of grain. Three days after the report was broadcast, the mayor of the county in which the closures occurred was fired.[47]

In 2002 the State Council General Office set up a supervision and feedback system to find out whether or not certain problems reported by *Focus* had actually been solved. That year, a total of forty-one incidents reported by *Focus* were checked out by the office.[48] The government's support for *Focus* is reflected in the fact that since it began, every prime minister has visited the set of the show. Owing to its exceptional impact, *Focus* receives a large number of tips from viewers who see it as their best chance to get a problem solved. At the same time, errant local governments have become vigilant as the show has gained in popularity. Once they find out they are being investigated by *Focus*, they usually send a representative to Beijing to speak with officials who are able to stop the report from being broadcast. Consequently, some people say that there are always two waiting lines outside the *Focus* studios: one for people who report problems and the other for people who try to cover them up. Moreover, cover-up appeals have not been completely ineffective; many reports have been suspended for various reasons, and the show has become less hard-hitting in recent years.

The producers and journalists at *Focus* operate with a sense of social responsibility and professionalism, and have made great efforts to carry out their watchdog function. However, the program's producers are still confined by political restrictions. They are frequently not allowed to report on social injustices and crises, let alone cases of corruption and scandals involving higher officials. Each program has to go through several rounds of rigorous examination with the deputy director of CCTV prior to broadcast.

Television experts have closely analyzed the operation of the program. A 2006 article by Ouyang Guozhong reported that about 30 percent of produced reports are not allowed to be broadcast.[49] According to some statistics, investigative reports on *Focus* accounted for approximately 30 percent of the total reports before 2002. The numbers between 1994 and 2001 were 28, 29, 32, 27, 38, 29, 34, and 25 percent, respectively.[50] But the number suddenly dropped to 17 percent in 2002.[51] As an anonymous insider explained, at that time the authorities issued a rule that investigative reporting could be no more than 20 percent of total programming.

Highlighting this change is a book written by the production team of *Focus* called *The Focus Series*.[52] It includes scripts of 581 episodes that aired between 1994 and 1998; of those selected, 396 (68 percent) were investigative reports. From this it is fair to infer that the production team believes that the investigative reports defined the character and value of the show.

While this may be the case, study of this book revealed that in those 396 reports, relatively few big state-owned enterprises or provincial-level officials were investigated. Clearly, few cases involving corruption at high levels were being investigated and disclosed.[53] Not surprisingly, "with the advantages of being a prime time show and the attention from the authorities, this program only reported on small potatoes. It is like killing a mosquito with a gun."[54] The producers of *Focus* have responded by saying that "it is necessary to follow the CCP's propaganda guidelines when we play the role of a watchdog."[55]

Nevertheless, *Focus* is so far the only successful television program in China to fulfill the function of media watchdog. In the late 1990s many provincial and municipal television stations produced similar programs. However, none of these programs lasted long. Either they quickly became something more akin to a general news show, or they disappeared.

CONCLUSION

Television remains the most widespread and influential medium in China today, particularly for poorer and less educated demographics. According to one 2002 survey, 95.8 percent of respondents said that they watched television "often" or "almost every day."[56]

As mentioned above, because propaganda departments exert strict control over Chinese television, official news has been unable to win the public's interest and trust. In addition, fierce competition between television stations is forcing a gradual shift toward simple entertainment of the public. As other more credible news has become available, particularly on the Internet, the younger and more educated public has abandoned television news. This trend has also occurred in many Western countries.

Cui Yongyuan, the most famous talk show host in China, once said, "If Chinese television is public television, it is the dirtiest one; if Chinese television is commercial television, it is the worst one. Our programs are boring and don't make money."[57] Under the pressures of propaganda, ratings, and fierce competition from newspaper, radio, and the Internet, the fortunes of Chinese television have taken an unfavorable turn. However, as an important tool for official propaganda and an industry with substantial annual advertising revenue, Chinese television is still a giant and will continue to have great influence for many years to come.

1. Quoted from the report submitted by the Central Broadcasting Bureau to the CCP Central Committee on 29 April 1958 in Yang Weiguang, *The History of CCTV's Development* (Beijing: Beijing Press, 1998), p. 5.

2. *Qiushi Online*, no. 1 (9 January 2009).

3. *Nan Fang Dian Shi Xue Kan*, no. 5 (2003): pp. 43, 47.

4. Zhang Haichao, *The Eye Is the King* (n.p.: Hua Xia Press, 2005), p. 85.

5. Yang, *History of CCTV's Development*, p. 138.

6. Hu Ruining, *Secrets of the War of Commercials* (n.p.: Nan Hai Press, 1994), p. 243.

7. Yang, *History of CCTV's Development*, p. 747.

8. *The Yearbook of CCTV, 2002* (Beijing: China Television and Broadcast Press, 2002), p. 413; and Yang, *History of CCTV's Development*, p. 750.

9. Xie Gengyun and Dang Fangli, "Current Competition Status of Chinese TV Commercial," *Xin Wen Jie*, no. 1 (2005): p. 4.

10. Liu Zai Xing, "The New Rules of TV Drama," *Shi Chang Guang Cha·Mei Jie*, no. 2 (2006): pp. 22–23.

11. Wei Xiying, "Why CCTV's Reading Time Is Gone," *Zhong Hua Du Shu Bao*, 29 October 2004.

12. One example is *Subculture of Homosexuals*, which depicts the status of homosexual people in China. Li Yinhe, *Subculture of Homosexuals* (n.p.: China Today Press, 1998).

13. Duan Peng, "An Evidential Study of Innovations on Diffusion Theory—a Survey on Disseminating Innovative Knowledge and Technology in Poor Rural Areas in China," *Dang Dai Chuan Bo*, no. 3 (2006): pp. 49–53.

14. *Zhong Guo Guang Bo Ying Shi*, no. 1 (March 2006): p. 19.

15. "SARFT's Ten-Point Ban Received Various Comments," *Beijing Times*, 14 May 2004.

16. Qu Jing Chun, *Comparative Studies of Chinese TV Drama and American TV Drama* (Shanghai: San Lian Press, 2005), pp. 33–34.

17. The show quoted someone saying that "retired government officials are those who shed blood in the revolutionary era; who shed sweat in constructional era and who shed saliva nowadays (meaning being jealous about the wealth of others)."

18. The general secretary of CPC, Hu Jintao, said in an address to CCTV soon after the 2002 Sixteenth Party Congress that "as long as a TV program is harmless, it is a good one." Du Ping, "Journalistic Reform Got a Green Light from Zhongnanhai," *Xinjiapo Zaobao* [*Singapore Morning Post*], 3 April 2003.

19. Huang Zhenwei, "Secrets of Fortune behind *Super Girl*," *Caijing Times*, 13 August 2005.

20. *Interviewing the Focused*, 1 August 2005.

21. Chang Ping, "*Super Girl* Makes People Happy," *Beijing News*, 25 August 2005; "A Citizens' Celebration Show," *Southern Metro Daily*, 25 August 2005.

22. Coverage in *China Times*, 21 April 2006; and *Fa Zhi Wan Bao*, 29 April 2006.

23. Shen Jianli, "SARFT Stops Taking CCTV's Revenue," *Beijing News*, 30 March 2006.

24. Xinhua News Agency, 26 August 2005.

25. "The Rating Ranks of National Satellite TV in 2005," *Zhong Guo Guang Bo Ying Shi*, no. 1 (March 2006): p. 33.

26. Coverage in *Hua Shang Bao*, 15 March 2006.

27. Xie Gengyun and Zhou Hongfeng, "Report on Competitions of Chinese TV News Programs," *Shi Ting Jie*, no. 1 (2005): p. 9.

28. Zhang Jianmin, "Strategy of TV News Reporting—Analysis of Production Theory of News Talk by Ar Liu Tou," *Zhong Guo Bang Bo Dian Shi Xue Kan*, no. 12 (2006): p. 34.

29. Chen Lidan, "Hu Jintao's Speeches on Propaganda Principles and Respect for Rules of Propaganda," *Jin Chuan Mei*, no. 3 (2006): p. 15; *Selections of Key Documents since CPC's 16th Congress* (Beijing: Renmin Press, 2005), pp. 288–290.

30. Li Xiang was quoted as saying, "*Just in Nanjing* doesn't belong to political news, neither can I say it falls in the category of social news." In Wang Yonggang, "Let *Just in Nanjing* Be the First Brand Name of News Programs—an Exclusive Interview with Mr. Li Xiang, Director of Jiangsu TV's Metro Channel," *Jiang Nan Shi Bao*, 1 January 2004.

31. Chen Lidan, "Hu Jintao's Speeches on Propaganda Principles and Respect for Rules of Propaganda," *Jin Chuan Mei*, no. 3 (2006): p. 16.

32. Tan Yunming and Yi Qianliang, "People's News: Chinese TV Programs Seeking Localization," *Dang Dai Chuan Bo*, no. 2 (2006): p. 32.

33. Li Jianqiu, "Analysis on Some Mistakes of People's News TV Programs," *Dang Dai Chuan Bo*, no. 6 (2005): p. 41.

34. Chen Fuqing and Zhou Jiong, *Ideology and Mainstream Media Constructing—Chinese People's News under the New Ideology*, no. 7 (2004): p. 59.

35. According to a market survey by CSM Media Research, from January to May 2006, the average rating of *CCTV News* was 5.6 percent in thirty-five major cities, which means 72.8 million people were watching this program each day. Guo Li, "Is CCTV News Changing?" *Nan Fang Zhou Mo [Southern Weekend]*, 15 June 2006.

36. *The Firsts in CCTV and How CCTV Changes Over Time, 1958–2003* (Beijing: Dong Fang Press, 2003), p. 25.

37. Zhang Tongdao, *Television Viewers: Chinese Television Audiences Investigation* (Hefei: Anhui Education Press, 2003), p. 23.

38. Zhou Xiaopu and Xu Fujian, "Studies on CCTV News," *Xian Dai Chuan Bo*, no. 3 (2002): p. 24.

39. A political slogan created by former CCP General Secretary Jiang Zemin.

40. "Statistics on Disasters in China," www.nptc.edu.cn/gljg/zhongwen/bianjixue/.

41. If you search "Dictionary of CCTV News" on a Chinese search engine called Baidu, at least 55,000 related Web pages would appear in the results.

42. Guo Li, "Is CCTV News Changing?" *Nan Fang Zhou Mo [Southern Weekend]*, 15 June 2006.

43. Liao Huailing, "Honesty Has Succeeded—Debates over SARS Pathogen," *Nan Feng Chuang*, last issue of May 2003, p. 19.

44. Guo Li, "Is CCTV News Changing?"

45. Miao Di and Fan Zhongli, *Television Culture Studies* (Beijing: Beijing Broadcast College Press, 1997), p. 289.

46. Sun Kewen, *Behind Focus* (Shanghai: San Lian Press, 1997), pp. 393–396.

47. Ibid., p. 101.

48. Liu Chang, "Things That You Don't Know about *Focus*," *China Youth Daily*, 29 March 2004.

49. Ouyang Guozhong, *Focus* (Guangzhou: Nanfang Daily Press, 2006), pp. 37, 48.

50. Yu Weili, *Quantitative Analysis of Focus's Investigative Reports*, no. 9 (2002): p. 45.

51. Liu Chang, "Things That You Don't Know about *Focus*."

52. *The Focus Series* (Beijing: China University of Politics and Law Press, 1999).

53. Ke Huixin, *Statistics in Communications* (Beijing: Beijing Broadcast College Press, 2003), pp. 500–504.

54. Liu Chang, "Things That You Don't Know about *Focus*."

55. Liang Jianzeng, "Our Key to Success Is Choosing Right Topics," *Dian Shi Yan Jiu* [*Television Research*], no. 5 (2004): p. 10.

56. The figures from the study were reported by Xinhua News Agency, Beijing, 19 December 2002 (reporters: Qin Jie, Shen Lutao).

57. Yi Lijing, "An Exclusive Interview with Cui Yongyuan: I Have Something to Say," *Nan Fang Ren Wu Zhou Kan*, no. 15 (2005): p. 25.

5

Environmental Journalism
in China

Zhan Jiang

A FTER THIRTY YEARS of market reforms and development, China's media have experienced big changes in terms of communication models, management philosophy, and ownership. But more important than that, these changes have also altered the way in which the government, media, and public interact. Environmental journalism provides a good window for understanding how the relationship between these actors is changing. In particular, it highlights how an alliance between the media and public intellectuals can exert pressure on the government.

DEVELOPMENT, REFORM, AND AN EVOLVING
RELATIONSHIP

To offer a more complete picture of how the relationship between the Chinese state and media has changed, it is worth considering how reform and development have led to the expansion in the number, variety, and ownership of media outlets.

China presently has over 3,000 television stations with more than 1 billion viewers, 1,943 newspapers with more than 100 million readers, 9,549 magazines, and 384 million Netizens. In addition to traditional media owned by the Chinese Communist Party (CCP), citizens now have access to many commercial newspapers, magazines, and radio and television stations, as well as Web-based media. It is in this environment that media outlets now find themselves competing for attention from the world's largest domestic audience.

Although even commercial print media are still primarily CCP or government owned, these publications cannot rely on subsidies for their continued operation; their operations are subject to market logic. They must provide content that can attract audiences, sell subscriptions, and ultimately turn a profit. Ownership of Web-based media is more diverse: portals such as Sina.com, Sohu.com, QQ.com, and 163.com are publicly traded with private majority shareholders. Even the official Web site of *People's Daily* (people.com.cn) has received investment by Australian-born international media mogul Rupert Murdoch. As public companies, these online media outlets are subject to even stronger market pressures than their print counterparts.

Media outlets have adjusted to this new competitive environment where providing the old style of content is no longer an option. The state advocacy system has changed to one with an equal emphasis on advocacy and information; commentary-oriented journalism has gradually shifted to information-oriented journalism; traditional propaganda writing styles are declining; international-style investigative reporting and features are booming; and as opinion writing dominated by the official ideology is fading away, opinion writing with pluralistic values and perspectives is flourishing.[1]

Public Intellectuals and the Public Sphere

Yet in the evolving relationship between the state and the media, a third actor needs to be mentioned: the public. Today's Chinese public is becoming more aware and assertive in claiming their civil rights. Moreover, individual citizens are seeking ways to use the emerging public sphere to criticize and condemn injustice and scandals. While the watchdog journalism of the past was conducted by traditional, state-owned media organizations and professionals, the spread of the Internet and the growth of commercial media have given individual citizens or "public intellectuals" opportunities to shed light on abuses perpetrated by powerful interests and to set the agenda for traditional media.

According to the classic theory of civil society, between the state and family exists an intermediate community space: the public sphere. It is in this sphere that people interact with the state. China has not yet developed a true civil society in the sense of being based on associations wholly independent of the state. Nevertheless, with the retreat of the state from many aspects of life during the reform era, space for a public sphere has begun to open.

Socially active citizens in such developed metropolitan areas as Beijing and Guangzhou have begun to step into this space. This small but growing group of socially active citizens, or public intellectuals, is concerned with the rule of law, human rights, and social justice. These citizens strive to set up nongovernmental organizations (NGOs) and to engage in the criticism of specific phenomena and events. In these endeavors, they have found the use of modern media essential.

Although the constitution of the People's Republic of China formally protects the right to associate, it remains difficult for citizens to legally establish NGOs. One result is a lack of accurate information on how many environmental NGOs exist. According to available figures, at present there are more than 3,500 environmental NGOs in China. Yet the accuracy of these figures is questionable; for as many environmental NGOs as are registered with and recognized by the state, probably as many remain unregistered and unrecognized.

Despite registration requirements, Chinese authorities do seem to be more lenient in granting legal status to NGOs that advocate environmental protection and awareness than to those that advocate for other social causes. The first legal environmental NGO was registered on 18 April 1991 in Panjin City, Liaoning Province. Called the Society for Protecting Black-Beaked Gulls, this NGO was actually founded by a journalist, Liu Detian of the *Panjin Daily News*. While the stated focus of the society was narrow, its founding was nonetheless an important milestone in the development of Chinese civil society.

Since the establishment of the Society for Protecting Black-Beaked Gulls, other public intellectuals have gone on to found similar organizations that advocate environmental protection and awareness. For example, in 1994 Liang Congjie, Yang Dongping, and Liang Xiaoyan co-founded the Friends of Nature in Beijing. As a longtime member of the Standing Committee of the Chinese People's Political Consultative Conference (CPPCC) and a grandson of Liang Qichao, a famous reformist in the late Qing Dynasty, Liang is the very image of a public intellectual. At the sessions of the CPPCC in 1995 and again in 1996, Liang submitted proposals suggesting the relocation of Beijing-based Capital Iron and Steel Group in order to reduce air and water pollution in the city. The Friends of Nature also went on to head up a major media campaign against the illegal hunting of endangered Tibetan antelope for the cashmere trade. In this campaign, the Friends were able to draw attention and pledges of support from international figures such as then British Prime Minister Tony Blair.

While none of three co-founders of the Friends of Nature have backgrounds in journalism, the founders of other prominent environmental NGOs, such as Liao Xiaoyi of Global Village and Wang Yongchen of Green Earth, do have backgrounds in journalism. From their beginnings, these NGOs have paid attention to actively promoting environmental protection and influencing elite opinion through the use of television, newspapers, and Web sites.

Both convenient and anonymous, the Web provides a virtual space for sharing information and forming public opinion through Web logs and forums. By building public support for environmental protection, public intellectuals use the Web to set the agenda for the traditional media's coverage of environmental issues.[2] Always hungry for stories that will draw large audiences in an ever more competitive market, the Chinese media take cues from these public intellectuals to expose the abuses of powerful interests.

The opinion pages of commercial newspapers and current affairs magazines perform a similar function. These media attract free thinkers whose critiques of powerful interests activate public participation led by the elite. Public intellectuals have gradually forged an informal alliance with the market-oriented and Web-based media. Through their activities, these individuals can bring pressure on state officials to change policy and are capable of constraining the government with their criticisms.

Public Intellectuals and the Nu River Hydroelectric Project

Consider the following example of public intellectuals using media to raise awareness of environmental concerns and influencing policy decisions despite powerful countervailing interests. At the first China Environmental

Cultural Promotion Association (CECPA) panel held on 3 September 2003 and sponsored by the State Environmental Protection Administration (SEPA), Wang Yongchen of Green Earth, Professor He Daming of Yunnan University, and other environmental experts voiced strong protest against the proposed construction of hydroelectric dams on the Nu River in Yunnan Province. A dozen journalists who were invited by Wang Yongchen were also present at the forum. This was the first time the media and an NGO had participated in a government-sponsored seminar on water resources.

On 11 September 2003, reporter Zhao Yongxin of the *People's Daily* first reported on the controversy. Following the second session of the CECPA on 25 October 2003, Wang Yongchen collected the signatures of sixty-two prominent activists from the arts, sciences, media, and other environmental NGOs to protest proposed construction plans. In March 2004, they submitted two motions protesting the building of dams to the committee members of CPPCC and the deputies of the National People's Congress. At the request of the Friends of Nature, nearly a hundred activists and sixty-one NGOs signed a petition letter. Although a long time in coming, the permanent suspension of the proposed project was assured by Premier Wen Jiabao in February 2009.

Make no mistake: traditional authoritarianism has left a deep imprint on the relationship between the government and the media. Branches of the CCP and government retain the ability to control and limit reporting of environmental issues. It is nonetheless undeniable that market-oriented and Web-based media have boosted the growth of civil society in China.

CHINA'S DEVELOPMENT, ENVIRONMENTAL COSTS, AND THE PUBLIC SPHERE

How does change in the relationship between the government, media, and the public relate to environmental issues? The simplest answer is that the alliance between public intellectuals and the new media has begun to exert pressure on government and business interests to address the adverse environmental effects of economic growth. The following section lays out some of the damage three decades of breakneck growth have done to China's environment and why containing the cost of this damage is difficult.

The past three decades of rapid industrial growth have come at a substantial cost to the Chinese environment, a cost that is being passed on to Chinese citizens. In 2006, Vice Minister Pan Yue of China's Ministry of Environmental Protection (MEP), which before 2008 was SEPA, attested that one-third of Chinese land has been polluted by acid rain and that two-fifths of China's major water sources contain "bad water." This means that more than 300 million rural residents are without clean drinking water. China is home to five of the ten most polluted cities in the world. From an economic perspective, it is estimated that pollution caused China to suffer losses of RMB 511.8 billion (USD 64 billion, or 3 percent of GDP) in 2004 alone.[3]

While the costs of pollution may be counted in dollars, they may also be counted in lives. For example, a report by the World Bank suggests that each year half a million Chinese citizens die prematurely as a result of air and other forms of pollution.[4] Furthermore, in a 2008 joint report by the Ministry of Health and the Ministry of Science and Technology, the Chinese government recognized that cancer has become one of the leading killers of China's rural residents: in the past thirty years, rates of lung and breast cancer have increased 465 percent and 95 percent, respectively. This same report goes on to predict that the number of cancer-related deaths could double in next twenty years.

While increased cancer rates could partially be the result of better detection by public health authorities or different lifestyle choices by citizens, the clustering of similar cases within certain towns and villages— so-called villages of cancers and villages of abnormal illnesses—suggests that the causal factors are environmental. Since 2002, such cases have begun to appear frequently in coastal areas that have seen the most rapid growth, such as Guangdong, Zhejiang, and Jiangsu provinces. Worse is that since 2007, there has been a new trend of the spread of such cases to inland provinces.

Although the causal link between environmental pollution and mortality remains unclear, the link between manmade environmental crises and mortality is more readily apparent. In one example, on 23 December 2003 an oil well owned by the East Sichuan Oil Drilling Company burst in Chongqing Province. As a direct result, 243 villagers died. They had been living less than 100 meters from the well. In another example, in November 2005, a benzene plant owned by the Jilin Petrochemical Company, a division of the China National Petroleum Company (SINOPEC), exploded. A large amount of benzene flooded into the Songhua River, and water rationing had to be imposed in downstream cities to keep citizens from drinking contaminated water.

The costs of mass pollution and manmade environmental crises can also be counted in terms of the important goal of social stability. Protests or "mass incidents" directed specifically against local environmental policies and officials are on the rise and represent an immediate and dynamic political challenge.[5] When the public becomes aware of the negligence and corruption that are often behind manmade environmental crises, it adds a political component to what is already a significant health problem. Zhou Shengxian, minister and secretary for the Party Leading Group for the MEP, has stated that "in recent years, the number of mass incidents caused by environmental problems has been increasing at a rate of 29 percent each year." In 2005 alone, 51,000 environmental conflicts were reported nationwide.[6]

Local Negligence, Collusion, and Manmade Environmental Disasters

Local governments show little regard for containing the environmental costs of economic growth and have almost no incentive to do so. It is costly for local officials to implement environmental protection policies because they may slow down growth. Since local growth is tied to promotions for local officials in China, these officials have strong motivation to shirk their environmental responsibilities.

In more extreme cases, the failure of local officials to implement environmental protection policies stems from corrupt or collusive arrangements between local government and business interests. "Comrades inside a trench" is how Zhang Qi, the executive director of the China Development Institute, characterized the relationship between local government officials and the managers of factories located on the banks of the Yangtze.

These types of situations draw the most anger from the Chinese public. As one environmental protester from Xinchang, Zhejiang Province, expressed, protesting "is the only way to solve problems like ours. . . . If you go to see the mayor or some city official, they just take your money and do nothing."[7]

Local officials are charged with implementing the environmental protection policies adopted by the CCP and central government, but it is difficult for the center to monitor implementation by local officials. In August 2006, an official SEPA spokesman acknowledged that there was no comprehensive investigation of "villages of cancers," and no real investigations of many environmental accidents. This official told the media that it was SEPA's ignorance of the basic situation and lack of data on environmental pollution that made it difficult to evaluate the relationship between China's ecology and human health.

A CASE STUDY IN ENVIRONMENTAL JOURNALISM: THE SONGHUA INCIDENT

The November 2005 Songhua River incident illustrates how the government, media, and public interact when faced with environmental crises that could provoke threats to social stability. Not only does it reflect the severity of China's environmental problems, but it also epitomizes the characteristics of Chinese media in environmental advocacy and reporting.

On 13 November 2005, an industrial accident occurred in which one of Jilin Petrochemical Company's factories exploded. According to official reports, five people died in the explosion. During the fire, a large amount of poisonous liquid benzene—which had not been burned or had been inadequately burned—flowed directly into the Songhua River. The leaked chemicals included benzene, its intermediate product, nitrobenzene, and the finished product, aniline, all of which are extremely harmful to the human body. Benzene has been known to cause leukemia and is a potential cause of cancer in blood-forming organs.

Over 3 million people get their drinking water downstream from the chemical plant. Following the explosion, the large northern city of Harbin in Heilongjiang Province had to cut its water supply for five days. This in turn led to a collective panic involving millions of people. A water pollution disaster of this magnitude had never happened before in China. To further complicate matters, the Songhua River merges into the Heilongjiang River, which flows into Russian territory. With the contaminated water threatening millions of Russians, the incident became a significant diplomatic crisis as well.

After the explosion of the plant in Jilin, the Songhua incident drew the immediate attention of media from all over the country. A slew of reporters rushed into Jilin. In addition to journalists from the official Xinhua News Agency, *People's Daily*, and *China Youth Daily*, journalists from market-oriented media gathered in Heilongjiang from all corners of China in direct violation of the Central Propaganda Department's ban on cross-regional oversight (*yidi jiandu*).

At the same time, China's official news control machine also sped into gear. The nationally influential, Guangdong-based *Southern Weekend* was among the first publications to investigate the explosion, but when the Jilin CCP Propaganda Department asked its counterpart in Guangdong to cover up the story, the *Southern Weekend* article was killed. As a result of a comprehensive local cover-up, no news agency was allowed to publish a timely or comprehensive report about the incident. On 26 November, nearly two weeks after the explosion, the Central Propaganda Department issued instructions to the media prohibiting any retrospective reports or any pieces attributing responsibility for the incident. The directive also requested that central news agencies cut their reports and asked local media to pull back their reporters. Most of the local media who had rushed to Heilongjiang were shut out, and the report of the centrally controlled Xinhua News Agency became, for a while at least, the sole, standard account of the incident.

On 28 November, Xinhua published a report titled "What Did We Learn during the Time without Water?" The report concluded that the Harbin residents "learned to calm down, to appreciate, and to understand." This article reported the line of the Central Propaganda Department, which asked the public to appreciate what the government had done to remedy the situation and to understand the difficulties facing the government. The article implied that the incident was in some respects a good thing because it helped residents better understand the government's predicament and appreciate its efforts. The article failed to address such key issues as why the incident happened and how such events might be prevented in the future. Useful information, accountability, and constructive analysis all were lacking.

The Media Fight Back

In the face of a political blockade, China's media and public intellectuals did not easily give up on the Songhua incident. For example, *Southern Weekend* sent two reporters to follow up on its original investigation, but was again forced to pull back from publishing articles. Given the hindrances facing the print media, the Web filled in as a crucial medium for both circumventing and exposing the cover-up. On 24 November, two days before the Propaganda Department's announcement of tightening control over media coverage, local reporters in Harbin sent news of the incident to *Asian Weekly* in Hong Kong. Soon, news of both the Songhua incident and the subsequent cover-up led by the provincial government were discovered and exposed on the Web. Some local reporters also posted observations on their personal blogs.

At the same time, the well-known commercial magazine *Caijing*, then led by crusading editor Hu Shuli, ignored the Propaganda Department's announcement and published an investigative report. The report explicitly stated, "In the first ten days after the occurrence of the big pollution incident, the truth was controlled by a few people," and also described what it characterized as the Jilin provincial government's "beggar-thy-neighbor" actions, conducted without care for the potential damage to those located downstream of Jilin.

Interestingly, *Caijing* was not significantly penalized for publishing the investigative report. This fact is indicative of two dynamics that shape China's media control regime. The first involves the dual nature of the media's watchdog function over local political elites and policies. While the Central Propaganda Department strictly prohibits independent media from using their own reports on nationally sensitive issues, it is often more flexible toward the media's monitoring of other issues directly concerning the public interest and social stability, including environmental problems. Though the Central Propaganda Department may still issue prohibitions and reserves the right to shut down coverage as it chooses, treatment varies from case to case. As a general rule, the central government has an interest in reducing the information gap between the center and localities regarding potentially volatile problems that result from negligence by local officials.

New media outlets like the Web have enhanced the central government's ability to detect local environmental crises and manage social unrest. As the *International Herald Tribune* reported in 2005, "Chen Xiwen, an economics vice minister who oversees agricultural affairs, saluted the Internet's role in allowing central government authorities to learn of unrest more quickly and praised demonstrating farmers for 'knowing how to protect their rights.'"[8]

The second dynamic stems from the differences in the intensity of oversight of official versus commercial media. For media that are part of official media groups like *Southern Weekend*, the censorship rules are expected to be followed strictly; but for more independent commercial media, like *Caijing*, the limits are more difficult to identify. Employees of official media outlets risk losing their salaries, health insurance, housing subsidies, and other benefits if they defy orders from the censors. Commercial reporters who earn their living independently are often willing to take more chances.

Professionalism in the Media

Despite the attempted cover-up of the Songhua incident, the surge of news interest described above brought pressure on the central government. In response, they dispatched an investigation team to Heilongjiang. Upon the arrival of the inspection team, the governor of Heilongjiang acknowledged the mistakes of initially lying about the incident and its causes and harmful effects. On 2 December 2005, China's authorities also announced the resignation of the head of SEPA, Xie Zhenhua, who became the highest ranked Chinese official to be fired due to an environmental disaster.

Yet this resignation was little more than a token gesture: Xie Zhenhua was reappointed as vice minister of the National Development Planning Commission in January 2007 and also serves as China's international climate change negotiator. Furthermore, charges were never brought against Jilin Petrochemical Company's parent company, SINOPEC, the primarily responsible party, nor were charges raised against the Jilin provincial government, which had allowed the factory to be built on the banks of the Songhua River. Moreover, there does not appear to be a viable long-term solution for preventing such crises from happening again. Firing the culprits gives the illusion of accountability, but leaves the political and incentive structures that bring about these crises in place.

The media and civil society can better protect citizens through raising awareness and coverage of potential environmental crises. An often overlooked aspect of media professionalism is the obligation of local media to find and report potential health risks before disaster strikes. Prior to such disasters as that at the Jilin Petrochemical Company, local journalists should have a clear perception of the potential pollution risks caused by a poorly managed petrochemical plant situated alarmingly close to a water source like the Songhua River. Local media who have done their homework could produce preliminary investigative reports concerning what would happen were an accident to actually take place in the plant. This may in turn influence local residents to try to prevent a problem before it arises.

To summarize, while the quantity of reports on the Songhua incident was ample, the quality of investigative reporting was largely poor. Many reports simply repeated each other. Incredibly, some reporters even reprinted the Jilin Petrochemical Company's claims that leaked benzene, after combustion, is entirely harmless. For China's media to become formidable and influential, more attention must be paid to accurate and analytical reporting, rather than the necessity to beat competitors by reporting on hot button issues as spectacularly and quickly as possible.

CONCLUSION

Since 1979, reform and development have changed how the government, media, and public interact. And nowhere is this clearer than in the realm of environmental journalism. Due to the rise of commercial and Web-based media as well as the rise of a civil society, environmental problems in China have more frequently become breaking news in recent years. This is putting pressure on the government to be more responsive to public concerns about the environment when formulating policy.

How will this relationship continue to evolve in the coming decades and how will it affect environmental policy? In September 2009, Chinese President Hu Jintao promised at the UN Summit on Climate Change that by 2020 China would cut emissions from 2005 levels by "a notable margin." On 26 November, the government released this target: reductions in the intensity of carbon dioxide emissions per unit of GDP in 2020 by 40 to 45 percent compared with the 2005 levels. Hu's promise appears to have been in response not just to international but also to domestic voices. While China's civil society as a whole remains weak and the media are still subject to government controls, together they are raising the priority of environmental policy and nudging the government in a more environmentally conscious direction.

Notes

1. Zhan Jiang, "Watchdog Journalism in China," *Young Journalist* (Jinan), November 2009.

2. Huang Dan, "The Public Space of China's Media and Its Future," *Communication and Society* (Hong Kong), Vol. 6, 2008.

3. "Environmental Pollution Costs China 511.8 Billion Yuan in 2004," *Xinhua General News Service*, 7 September 2006.

4. World Bank, Rural Development, Natural Resource and Environmental Management Unit, *Cost of Pollution in China: Economic Estimates of Physical Damages* (Washington DC, 2007), pp. 19–32.

5. "China Focus: 'Mass Incidents' on Rise as Environment Deteriorates: Official," *Xinhua General News Service*, 5 July 2007.

6. Excerpt from Sina.com posting of "Investigating China's Water Pollution: The Disasters Are Not Natural, but Manmade," *China Digital Times*, excerpt posted on 15 August 2007, http://chinadigitaltimes.net/2007/08/investigating-chinas-water-pollution-the-disasters-are-not-natural-but-manmade-sinacom/ (accessed 19 March 2009). The article was originally printed in the biweekly magazine *Observation and Reflection*, published by the Academy of Social Sciences of Zhejiang Province. Excerpts translated by *China Digital Times*.

7. Howard W. French, "Protesters in China Get Angrier and Bolder," *International Herald Tribune*, 20 July 2005, http://www.iht.com/articles/2005/07/19/news/china.php.

8. Ibid.

6

Engineering Human Souls: The Development of Chinese Military Journalism and the Emerging Defense Media Market

Tai Ming Cheung

WHEN CHINA SHOWED off its newest generations of tanks, missiles, and aircraft at the sixtieth anniversary National Day parade in October 2009, it was a tightly choreographed display designed to impress the hundreds of millions of Chinese citizens watching on live television but not alarm the rest of the world. To achieve this delicate balance, the propaganda maestros in the People's Liberation Army (PLA) conducted an intensive charm offensive to promote the message that its warriors had the means and will to defend the country's sovereignty and stability but were politically subservient and did not pose an expansionist threat to China's neighbors. PLA officers appeared on television shows and participated in online chats; military bases were opened to foreign journalists; and media outfits with close military ties were given nuggets of information.

This carefully scripted media management of the National Day parade shows the central role that the military media and affiliated civilian defense news apparatuses play in defining the relationship and place of the military in contemporary Chinese politics and society. This is a difficult and complex undertaking because of the inherent conflicts that arise when the insular and tradition-bound military seeks to adapt to a modern and more permissive environment. These dueling tensions were not far from the surface when Hu Jintao, the Chinese Communist Party (CCP) General Secretary and Chairman of the Central Military Commission (CMC), paid a visit to the *Liberation Army Daily* (LAD), *Jiefangjun Bao*, the PLA's flagship publication and official mouthpiece, in 2006 to celebrate its fiftieth anniversary. To make clear what their primary duties were, Hu told the assembled military journalists and propaganda workers that their overriding responsibility was to serve as a loyal and effective conduit of propaganda for the CCP and PLA leaderships. A subsequent LAD editorial pointed out that the principle of "running the newspaper as politicians" should be firmly upheld.[1]

Fulfilling their role as propagandists and remaining relevant in the information age is a daunting challenge for the country's uniformed scribes. The rise of the market economy and of a more open and connected society has increased the demand for more substantive news on military affairs. The PLA press and propaganda apparatus has made some efforts to liven up and expand its reporting to meet these new requirements, and the military has assisted by providing exclusive information, such as the participation of female pilots in the aerial fly-past in the October 2009 parade. An especially important innovation has been to broaden the appeal and outreach of the military media beyond their traditional military audience to the rest of the population through television broadcasting, the Internet, and regular press briefings by PLA spokespeople. But these moves have fallen short of satisfying a growing public appetite for knowledge of defense matters that has been driven by high-profile news events such as the flexing of Chinese military muscle over Taiwan and the U.S.-led invasion and occupation of Iraq and Afghanistan.

Other more commercially minded and less strictly controlled media groups have moved to fill this information gap. This is especially true for topics that are not politically sensitive. At the forefront of these efforts are media outfits affiliated with the civilian-run defense industrial complex. They publish military magazines and other types of specialized defense media products that have wide-ranging popular appeal and help stimulate public demand for a modernized military of which China can be proud. A small number of civilian media outfits have also begun to provide their own military coverage, in addition to a fast-expanding online community of defense-related Web sites, Internet chat rooms, and blogs.

THE ROLE OF THE MILITARY MEDIA IN CHINA'S CIVIL-MILITARY RELATIONS

The principal-agent framework provides a useful approach to examining the place of the Chinese military media system in the broader context of the PLA's relationship with the CCP. Political scientist Peter Feaver argues that the essence of civil-military relations is a "strategic interaction between civilian principals and military agents" in which civilian leaders delegate power and authority to their uniformed subordinates but seek to carefully and intrusively monitor their behavior.[2] In democracies, an important monitoring mechanism is the news media, which can alert the principal when questionable activities take place.

The CCP, however, is unwilling to allow the news media and civil society groups to serve as watchdogs of the military. Instead, over time they have established a comprehensive, centralized, and highly intrusive internal monitoring system for the military; the government and military bureaucracies are overlaid by a parallel hierarchy of party committees that enables the ruling party to supervise their work.[3] In addition, all the top military and government leaders are party members and are appointed by the party. The news media do not monitor the military and their role is to serve as propaganda mechanisms.

Despite its lack of autonomy or monitoring responsibilities, the military media apparatus nevertheless occupies a strategic position within the PLA hierarchy. First, as one of the few conduits between the opaque Chinese military system and the outside world, the military media represent an important, though not particularly insightful, window into the country's military activities. This is because the military media project a sterilized image of the PLA that is determined by the military authorities. Second, the military media are situated at the very heart of the political lines of communications between the CCP and the PLA. The military media report directly to the Propaganda Department of the PLA General Political Department (GPD), which holds the rank of a group army-level unit, and is viewed by the PLA top brass as a critical instrument for disseminating propaganda and instructions to all levels of this huge behemoth.

The military media's key position is reflected in the career tracks of officers who have been assigned to oversee this apparatus. A number of political commissars who have run the LAD and the GPD Propaganda Department have subsequently been elevated to the highest echelons of the PLA high command. They include General Chi Haotian, who was defense minister and a vice chairman of the Party CMC during the 1990s, General Sun Zhongtong, a deputy director of the GPD, and most recently General Xu Caihou, who took over as a CMC vice chairman and member of the Politburo at the Seventeenth CCP National Congress in 2007.[4] Xu served as director of the LAD between 1992 and 1994 and later became GPD director in 2002.[5]

The military media system is highly regimented and disciplined. It rigidly adheres to the political line set by the civilian and military authorities. The rare occasions when the military media have appeared to stray from their official mandates have fueled speculation about civil-military tensions or leadership disputes. This is because these discordant events, which are often subtle and easy to miss, have usually coincided with periods of transition and upheaval within the politico-military leadership. Chinese officials and military officers, as well as foreign China analysts, follow the military press to keep abreast of the official line and to watch for hints of internal differences.

There have been just two occasions over the past two decades when the LAD has published articles that appeared to stray from the party line. In one of the most dramatic incidents in the otherwise uneventful history of the LAD, its director and chief editor were dismissed in 1993 for relegating a story about Jiang Zemin being interviewed by the foreign press onto the back page of the newspaper at a time when the CMC chairman was engaged in a major propaganda effort to assert his authority within the PLA.[6] The second event occurred during the extended handover of civilian and military leadership authority from Jiang Zemin to Hu Jintao between the Sixteenth CCP National Congress in late 2002, when Hu took over as CCP general secretary, and the Fourth Plenum of the Sixteenth CCP Central Committee in late 2004, when Jiang finally handed over the leadership of the CMC to Hu. There was intense speculation about whether there were one or two power centers in charge of the running of the country. During this period, the military media, led by the LAD, stood resolutely behind Jiang in his continuing role as CMC chairman. But in a subtle hint that this division of power between Jiang and Hu was causing concern among the military brass about a lack of clarity over the lines of command, a senior LAD journalist, Wang Wenjie, wrote an article that, according to James Mulvenon of the Rand Corporation, "could be interpreted as an indirect but shockingly heterodox attack on divided civilian leadership in the CMC."[7]

Another way in which the military press signals underlying political tensions within the military establishment is when articles are published that allude to internal debates or political concerns that the CCP and PLA leaderships may have on sensitive political issues. One topic that has received periodic attention in the LAD since the 1990s concerns the concept of an army under the control of the government instead of the CCP, as is the case in most other countries, including the former Soviet Union. The LAD claims that "Western hostile forces" have sought to divide the political relationship between the CCP and the PLA and seek to have the military placed under state control (*guojiahua*).[8] One typical commentary in the LAD in 2003 pointed out that the PLA "should resist and repudiate, in a clear-cut manner, the influence of the erroneous viewpoints" such as "separating the army from the party," "depoliticizing the army," and "nationalizing the army."[9] So far, this appears to be a one-sided debate as no articles have appeared in the PLA or official media arguing the case for a depoliticized, state-controlled army.

THE MILITARY MEDIA'S MISSION IN THE REFORM ERA

Jiang Zemin once described military journalists as "engineers of the human soul" because of their mission to provide ideological education.[10] This role has not changed with Hu Jintao despite the gales of commercialization that have swept across the media industry. In his address to the LAD in 2006, Hu said that the military media should adhere to four key requirements:[11]

- Remain a loyal servant to the party and military authorities and strictly promote the official ideological line. This is especially important as the country's opening up and prosperity leads to a more pluralistic society.
- Be clear that the military media owe allegiance to the center even as they seek to cater to a broadening and more diverse audience.

The center refers to Hu, the Party Central Committee, and the CMC.

- Give prominence to grassroots units left out in the military modernization drive. Like the consequences of economic development on the rest of the country, there are winners and losers in the PLA. Military units stationed in coastal areas and cities have had priority access to resources. This is the military dimension of Hu's "scientific development concept."[12]
- Promote innovation in military journalism and propaganda in a more effective, down-to-earth manner. This refers to addressing the real-life economic and social concerns of military personnel and their family dependents.

The PLA propaganda authorities also added a lengthy list of requirements for the military media. One of these cardinal duties is to support the country's economic development by reporting positively about economic reforms and offering guidance to troops about how to contribute to economic construction. However, no mention was made about whether there is any role for the military press to participate in the country's growing prosperity through commercialization.

During the 1980s and 1990s, when the PLA was extensively engaged in commercial activities, the military media apparatus did join the rush. But this commercialization was constrained compared to the freewheeling activities undertaken by other parts of the military system because of the conservative culture that permeated the military propaganda system and also by the lack of resources available to exploit business opportunities.[13] Among the commercial initiatives that the LAD did undertake was allowing advertisements to appear in its newspapers, offering its archives for sale, and expanding its publishing operations.

When in 1998 the PLA was ordered to divest its commercial interests because of rampant malpractices, this decision had a considerable impact on the military media's revenue-generating operations. But military media units were permitted to continue with business operations that were deemed politically acceptable, such as advertising, as long as it did not interfere with their primary duties. Since then, the guiding operational model for the military media apparatus has been "propaganda first, profitability second."

THE NATURE OF THE CHINESE DEFENSE MEDIA MARKET AND THE IMPACT OF COMMERCIALIZATION

The PLA-owned journalism system consists of newspaper and print organizations along with entities concentrating on television and audiovisual operations. Around sixteen PLA-owned newspapers are published on a weekly basis while another 260 are printed less frequently.[14] The largest and most prominent of these is the *Liberation Army Daily*, which is published daily and has a print run estimated at 500,000 copies in 2005.[15] Though a substantial printing, it is modest when compared to national dailies such as the *People's Daily*, which has a daily circulation of 1.8 million. Moreover, the LAD's daily circulation has fallen precipitously since the beginning of economic reforms at the end of the 1970s. In 1981, its circulation was 1.7 million.[16]

A number of factors have contributed to the steady decline of the LAD's readership base. First, the size of the military establishment, which accounts for the overwhelming majority of its subscribers, has shrunk significantly over the past quarter century. At the beginning of the 1980s, the PLA had more than 4 million troops; today that number is 2.2 million. Second, the LAD's distribution system is badly outdated. The newspaper often takes days to reach its readers, especially if they are in outlying posts, because the LAD continues to use the slow and cumbersome state-owned postal system as the principal means of distribution.[17] A third reason for the LAD's shrinking audience is its dismal content, which remains overwhelmingly propagandistic in focus and lacking in real news.

The LAD and other military newspapers have been able to remain in business because of a long-standing PLA General Political Department policy that requires military units to subscribe to them. In 2004, however, this rule was rescinded and military units could, in principle, freely choose which newspapers they wanted to order. But when units stopped ordering the LAD in favor of tabloid publications, the newspaper responded indignantly that military units "should do a good job" in maintaining their military newspaper subscriptions. The LAD pointed out that it was "an important mass media tool that propagates the instructions and policy decisions" of the party and military authorities.[18] Nevertheless, the exodus of subscriptions appears to have continued unabated through 2006, when the GPD issued an order that all military units were required to adhere to mandatory subscription quotas.[19]

While the LAD has remained focused on its core mission of ideological education, some limited adjustments have been made to its content to include more coverage on social, economic, and legal issues that directly impact the welfare of soldiers and their dependents. This focus on livelihood issues will likely increase, as it was one of the four requirements outlined in Hu's January 2006 speech to the LAD.

In response to its steadily falling print circulation and the distribution problems in reaching its audiences in a timely manner, the LAD has created an Internet version called China Military Online (CMO) or *Zhongguo Junwang*.[20] This news site appears to have been successful in reclaiming the LAD's readership. In 2002, the LAD claimed to have a daily average of 710,000 hits.[21] This figure more than doubled to 1.5 million daily hits in 2003.[22] However, in comparison with the growth of other major national news sites, CMO's expansion is considered too slow by military media analysts.[23]

One reason for CMO's slow growth is a paucity of investment in the development of the Web site that has severely restricted its ability to attract readers with fresh, constantly updated content. A good comparative example is found in the interactive forums that are considered an important tool to promote traffic to news Web sites. One popular site, the Strong Country (*Qiangguo*) forum of the *People's Daily*, was managed by more than twenty staff members in 2007, while the defense forum on CMO had only one Web manager.[24] CMO has also lagged behind in developing services that are standard on major Web sites, such as online chat rooms, e-mail communications, and blogs.

The only other PLA newspaper with a sizeable circulation, *China Defense News* (CDN) or *Zhongguo Guofang Bao*, is also part of the LAD publishing stable. The principal audiences for CDN are the military and civilian units involved in civil-military activities such as mobilization work. When CDN celebrated its tenth anniversary in 2003, GPD director Xu Caihou visited the newspaper's headquarters and pointed out that CDN should "provide a powerful public opinion support for pushing military change with Chinese characteristics, deepening education on defense by the whole people, and promoting the defense modernization drive."[25]

Since the 1990s, the PLA media apparatus has also made a concerted effort to expand its reach into television broadcasting. In 1996, China Central Television (CCTV) established its No. 7 Television Channel and allocated three hours of daily broadcasts to military propaganda issues, with the remaining time devoted to agricultural and children's programming.

Previously, the broadcast of military programs was conducted on an ad hoc basis.

To facilitate this expansion, the PLA established a television propaganda center in April 1996 that has a staff of around three hundred military and civilian specialists.[26] In 2005 a state-of-the-art military television complex was completed to provide more advanced programming and distribution capabilities.[27] According to polling research conducted in 2005 on the audience of *Military Reporting*, CCTV-7 Channel's flagship military program, more than 90 percent of its viewers were civilians.[28] In 2002, CCTV-7 claimed that more than 50 percent of the country's population (or 650 million people) have access to its programming, although no figures showed what the actual audience size was.

COMMERCIAL OUTPUT FROM THE DEFENSE INDUSTRIAL COMPLEX

Defense-related magazines published by defense industry–affiliated media outlets proliferated in the 1990s, and they appear to have successfully carved out a niche that is distinct from the PLA media and propaganda apparatus. One 2004 industry analysis estimated the number of defense science and technology-related publications at 210.[29] They range from popular magazines featuring foreign weapons to more serious professional journals intended for the military and defense industrial communities (see table 6.1). By highlighting the technological advances of U.S., European, and other Asian militaries, these publications have helped to create public support for China's own military spending.

Most of these publications originate from defense industrial research institutes that have seen their state funding retrenched significantly in the reform era and are seeking opportunities to generate independent revenues and provide employment for underutilized staff. Many are printed on a monthly or more frequent basis and their circulation numbers are in the tens of thousands. *Ordnance Knowledge* (*Bingqi Zhishi*), one of the oldest and best-known of these publications, reportedly has a print run approaching 400,000 per issue.[30] The LAD Publishing House has also ventured into this emerging market through *Global Military* (*Huanqiu Junshi*), a glossy full-color monthly that focuses its reporting on foreign militaries and their weapons systems.[31]

TABLE 6.1   Leading PLA and Defense Industry Periodicals

Title	Affiliation
Military World Pictorial (Junshi Shijie Huakan)	PLA General Armament Dept. China Defense Science and Technology Information Center
Conmilit (Xiandai Junshi)	PLA General Armament Dept. China Defense Science and Technology Information Center
Weaponry (Bingqi)	China Ordnance Science Research Institute
Ordnance Industry Science and Technology (Bingqi Keqi)	Shaanxi Science and Technology History Association and Shaanxi Provincial Commission of National Defense Industry Communist Youth League
Ordnance Knowledge (Bingqi Zhishi)	China Ordnance Society
Naval and Merchant Ships (Jianchuan Zhishi)	Chinese Society of Naval Architecture and Marine Engineering
Military Digest (Junshi Wenzhai)	2nd Academy, China Aerospace Industry Corp.
Modern Weaponry (Xiandai Bingqi)	No. 201 Research Institute, China Ordnance Industry Enterprise Corp.
Modern Navy (Dangdai Haijun)	PLA Navy Political Dept.
PLA Pictorial (Jiefangjun Huabao)	LAD Publishing House
Chinese Air Force (Zhongguo Kongjun)	PLA Air Force Political Dept.
Defense Science, Technology and Industry (Guofang Keji Gongye)	State Administration for Science, Technology and Industry for National Defense
International Aviation (Guoji Hangkong)	China Aviation Media Group
Aerospace China (Zhongguo Hangtian)	China Aerospace Science and Technology Enterprise Group Aerospace Information Center
Global Military (Huanqiu Junshi)	LAD Publishing House
Kanwa Defense Review (Hanhe Fangwu Pinglun)	Kanwa Information Center (Canada-registered but Hong Kong–based independent media firm)

One of the best-known and most widely circulated defense magazines is *Conmilit* (*Xiandai Junshi*), which is published by the No. 201 Research Institute of the China Ordnance Industry Enterprise Group (COIEG), one of China's leading defense industrial conglomerates. Established in 1979, the magazine has helped to pioneer the development of the independent defense media sector with innovations such as an overseas edition published in Hong Kong. While the magazine is primarily a commercial venture, it still has the important function of acting as a propaganda conduit for COIEG.[32]

By focusing almost exclusively on issues related to technology and operations that are not politically sensitive, and by predominantly covering foreign countries, these publications have largely avoided attracting the attention of official agencies dealing with political, propaganda, or secrecy affairs. Moreover, their largely technical content has drawn a large civilian readership, especially among high school and college-level students, which is regarded as an especially attractive group not only for advertisers but also for the military and defense industrial establishments that see them as good recruitment targets.[33]

An important innovation in this media sector has been publishing outside of China. These efforts are aimed at circumventing China's stringent secrecy restrictions and licensing controls, as well as reaching out to markets in Hong Kong, Taiwan, and the Chinese Diaspora. *Conmilit* was the first magazine to do this in the 1980s, and in 2004 a new bilingual Chinese-English publication, *Kanwa Defense Review*, appeared. Unlike its competitors, *Kanwa* is published by a private Canadian-registered but Hong Kong–based company that is operated by a former Chinese national.[34]

This niche defense magazine market appears to offer plenty of growth potential. The LAD's *Global Military* magazine, for example, claimed that its 2004 readership numbers had soared by 27 percent compared to the previous year.[35] However, the large number of publications crowding into this marketplace means that competition is fierce, and this undoubtedly has had a major impact on profitability. Because of a dearth of advertisers, many of these publications are heavily dependent on subscription income. But there is significant price sensitivity because of the market competition and limited earning power of their main audiences.[36]

In contrast to the print sector, the commercial television industry has been far less inclined to develop military-related programming. This may be due to the high cost and difficulty in getting access to the military establishment. This has allowed CCTV-7 to dominate the market. However, Hong Kong–based Phoenix Television Co., which can be viewed in China and has excellent ties with the central authorities in Beijing, has moved into this domain by broadcasting a weekly defense-related program called *Military Observation Post* that discusses military and broader geostrategic issues to do with China and other countries.

MILITARY COVERAGE IN CIVILIAN MEDIA OUTLETS AND ON THE INTERNET

Before the reform era, military topics were generally taboo for the civilian media industry and there was little original coverage of this area. In the reform era, though, a growing number of civilian newspapers, news agencies, and broadcasting outlets have been willing to devote resources to military reporting in recognition of the general public's intense interest in international security and military matters. As one senior military journalist pointed out, "military news has always been 'high-grade ore' that the various media have fallen over each other to mine. 'Military news fever' never subsides. Numerous news media, including Internet sites, have set up special pages and columns for military news."[37]

Major national newspapers such as *People's Daily* (*Renmin Ribao*), *China Youth Daily* (*Zhongguo Qingnian Bao*), and *Science and Technology Daily* (*Keji Ribao*) regularly publish special features and sections on defense affairs that include reporting from their own correspondents. Xinhua News Agency has its own small stable of military correspondents. This extends to the online versions of these news services. The Web sites of *People's Daily* and Xinhua have military sections that provide extensive coverage of a wide range of defense issues.[38] In addition, major Internet service providers such as Sina.org, Tom.com, Qianlong.com, and China.com have detailed military media Web sites.[39]

For secrecy and political reasons, civilian media organizations are careful about how they report military matters. Little, if any, independent investigative reporting takes place, and much of the coverage focuses on foreign issues and on Taiwan. But civilian newspapers have discovered that military news is lucrative, with demand soaring during periods of military tension. For example, in 1999 the *China Business Times News Weekly* reportedly saw a fourfold increase in its street sales after a serious outbreak of tensions between Beijing and Taipei. The circulation of the *Global Times* also doubled during this period.[40]

A small number of independent Web sites and bloggers specializing in defense themes have also appeared in the past few years. They have been an important source of new insights and occasional leaks.[41] Though some of these Web sites and blogs are temporary, they appear to be written by current or former PLA soldiers. In addition, CMO and other Internet providers such as Tom.com provide bulletin boards that allow readers to post messages on defense issues.

THE AUDIENCES OF THE PLA AND DEFENSE MEDIA

The PLA and defense media play a key role in shaping public attitudes toward national security and military affairs, with various parts of these media machines targeted at different constituencies within the country's diverse population. As previously noted, the official military media are the principal propaganda instruments that ensure that the correct ideological line is transmitted throughout the armed forces. Their most important audience is the rank-and-file military and civilian personnel employed by the PLA and the party and government officials who deal with military affairs. The LAD is aimed at the entire military establishment, while other military newspapers serve more narrow constituencies. Each service arm and military region has its own newspapers.

Surveys suggest, however, that the percentage of PLA personnel who actually read military newspapers is small. A survey of soldiers in ten regiments, companies, and platoons found that most preferred to read local civilian newspapers. Another survey of three hundred soldiers found that when they were required to read military newspapers, more than 60 percent spent less than five minutes doing so.[42]

As the mouthpiece of the political-military leadership, the LAD has traditionally acted as the official voice of the PLA through editorials and commentaries. These pronouncements are equivalent to the press releases and public announcements that are usually handled by the press offices of defense ministries in other countries. The LAD regularly publishes official commentaries and opinions concerning Taiwan, China-Japan ties, and China-U.S. relations.

The audience of the defense technical press is predominantly young, mainly male high school and university students who are interested in military affairs or going into a military career, former and current military personnel, militia and reservists, military dependents, and defense industry personnel. They have become increasingly well informed on topics that would have been taboo in the past. A consequence of the efforts of the defense technical media to provide detailed knowledge on foreign hardware and operational issues is that it has stimulated popular demand for the PLA to release more information about its own capabilities and intentions.

When circumspection is preferred to bluster in communicating to the outside world, the PLA authorities use pro-Chinese media outlets in Hong Kong to broadcast their messages and signal intentions. *Wen Wei Pao* and *Ta Kung Pao* have been favorite dissemination channels.[43] During the 1996 Taiwan Strait tensions, unidentified Chinese military officials were often quoted in these newspapers about possible Chinese military actions to oppose Taiwanese independence.

The PLA broadcasting system is targeted toward a general civilian audience. Programming portrays a positive and strongly patriotic image of the military as the defenders of the country's sovereignty and ideological purity. This slant is reflected in all programming, whether it is documentaries on military life, soap operas, or general news propaganda features.

HOW THE MILITARY MEDIA SHAPE PUBLIC ATTITUDES TOWARD THE PLA'S ROLE IN CHINESE SOCIETY

As China goes through a period of unprecedented socioeconomic change in its transition to being a modern, prosperous, and increasingly integrated world power, the PLA leadership is keen to portray itself as an anchor of stability, integrity, continuity, and strength for the country and the party. Furthermore, the military media are seen as playing an important role in projecting this image. As an editorial in the LAD on the role of military journalism pointed out, "as one of the most advanced groups in society, the army has always had a notable advantage in the construction of spiritual civilization," referring to the building of a homegrown socialist culture.[44]

Recognizing the need for a dedicated and responsive media apparatus to meet the demands of this increasingly information-driven society, in 2008 the PLA assigned its first-ever information department to the Chinese

Ministry of National Defense (MND).[45] PLA spokespeople began to organize regular public press briefings in the wake of the May 2008 Wenchuan earthquake in Sichuan, in which military units played the central role in rescue and recovery operations. While the PLA faced major difficulties in mobilizing and deploying troops in this operation, its reputation was considerably enhanced by the extensive positive coverage of its role in the crisis, which can be attributed in large part to the PLA briefings. Military press conferences have now become a routine dimension of the PLA's public relations efforts. In August 2009, the MND launched its own Web site, which has attracted considerable attention. In the first three months of operation, the site received 1.25 billion hits, 40 percent of which came from Beijing, Guangdong, and Jiangsu. In addition, the site suffered 2.3 million hacking attacks in the first month. An MND spokesman said these attacks were caused by hackers looking for military secrets or seeking to disrupt the Web site's operations.[46]

In its efforts to shape public attitudes about the core values of the military and its role in Chinese society, the military media have focused on a number of themes:

- Portraying the PLA as a strong, principled defender of the country's national security and territorial integrity. This is most obviously exemplified in the coverage of Taiwan.
- Instilling a strong sense of patriotism and nationalism within the general public and linking this with the notion that a prosperous country requires a strong army (*Fuguo, Qiangbing*).[47] In an editorial a few months after the accidental U.S. bombing of the Chinese embassy in Belgrade in 1999, the LAD analyzed the fierce populist backlash against the United States and assessed that military journalism had a vital role to play in keeping the Chinese domestic audience informed about military events and "enhancing their defense consciousness" because "the entire nation became extremely indignant [over the bombing] and began to spend more time thinking about how to protect national security and how to beef up the country's defense capability. They shouted out a common wish: the country must be strong, our army must be strong."[48]
- Stressing the PLA's complete loyalty and obedience to the CCP and the core leadership.

- Emphasizing the military's readiness to aid communities that are hit by natural disasters, such as floods or earthquakes.
- Showing off the technological progress that has been achieved in the military's modernization drive, such as through public parades and the military-managed space program.
- Painting the PLA as a peaceful force that does not represent a security threat to any other country unless China's national interests are challenged.
- Spotlighting the PLA's commitment to support the country's economic development. This ranges from military participation in construction projects to the conversion of military facilities to civilian factories. Regular media campaigns have also promoted idealized military role models. The most famous of these hero figures was Lei Feng, a soldier who served during the Cultural Revolution, but more contemporary examples include soldiers such as Li Guoan, Xu Honggang, Bai Yaoping, and Fan Kuangfu. Although the use of these exemplary role models has "increased the prestige of the armed forces' news reporting work," one senior military propaganda official warned that "excessive emphasis on publicizing model examples may result in neglect of regular military news reporting."[49]

CHINA'S MILITARY MEDIA IN COMPARATIVE PERSPECTIVE

The Chinese military media's role as a loyal servant of its military and civilian masters is not unique, although its single-minded and unwavering dedication to its political and propaganda duties is unsurpassed, with perhaps the exception of military-dominated regimes such as North Korea and Myanmar. But it is the Chinese military media's struggle to balance their political responsibilities with countervailing pressures from an information-savvy, market-oriented, and sophisticated population that is worth considering from a comparative perspective.

The post–cold war Russian military media may offer some useful insights as to whether a postcommunist but still heavily politicized and secretive military institution will allow its journalists to become more autonomous and monitor it. Under communist rule, the roles, practices, and institutional relationships of the Soviet military media with the Soviet Communist Party and armed forces were similar, if not identical, to the Chinese system. In postcommunist Russia, the military media continue to preserve military secrecy, protect the military's reputation, and serve as a key champion of patriotism. Their character as a propaganda tool has outlived the one-party system. This continuity is closely associated with the military's vision of itself as the guardian of the country's national identity and security.[50]

For democracies such as the United States, the relationship between the military, its media and public affairs apparatus, and the independent media appears on first impression to be fundamentally different from the Chinese case. This is because the historical and contemporary relationship between the military and civilian media has been adversarial in nature. According to Douglas Porch, the military prefers to operate behind closed doors and views "the media as a subversive, rather than a positive, element. The press, however, responds to the requirement of democracy to expose the actions" of the military to public scrutiny.[51] In this regard, the media are considered the "most prominent fire alarm on defense policy."[52]

But the interactions between the media and military in the United States and China do share some similarities, especially during wartime. One area of common thinking is the use of both the military and civilian media for information operations. Under the administration of George W. Bush and especially in its extended military campaigns in Iraq and Afghanistan, the civilian Defense Department and the military services viewed the media as useful tools for psychological operations.[53] This is an approach that the PLA shares.[54]

A Chinese military analysis of the U.S. media effort before and during the 2003 invasion of Iraq admiringly pointed out how carefully organized and strategically implemented it was. The assessment noted that "after the decision was made to attack Iraq," the White House Office of Global Communications

> was in charge of planning, coordination, and managing news and public opinion, formulated a public opinion and propaganda plan based on the war plans, and provided unified arrangements for news and public opinion efforts in this war. A highly modernized, global news and information broadcasting network quickly went into full-load, supra-conventional operating status to issue relevant information

quickly and in great quantity and cover the whole world with the sound of the US voice. After the war started, under the direction, coordination, and control of news and public opinion administration organizations at all levels, the US news media and the military acted in concert with each other to provide support for the military strike.[55]

The Pentagon also developed a highly sophisticated information/propaganda apparatus to support the 2003 Iraqi invasion and occupation aimed at achieving "information dominance" in the highly competitive and overloaded news environment in the United States. One innovation was the recruitment of former senior military officers as military media commentators, many of whom subsequently became highly respected opinion makers.[56] The PLA apparently incorporated some of the lessons learned from the U.S. military media in the 2003 invasion of Iraq into its revised Regulations on Political Work that were issued at the end of that year, especially the importance of shaping domestic and international public opinion in the support of military operations.[57]

CONCLUSION

As the chapters in this volume testify, media institutions operating in different political, economic, and social spheres have found diverse balances between the competing and often volatile pressures of political control, propaganda, and commercialization. For China's military media, especially its LAD flagship and associated operations, their role as purveyors of propaganda and ideological education will take precedence over any commercial opportunities that may arise in the foreseeable future. The dissemination of military-related news and information is unlikely to change significantly from the highly conservative and propagandistic style that has existed over the past sixty years.

The popular demand for information on defense matters is being met by the development of a market-driven and independent defense media sector that focuses on technological and professional issues rather than politically sensitive matters. In general, this trend will be positive for the PLA and the defense industrial complex as they will be able to use the media as a recruitment tool and, perhaps more important, to cultivate grassroots support for ample military budgets. The continuing development of this quasi-autonomous defense media will also help to stretch the restrictive boundaries for coverage and discussion of defense affairs. This in turn will help to gradually nurture a more transparent attitude toward military affairs in the country. However, it is questionable whether the civilian defense media will eventually emerge as a watchdog in the same mode as counterparts operating in democracies.

Notes

1. "Jiefangjun Bao Commentator on Hu Jintao's Important Speech on Jiefangjun Bao," *Jiefangjun Bao* [*Liberation Army Daily*], in Foreign Broadcast Information Service (FBIS), 11 January 2006.

2. Peter Feaver, *Armed Servants: Agency, Oversight, and Civil-Military Relations* (Cambridge, MA: Harvard University Press, 2003), pp. 75–87.

3. Susan Shirk, *The Political Logic of Economic Reform in China* (Berkeley: University of California Press, 1993), pp. 57–62.

4. Zhang Xin, "A Personnel Change at Jiefangjun Bao High-Level Leadership," *Hong Kong Wen Wei Po* [*Hong Kong Wen Hui Daily*], in FBIS, 25 June 2005.

5. "Xu Caihou—Politburo Member of CPC Central Committee," *Xinhua News Agency*, 22 October 2007.

6. Interview with senior *Jiefangjun Bao* journalist, Beijing, 1993, and "Editor 'Fired for Putting Jiang on Back Page,'" *Straits Times*, 3 June 1993.

7. Wang Wenjie, "Advance Development by Leaps and Bounds in Our Military Modernization under the Guidance of the 'Three Represents': Report on Efforts by the Military Deputies to the NPC to Study President Jiang's Important Speech at the Military Delegation," *Jiefangjun Bao* [*Liberation Army Daily*], 11 March 2003, p. 5; and James Mulvenon, "Party-Army Relations Since the 16th Party Congress: The Battle of the 'Two Centers'?" in Andrew Scobell and Larry Wortzel (Eds.), *Civil-Military Change in China: Elites, Institutes, and Ideas After the 16th Party Congress* (Carlisle, PA: US Army War College, 2004), pp. 24–27.

8. See David Shambaugh, *Modernizing China's Military* (Berkeley: University of California Press, 2003), pp. 46–54; and Andrew Scobell, "China's Evolving Civil-Military Relations: Creeping Guojiahua," in Nan Li (Ed.), *Chinese Civil-Military Relations* (London: Routledge, 2006), pp. 25–39.

9. Jiang Yong, "Fulfilling Task of Primary Importance and Facilitating New Advances in Army Building," *Jiefangjun Bao* [*Liberation Army Daily*], 18 February 2003, p. 7, in FBIS, 14 April 2003.

10. *Xinhua News Agency Domestic Service*, 2 January 1996, in BBC Monitoring Service, Asia-Pacific, 4 January 1996. The phrase was originally used by Joseph Stalin.

11. "President Hu Jintao Congratulates 50th Founding Anniversary of PLA's Newspaper," *Xinhua News Agency*, in FBIS, 3 January 2006; and "JFJB Commentator

on Hu Jintao's Important Speech on Jiefangjun Bao," *Jiefangjun Bao* [*Liberation Army Daily*], in FBIS, 11 January 2006.

12. Joseph Fewsmith, "Promoting the Scientific Development Concept," *China Leadership Monitor*, no. 11, 2004.

13. See Tai Ming Cheung, *China's Entrepreneurial Army* (Oxford: Oxford University Press, 2002). Some GPD propaganda units, though, did jump onto the commercial bandwagon, such as the principal military film producer, the August First Film Studio, which produced popular entertainment products for money-making reasons. Wang Jingyang, "Shooting Begins on Monumental Movies on History of Revolutionary War," *Jiefangjun Bao* [*Liberation Army Daily*], in FBIS, 10 January 2005.

14. Wu Changde, "Views on Some Issues in Military News Coverage," *Zhongguo Junshi Kexue* [*Chinese Military Science*], February 2002, 101–106, in FBIS, 1 February 2002. Major-General Wu is identified as a deputy director in the GPD's Propaganda Department. Other PLA media experts say that the armed forces publish as many as 30 newspapers on a weekly or more frequent basis while another 270 are printed less frequently. See Wu Yangbo and Cao Yongqing, "Analysis of the Strategy and Functions of the Army's Media Innovation System," *Journal of PLA Nanjing Institute of Politics*, no. 6, 2005, p. 122.

15. Xu Lei and Wang Yongliang, "Success in Achieving Innovation," *Junshi Jizhe* [*Military Journalist*], January 2005, p. 24.

16. Todd Hazelbarth, *The Chinese Media: More Autonomous and Diverse—Within Limits* (Washington, DC: Central Intelligence Agency, September 1997), p. 8, www.cia.gov/csi/monograph/425050797/index.htm.

17. Wu and Cao, "Analysis of the Army's Media System," p. 122.

18. Zhang Xianglin, "Military Newspapers Should Be Subscribed to According to Rules," *Jiefangjun Bao* [*Liberation Army Daily*], 7 November 2003, p. 2, in FBIS, 23 December 2003.

19. "Notice from the General Political Department to the PLA and Armed Police: "Ensure Strict Adherence to the Standard of Subscribing to Next Year's Liberation Army Daily," *Jiefangjun Bao* [*Liberation Army Daily*], 14 November 2006.

20. China Military Online (in Chinese). http://www.chinamil.com.cn.

21. Chinese Academy of Social Sciences Institute of Media and Broadcasting (Ed.), *China 2003 Media Yearbook* (Beijing: China Media Yearbook Press, 2003), p. 99.

22. Ibid., p. 143.

23. Zhang Feng, "21-Point Suggestion to Strengthen, Expand Military Networks, Websites," *Junshi Jizhe* [*Military Journalist*], 1 March 2007.

24. Ibid.

25. Tang Shuifu, "Our Paper Holds Forum to Mark 10th Anniversary of the Founding of 'Zhongguo Guofang Bao,'" *Jiefangjun Bao* [*Liberation Army Daily*], in FBIS, 28 September 2003.

26. Zhao Zhigang, "Examination of the Strategy to Carry Out the Strengthening of Military Television Media and Propaganda," *China Radio and TV Academic Journal*, December 2000, pp. 27–28.

27. See "Chinese Military Leaders Inspect Army Television Propaganda Center," *Xinhua News Agency*, 9 December 2005.

28. Zhang Wei, "Brief Talk of the Position of Military Media Television," *TV Research*, August 2005, p. 19.

29. Xu Yazhou, "The Development and Trends in Defense Science and Technology Publications," in Zhang Baohai and Tian Shengli (Eds.), *China Periodical Yearbook, 2003–2004* (Beijing: China Encyclopedia Publishing House, 2004), pp. 258–261.

30. Ibid.

31. Liu Shuchen, "Speaking of the Style of 'Global Military,'" *Junshi Jizhe* [*Military Journalist*], April 2005, pp. 9–12.

32. "Modern Weaponry Board of Directors Established," *Xiandai Bingqi* [*Modern Weaponry*], June 2007, p. 60.

33. Liu, "Speaking of 'Global Military,'" p. 9.

34. See Kanwa Information Center, www.kanwa.com.

35. Liu, "Speaking of 'Global Military,'" p. 9.

36. Xu, "Development in Defense Publications," p. 261. See also Liu, "Speaking of 'Global Military,'" p. 9, who reported that Global Military was operating in the red.

37. Wu Changde, "Views on Some Issues."

38. Renmin Wang's military Web site is http://military.people.com.cn/ and Xinhua's military Web page is http://www.xinhuanet.com/mil/.

39. See Taylor Fravel, "The Revolution in Research Affairs: Online Sources and the Study of the PLA," in James Mulvenon and Andrew Yang (Eds.), *A Poverty of Riches: New Challenges and Opportunities in PLA Research* (Santa Monica: RAND Corp., 2003), pp. 49–118.

40. "China's Newspapers Cash in on Row with Taiwan," *Reuters News*, 13 September 1999.

41. Examples of such Web sites include www.war-sky.com, a military enthusiast Web site, and http://junshi.xilu.com, the Web site of a Chinese information technology company with an extensive series of military bulletin boards.

42. Tao Ke, "Strengthening the Readability of the News from a Reader's Perspective," *Junshi Jizhe* [*Military Journalist*], January 2005, pp. 19–21.

43. "Taiwanese, Chinese Militaries Slug It Out on Television, Newspapers—Not Battlefields," *Associated Press*, 4 September 2001.

44. Editorial Department, "Military News Reporting Can Accomplish Much in Peacetime," *Jiefangjun Bao* [*Liberation Army Daily*], in FBIS, 5 October 1999.

45. Ni Erh-yen, "PLA Established News Release Channel," *Hong Kong Wen Wei Po* [*Hong Kong Wen Hui Daily*], 15 January 2008. See also Jian Zhou, "On the Establishment of a PLA Military Spokesperson's System in the Informationized Age" (master's thesis, National Defense Science and Technology University, Changsha, Hunan, December 2005); and Matthew Boswell, "Media Relations in China's Military: The Case of the Ministry of National Defense Information Office," *Asia Policy*, no. 8, July 2009, pp. 97–120.

46. "China Defense Website Gets 2 Mln Hack Attacks," *Agence France Press*, 19 November 2009.

47. Zhou Yongming, "Informed Nationalism: Military Websites in Chinese Cyberspace," *Journal of Contemporary China*, Vol. 14, no. 44, 2005, pp. 543–562. See also "Military Launches Initiative against Colonial Culture in the Names of 'National Defense Consciousness,'" *Inside China Mainland*, October 1996.

48. "Military News Reporting Can Accomplish Much," *Jiefangjun Bao* [*Liberation Army Daily*], 5 October 1999.

49. Wu, "Views on Some Issues."

50. Ivan Safranchuk (Ed.), *Contemporary Russian Military Journalism* (Washington, DC/Moscow: Center for Defense Information and Center of War and Peace Journalism, 2004).

51. Douglas Porch, "No Bad Stories," *Naval War College Review*, Vol. 55, no. 1, 2002, pp. 85–107.

52. Feaver, *Armed Servants*, p. 80.

53. Charles Zews, "'Infoganda' in Uniform: The Bush Administration Creates Media Outlets to Tell Its Story," *Niemen Reports*, Vol. 58, no. 3, September 2004.

54. Laura Murray, "China's Psychological Warfare," *Military Review*, Vol. 13, no. 5, September 1999.

55. Cai Huifu et al., "Research into News and Public Opinion Warfare during the Iraq War," *Zhongguo Junshi Kexue* [*Chinese Military Science*], no. 4, 20 August 2003, in FBIS, 28 January 2004.

56. David Barstow, "Behind TV Analysts, Pentagon's Hidden Hand," *New York Times*, 20 April 2008.

57. See Meng Fan-yu, "Investigation into Impact, Effect of Media Warfare on War," *Hai-chun Hsueh-shu Yueh-Kan* [*Navy Monthly Journal*], 26 September 2006. This was an assessment from a Taiwanese military publication.

7

Changing Media, Changing Courts

Benjamin L. Liebman

S HE XIANGLIN'S CASE helped to bring him back from near death; it also made him a wealthy man. In 1994, She's wife, Zhang Zaiyu, disappeared from their home village in rural Hubei Province; Zhang Zaiyu's family accused She of killing her. After local police found the body of an unidentified female in a nearby water tower, they charged She with murder. She Xianglin was sentenced to death; on appeal, the Hubei Province High People's Court sent the case back for retrial due to insufficient evidence. On retrial, a local county court sentenced She Xianglin to fifteen years in prison for intentional homicide.

In March 2005, the case received media attention when Zhang Zaiyu returned to the village—proving that her husband had not killed her. An initial report on Zhang Zaiyu's return ran in a paper in Wuhan, the capital of Hubei. Following the article, local authorities banned further reporting on the case pending an official investigation, and instructed the media to use only an officially approved report on the case. Nonetheless, news quickly spread online and to newspapers elsewhere in China, and a few weeks later, on 15 April, She Xianglin was released from custody. Media coverage of the case also appeared to assist She Xianglin in obtaining RMB 460,000 in compensation from the state for his wrongful incarceration—reported to be the largest such settlement in Chinese history.

She Xianglin was not alone: in numerous other cases, public opinion voiced on the Internet has had a direct influence on court proceedings. Deng Yujiao became a national celebrity in 2009—widely referred to as "the most virtuous woman in China"—after she stabbed a local official to death. Deng Yujiao, who worked in an entertainment complex in a small town in Hubei, claimed that three local officials had approached her seeking "special services." When she refused, one of the men attempted to push her onto a sofa and remove her clothes. She stabbed him, killing him, and wounded another official. After a popular outcry on the Internet, a local court, while convicting Deng Yujiao of causing intentional harm, exempted her from punishment because of diminished capacity resulting from mental illness. Likewise, Xu Ting, a migrant worker in Guangdong who had withdrawn more than RMB 170,000 from a broken ATM machine in 2006, had his sentence reduced from life in prison to five years after a popular outcry in the media and online.

Many Chinese journalists—and some Western observers—perceive the recently commercialized media as an important check on China's courts, serving to improve transparency and fairness in the system. According to this view, expanded coverage of legal issues is boosting not only the ability of individuals to obtain just decisions but also the role of law in China more generally. The Supreme People's Court (SPC) has echoed this view: in response to questions regarding the recent phenomenon of "media judgments," the court's spokesperson stated that the SPC believes that media supervision of the courts is helping to ensure just and fair outcomes.[1]

Over the past fifteen years the Chinese media have undoubtedly become one of the most important actors in the legal system. In numerous cases, the media are an important check on official abuses, coming to the assistance of victims of injustice, or pressuring courts to act fairly. However, the story is not so simple. In other cases, media coverage encourages party officials to intervene in the courts, predetermining the outcomes of cases and reaffirming Chinese Communist Party (CCP) oversight of the judiciary. In some criminal cases, media coverage has resulted in rushed trials in which assuaging populist demands for harsh treatment of defendants is more important than observance of procedural or substantive legal standards. Furthermore, courts are not merely passive recipients of media oversight. They have also developed mechanisms for resisting and managing media coverage. Journalists and newspapers are increasingly finding themselves in court as defendants in defamation cases brought by the targets of critical reports—frequently as the losing party. Thus, although Chinese media are changing the courts, the courts are also beginning to change the media.

This chapter examines court-media relations in China and argues that such relations are increasingly a two-way street. Media coverage is forcing the courts to act more carefully—and perhaps fairly. But pressure from the courts is also resulting in greater attention to factual reporting and professional standards in the media. This interactive relationship reflects the position of the courts and media as institutions competing for authority within the Chinese political system. It also suggests that there is significant room for ground-up development of both media and the courts.

The first section discusses the growth of media coverage of legal issues in recent years, as well as the effect of the Internet on this coverage. The second section examines the impact of media coverage on the courts, showing that although it may force courts to act more fairly and remedy unjust cases, the media also encourage courts to treat criminal defendants harshly—and may be reinforcing CCP oversight of the legal system. The third section discusses court efforts to resist and control the media. The conclusion discusses the implications of court-media relations for the continued evolution of both institutions.

COMMERCIALIZING MEDIA, EXPANDING LEGAL COVERAGE

One result of the commercialization of the media in the 1990s was wider coverage of legal issues. Traditional CCP legal newspapers such as *Legal Daily* and *Procuratorate Daily*—linked to the Ministry of Justice and Supreme People's Procuratorate,[2] respectively—developed commercialized offshoots. These subsidiary papers generally still focused on legal issues, but were designed to attract broader readerships, and thus greater revenue, than their official parent publications. Other legal publications, such as *Democracy and the Legal System*—published by the state-run China Law Society—and *Chinese Lawyer*, published by the All-China Lawyers' Association—similarly underwent significant editorial changes in an effort to attract more readers. More significantly, commercialization brought expanded legal coverage in nonspecialist papers, in particular in the municipal daily papers that have flourished since the late 1990s. Many mass-market papers dedicate extensive space to legal issues and often have reporters specializing in legal matters, dedicated legal pages, or weekly features focusing on law.

The growth of investigative journalism in the 1990s also resulted in increased coverage of the legal system, and in particular of the courts. As competition for readers developed, papers sought to expand critical reporting, generally referred to as *yulun jiandu*, or "popular opinion supervision." Critical reporting was not new: China's media have long served in part as investigatory arms of the state. But commercialization gave the media greater editorial autonomy and increased incentives to compete to provide critical reports. Many of these reports focus on improper action or inaction by low-level officials, or on egregious cases of injustice. Although not limited to law or the legal system, such reports often involve legal matters, and a significant number of them expose alleged wrongdoing or mishandling of cases by the courts. Newspapers such as *Southern Weekend* and *China Youth Daily*, which became well known in the 1990s for critical reporting that challenged the boundaries of permissible content, frequently devote extensive space to legal issues and to individual cases. More recently, mass-market urban newspapers such as *Southern Metropolitan Daily* and magazines such as *Caijing* and *Liaowang Dongfang* likewise became well known for hard-hitting legal reporting.

Reporting on the courts and the legal system follows the informal rules that govern investigative reporting more generally: the media only expose wrongdoing by low-ranking officials, targeting "flies, not tigers." Critical reports are published most often by media with a higher administrative rank than the target of criticism, or by media from another province or region. As noted in the other essays in this book, however, China's propaganda system is dynamic and inconsistent, with permissiveness varying across publication, media type, and time. Successful journalists and editors are often those most adept at judging and navigating the prevailing local and national political winds.

In addition to explicitly critical reporting, papers also compete to provide the latest details on major cases—in particular those involving celebrities or officials accused of wrongdoing. Coverage of legal matters helps to sell papers. Daily updates on high-profile cases are common, with journalists often relying on anonymous sources inside the courts or procuratorates for the latest details of prominent cases. Hence, for example, during the 2002–2003 detention and trial of professional soccer referee Gong Jiangping for accepting bribes to fix matches—referred to in the Chinese media as the case of the Black Whistle—papers competed to provide the latest news on the trial. Papers in Beijing, where Gong was detained, and elsewhere carried frequent reports, apparently obtained through leaks from the procurator-ate's office and the court. The details leaked included when Gong would be tried and what charges would be filed against him. Similarly, in 2009 the Hangzhou Drag Racing Case became a national sensation after an illegally modified Mitsubishi, driven by the son of a rich local businessperson, struck and killed a recent university graduate in central Hangzhou. The case went viral after pictures taken by anonymous observers were posted on the Inter-net within hours of the crash—including images showing friends of the driver, Hu Bin, smoking and laughing at the scene. Both the print media and Web portals competed to provide daily updates, with Web portals dedicat-ing special sections and discussion forums to the case. As debate swelled regarding the possible charges against the driver, the media ran reports based on apparent leaks from the procuratorate's office on what charges would be brought against Hu.[3]

Television stations have likewise discovered that legal news attracts viewers. China Central Television (CCTV) shows such as *Focus* and *News Probe*—the prime-time investigative programs—frequently cover legal issues. In the late 1990s, *Focus* and *Law Today*—a midday show that uses indi-vidual cases to educate viewers about the law—became two of the most profitable programs for the network. Such success led to numerous imita-tors, both on CCTV and on provincial and municipal television stations.

Commercialization was not the only factor that encouraged greater legal coverage. The party-state also encouraged the media to boost aware-ness of law and legal issues to strengthen the legal system. Commercial-ization played an important role, however: increased autonomy over content—because successful papers are often given a longer editorial leash by the CCP-led press groups to which they belong—in turn fostered even more financial incentives for the media to challenge limits on permissible content.

Increased media attention to the courts and law has come at a sensitive time for the judiciary. Although the media traditionally have served as both the mouthpiece and the eyes and ears of the CCP, the courts have long occupied a weak position in the political system. Courts possess only limited authority to review the actions of other state actors and often lack the power to enforce their own judgments. Courts have made significant progress in recent years by boosting the education of judges and taking modest steps toward professionalization. The number of cases courts hear has also increased significantly over the past fifteen years. The effectiveness of China's courts, however, continues to suffer from lack of autonomy, corruption, and incompetence. Emphasis on procedural law remains weak. Local governments control court budgets and judicial appointments, meaning that courts are unable to resist pressure from either local officials or persons with ties to such officials. In addition, CCP officials continue to have the authority to intervene in individual court cases, both formally and informally. Senior court officials have in recent years reemphasized courts' obligation to follow CCP leadership, although at the same time they have recognized the need for courts to win popular trust and have begun important reforms designed to centralize court finances (and thus lessen courts' dependence on local governments).

In the late 1990s and early 2000s, the dramatic growth of the Internet in China added a new dimension to media coverage of law. Internet news portals such as Sohu and Sina began to provide extensive legal coverage. Such sites post articles from traditional print media and supplement such coverage with online discussion forums, commentaries, and in some cases their own news content.[4] In addition, some of the traditional media, including *People's Daily*, include significantly more content on their Web sites than in their print editions. Such Web sites sometimes include articles that would not be allowed to run in print. More recently, blogs have played an important role in spreading information, at times fanning the flames of media coverage of high-profile cases. In the Deng Yujiao case, for example, one of the lawyers initially working on the case used his blog to release information about the case, including allegations that one of Deng Yujiao's alleged assailants had tried to remove her clothing. Another blogger visited Deng Yujiao in a psychiatric ward in the hospital where she was being detained—and then posted details of his encounter, and pictures of Deng, on the Internet.[5]

The growth of the Internet is having two major effects on the dissemination of information. First, it means that local news can instantly become national news. In the past, articles about individual cases that ran in the local media were unlikely to be noticed outside the immediate region, unless a paper with national administrative rank or circulation took notice of the case. The growth of Web portals that post thousands of news articles from across China each day means that information now spreads rapidly.

This rapid spread of information, and in particular the speed with which information spreads via blogs and social networking sites, makes it much harder for local authorities to cover up bad news. Although efforts to ban reporting on sensitive cases continue, the growth of the Internet makes these bans less effective: by the time a ban is imposed, news has often already spread. For example, in late 2005 and early 2006 a number of major Chinese media outlets covered the case of Zhou Yezhong, a Wuhan University professor accused of plagiarizing the work of another scholar, Wang Tiancheng. In an ironic twist, Zhou Yezhong was a prominent scholar known for his close links to CCP leadership; Wang Tiancheng was a former Peking University lecturer who had been imprisoned for his liberal leanings and attempts to form a rival political party.

After initial coverage of the plagiarism allegations in November 2005 in *Freezing Point*, a weekly supplement of *China Youth Daily*,[6] Peking University law professor He Weifang wrote a detailed dissection of Zhou Yezhong's article and his weak defense against the plagiarism accusations.[7] The article was originally scheduled to run in *Freezing Point*—despite the fact that the Central Propaganda Department had criticized the publication for its earlier report on the case, and had apparently banned the media from further reports on the scandal.[8] The publication in the end decided against publishing He Weifang's article, apparently yielding to higher-level pressure. But his article was posted on a legal Web site and widely discussed online. Likewise, although there was little subsequent media coverage of the case, Wang Tiancheng posted updates regarding the case to his blog. Although the blog was subsequently blocked in China, complaints and other documents relating to the case were posted anonymously elsewhere—and remained available even after most discussion of the case was removed from major Web sites.[9]

In March 2006, Wang Tiancheng sued Zhou Yezhong for infringing on his copyright, claiming more than RMB 70,000 in economic and emotional damages.[10] After the *Beijing News* reported on the case, Propaganda Department officials issued an instruction ordering punishment of the journalists and editors who had been involved in publishing the article on the case. The punishment suggested that the ban imposed after the November report by *Freezing Point* remained in place. Most media appeared to obey the ban, but the *Beijing News* article remained available on the *China Youth Daily* Web site, and a few other publications, including the *Shanghai Morning Post*, also reported on the case.[11] The willingness of the Shanghai paper to cover the case suggests that local authorities in Beijing may have been responsible for punishing the *Beijing News*. In addition, an internal notice from the *Beijing News* fining the editors and journalists responsible for the article and referencing the ban was posted and discussed on the Internet[12]—thus drawing further attention to both the ban and the allegations of plagiarism. Similarly, when the Beijing High Court decided the appeal in the case, in which it upheld the original verdict vindicating Zhou Yezhong of the plagiarism charge, mainstream media refrained from covering the outcome. But the court decision was posted to the Web,[13] and one Chinese Web site, Tianya, covered the decision. The Tianya report quoted Wang's lawyers as stating that the outcome was obviously the result of political interference, as such an opinion could not have been written by judges who understood the law.[14]

Still, the authorities do sometimes succeed in imposing near-total bans on discussion of cases on major Web sites, as was the case in the July 2009 detention of legal activist and scholar Xu Zhiyong. Yet even in such cases information appears to spread quickly via blogs and social networking sites. The growth of e-mail and the Internet also makes it possible for reporters blocked from reporting in their local areas to pass information along to colleagues elsewhere—often those working at media outlets not subject to the local propaganda department bans. Thus, for example, in 2003, the BMW Case—in which a woman in Harbin killed a farmer with her BMW following an argument about a traffic accident—generated nationwide public and media outrage when a local court did not sentence the driver to prison. After an initial report in the *Heilongjiang Morning News*, Harbin media were instructed to use only officially approved reports and were prohibited from carrying articles that questioned the local court's decision. But media from elsewhere covered the case—and posted articles to the Internet. These reports resulted in an enormous volume of postings to online discussion forums. The Central Propaganda Department eventually issued a nationwide ban on further reporting and discussion of the case, but not until after it had generated more online discussion on Sohu and Sina than even the SARS crisis earlier in 2003.

Likewise, in the 2005 She Xianglin case, discussed above, local media in Hubei Province were banned from investigating or reporting on the case pending an official investigation, but media from outside Hubei covered the case extensively, and reports again spread quickly online.[15]

The Zhou Yezhong, BMW, and She Xianglin cases highlight the challenge that the development of the Internet poses to China's traditional system of media control. Effective censorship depends on the ability of national and local propaganda officials to terminate discussion of topics. Although propaganda authorities remain able and willing to punish those who overstep the boundaries of permissible content, it is increasingly difficult to block all reporting on a particular case or topic—in particular when the ban is imposed by local or provincial authorities.

The growth of the Internet has also facilitated increased debate of legal matters. In the 1990s, reporting on legal matters in newspapers and magazines expanded to include coverage of a variety of views on legal controversies. The Internet, however, has much more dramatically facilitated broader discussion of legal issues. Seemingly minor cases can instantly become major topics of online debate, and such debates often go well beyond the boundaries of what would be permitted in the print media or on television.

In another example, in May 2003 a court in Zhengzhou, in Henan Province, issued an opinion stating that a provincial pricing regulation was "spontaneously invalid" because it violated the national Seed Law. The case might well have gone unnoticed but for the Internet. Following the decision, provincial authorities reacted angrily, arguing that the court lacked the authority to invalidate a local regulation. In October, the Standing Committee of the Henan Province People's Congress issued a notice seeking punishment of the court and the judges responsible for the decision. The Henan Province High People's Court obliged, ordering that Judge Li Huijian, who had written the opinion, and one other judge be removed from office.

The decision to punish the judges resulted in widespread media attention to the case, which had not previously been covered by the media. In what appeared to be an organized effort to generate media coverage, four lawyers wrote an open letter arguing for review of the regulation by the Standing Committee of the National People's Congress and protesting the punishment of Judge Li Huijian. Reports in *Southern Weekend* and *Legal Daily* discussed both the case and the letter—apparently the first media reports about the case. Within days, reports and discussion spread online, initiating extensive debate over whether the court's actions were permissible. The online discussion appeared to go beyond the boundaries of traditional print media, with Web sites carrying far-reaching discussions of the limited powers of Chinese courts and arguments for giving courts more authority. The case was controversial because courts in China lack the power to invalidate regulations or laws—such power lies exclusively with the National People's

Congress. Nonetheless, following the extensive discussion and outcry in the traditional and online media—and apparently after the intervention of the Supreme People's Court—Judge Li Huijian regained her position.

The following two sections investigate the way expanded media coverage of the courts has brought new scrutiny of, and hence pressure on, China's courts. But before proceeding, it should be noted that the growing availability of legal information and debate may also be making it easier for judges to do their jobs. Judges in less-developed areas of China, who only a few years ago frequently lacked basic legal training and information, now have easy access to a large volume of material online. Judges comment that they routinely go online to locate laws and regulations, to find examples of how courts elsewhere in China have handled similar legal issues, and to read academic opinion on novel or difficult legal issues. Furthermore, judges state that better access to information makes it easier for them to resist pressures from CCP officials and others because they can respond with improved legal arguments. The growth of the Internet thus appears to encourage greater innovation and standardization of the law across China.

EXPANDING SCRUTINY, RETAINING CONTROL

Increasing Oversight, Increasing Justice?

Without help from the media, Sun Zhigang's killers would have gone unpunished. In March 2003, Sun, a twenty-seven-year-old graphic designer, was beaten to death at a detention center for migrant workers in Guangzhou. Local police had detained him after he failed to produce the temporary residence permit that was at the time required of all migrant workers, including university graduates like Sun.

More than a month after Sun's murder, *Southern Metropolitan Daily*, the leading commercial paper in Guangdong Province, carried an extensive report on the case. The paper, which is part of a press group owned by the Guangdong Province Communist Party Committee, acted in response to appeals for help from Sun's family. The paper also printed a commentary condemning the killing, titled "Who Will Take Responsibility for the Abnormal Death of a Citizen?" Local propaganda department officials sought to ban further reporting on the case. But within hours of publication, the original report was posted to numerous Web sites and touched off a wave of outrage in Internet discussion forums. Other media soon took up the case, forcing the authorities to investigate Sun's murder and punish those responsible. Twelve suspects were sentenced in criminal trials: the principal defendant, who was a nurse at the detention center, received a death sentence. An additional twenty-three officials received administrative sanctions for their mishandling of the case.

Nevertheless, the most important effect of the media coverage was not punishment of Sun's killers. The media coverage contributed to fundamental changes to the detention system that had resulted in his death. Following the initial reports and subsequent arrests in the case, three young academics issued a petition to the National People's Congress seeking to abolish the custody and repatriation system for migrant workers. The system, under which Sun had been detained, permitted local police to incarcerate and send home migrant workers who lacked local residence permits. The timing of the petition was coordinated with journalists who used news of it to write further reports on widespread abuses in the system. Internet news portals again posted the articles in prominent positions on their sites, leading to further discussion and encouraging the press across China to carry similar reports. A second petition from a group of academics helped to keep the issue in the news. In June 2003—just three months after Sun's murder and two weeks after the trial of those allegedly responsible—China's State Council announced that the custody and repatriation system was being abolished and replaced by a system that would focus on assisting, rather than punishing, migrant workers.

The Sun Zhigang case is the most prominent example of the media's ability to expose injustice and force change in the Chinese legal system. Yet it is far from the only such example. In numerous other cases, the media have come to the assistance of aggrieved individuals, frequently claiming that courts have issued unjust decisions. Many public interest lawyers in China say that favorable media coverage of a client's plight is often the most important factor leading to a successful lawsuit.

Changing Media, Weakening Courts?

Media coverage is undoubtedly increasing transparency in the Chinese legal system. The threat of media exposure is a powerful weapon that can pressure courts to follow both substantive and procedural law. The increased relevance of law in China has provided journalists with standards to which they can point in criticizing the courts. Judges comment that it is far more difficult to conceal illegitimate decisions today than in the past because a single posting online can spark nationwide coverage. As a result, judges are paying more attention to issuing well-reasoned decisions that follow the law.

Yet the media do not function as simply a watchdog that checks court abuses. In many cases, members of the media themselves serve as fact finders. The party-state superiors—who oversee the courts and continue to issue written instructions to courts in individual cases—are frequently influenced by the media. They will treat media accounts as fact. Judges comment that they are not afraid of media scrutiny; they are wary of the ability of the media to influence party-state superiors. Judges also contend that the media suffer from many problems similar to those that undermine the courts: corruption and bias. The practice of journalists writing biased reports in exchange for payment has given rise to the saying among some lawyers and judges that "it is better to hire a journalist than to hire a lawyer."

The media's traditional position as both the mouthpiece and an investigative arm of the party-state means that when the courts and media are in conflict, media views are likely to prevail. Hence *Focus*, CCTV's investigative program, has been called "the highest court in the land" due to its ability to influence China's central leadership. The reliance of officials on media views is accentuated by the fact that national, provincial, and local media continue to issue internal reports, or *neican*. These are confidential reports prepared for leaders of a particular rank that often contain material deemed too sensitive for inclusion in public editions. Journalists use internal reports to apply pressure in court cases, either in place of or as supplements to public reporting. In some cases, internal reports pave the way for public reports. In the Sun Zhigang case, for example, the official Xinhua News Agency filed confidential internal reports on the case at the same time as its public reports.

Prominent CCP mouthpiece newspapers also have offices responsible for handling letters and visits from readers and viewers. Such offices sometimes refer complaints directly to the relevant party-state department, including the courts, with an implicit threat to publicize the complaint if the issue is not resolved. Journalists also use informal pressure to affect the outcome of cases, telephoning judges to express interest in a case even when the journalist has no intention of actually reporting on it. Journalists and lawyers say that such actions are sometimes sufficient to alter case outcomes. For some journalists, resolving problems and obtaining redress for aggrieved individuals is itself a goal, independent of the potential news value of the underlying grievance.

The ability of the media to affect outcomes is most apparent in criminal cases. Judges and lawyers report that media coverage of these cases often results in pressure to punish defendants harshly as courts try to "manage the emotions of society." Although in some cases media coverage can benefit defendants, as it did She Xianglin and Deng Yujiao, defense lawyers state that they generally avoid seeking media coverage of criminal cases. Media coverage often reflects populist demands for justice—or vengeance—in particular, in cases of alleged wrongdoing by officials. Hence, for example, one headline on the case of Zhang Jun, who was accused of multiple counts of murder, declared that the defendant should be "Sliced into 1,000 Pieces."

Convicted gangster Liu Yong found that media coverage of his case made the difference between life and death. An intermediate court in Liaoning Province convicted Liu of a long list of crimes, including intentionally causing harm and organizing a criminal syndicate, related to his role as a leading organized crime figure in Shenyang. The trial court sentenced Liu to death. On appeal, however, Liu's lawyers persuaded the Liaoning High People's Court to reduce his sentence to life in prison. Among the factors that apparently resulted in the lighter sentence was the argument that Liu's confession had been obtained through torture.[16]

A week after the appellate court's decision, a Shanghai paper, *Bund Pictorial*, issued an article titled "Doubts Regarding the Decision to Change the Sentence of Gangster Liu Yong to a Suspended Death Sentence." Online news accounts of the case quickly spread, with one major portal employing a much more direct headline: "Liu Yong Will Not Die." Reports suggested that Liu had received lenient treatment because of ties to CCP officials in Liaoning. Web sites filled with angry comments, expressing outrage at the perceived favorable treatment.

The public outcry led the Supreme People's Court to intervene in the case, apparently at the instruction of senior national CCP officials. The court invoked a rarely used procedure through which it may retry questionable cases de novo. The outcome of the carefully scripted retrial surprised no one: Liu was resentenced to death. He was executed the same morning that the court announced its verdict. The media claimed victory, noting that the decision was in line with popular demands.

The Liu Yong case reflects a pattern that has been replicated in numerous cases: media intervention leads CCP officials to issue instructions to the courts that result in rapid trials and harsh punishments. The media then declare victory, noting that the courts have acted in line with popular demands. Even in the Sun Zhigang case, in which the media were widely viewed as having played an important role in advancing justice, media pressure led to show trials of the alleged culprits. Only a small number of reporters were permitted to attend the three simultaneous trials in the case, and propaganda authorities ordered all media in China to use only officially sanctioned reports on the proceedings and verdicts. Commentators who sought to question the fairness of the trials—and in particular to ask whether the defendants were being made scapegoats for more senior officials who were responsible for the conditions at the detention center and who had encouraged the attack on Sun—were not permitted to do so.

The Liu Yong, Sun Zhigang, and perhaps even the Deng Yujiao cases demonstrate that increased media oversight does not necessarily result in fairer trials: under media pressure, courts have little, if any, autonomy to decide cases based on the facts before them. Judges argue that there is little they can do to combat media pressure—even in cases where the media misunderstand or misrepresent the legal issues or facts in a case. The media's ability both to stir up popular sentiment and to influence official opinion may reinforce the CCP's control of the courts by encouraging officials to intervene in individual cases. The media are not solely responsible for the powerful effect of populist views on the courts, but the media's traditional role has combined with their new commercialized mass appeal to make them particularly influential.

CHANGING COURTS, CHANGING MEDIA

Chinese judges often portray themselves as the victims of unfair or biased media scrutiny and complain that journalists are frequently corrupt or ignorant of the law. Yet courts have not been solely passive recipients of media scrutiny. Courts and judges are adept at managing and controlling media coverage. In addition, members of the media are increasingly finding themselves in court as defendants in defamation cases—the overwhelming majority of which they lose. These trends show that courts are developing the ability to resist media oversight. Pressure from the courts may also be altering how the Chinese media operate.

Controlled Transparency

Over the past decade, senior court officials have repeatedly emphasized the importance of greater transparency in China's courts. Addressing the National People's Congress in March 2006, then Supreme People's Court President Xiao Yang noted the importance of "public supervision" (*renmin qunzhong jiandu*) of the courts.[17] In another 2006 speech, this time to the heads of Provincial High People's Courts, Xiao noted that courts must voluntarily release information about important cases, cease being passive in response to media coverage, and strengthen their propaganda systems to "lead the media to report positively" about the courts.[18] Xiao's successor at the SPC, President Wang Shengjun, has likewise spoken of the importance both of courts opening themselves to media supervision and of balancing legal outcomes with the needs of the nation and the CCP.[19] And in May 2009 the SPC issued directions to lower courts concerning implementation of the concept of justice for the people, calling on courts to respond quickly to negative reporting, to improve relations with the media, and to voluntarily provide tips to the media so as to encourage positive coverage.[20]

The comments and rules reflect two tactics that courts have used in response to increased media pressure. Courts have spoken of the importance of supervision and have publicly welcomed greater coverage. At the same time, however, courts have stepped up efforts to manage information flows to the media, attempting to control access to the courts as well as the content of news reports about the courts. Regulations adopted by the SPC in 1999 state that most cases should be open to the public and the media—but also include numerous vague exceptions and require reporters to obtain advance permission from the court hearing the case. In practice, the regulations give judges and courts significant discretion to deny access to the media. Such restrictions are particularly helpful for local courts seeking to block coverage by national or nonlocal media.

Courts have also become adept at encouraging positive media coverage. They frequently draft articles for the media or provide details about cases to journalists. Courts reward judges with praise and bonuses for obtaining positive coverage or for authoring articles that help to strengthen the courts' public image. Many courts also require local media to seek approval of articles from either court propaganda officials or the judges hearing a particular case prior to running a report. Failure to seek approval—or running a critical article—can result in journalists being barred from further reporting on the court. In 2006, the SPC also announced that it was creating an official press secretary and that judges were henceforth forbidden from speaking to the media without prior approval. Local courts have taken similar steps. Media commentary has portrayed the system as an effort to restrict critical coverage because it restricts other judges from speaking to the media, and has criticized the courts for being afraid of media scrutiny.[21]

Following the 2003 Sun Zhigang and Liu Yong cases, courts in a number of provinces stepped up their efforts to control reporting. Regulations issued jointly by the Guangdong High People's Court and the Guangdong Propaganda Department bar reporting on cases prior to courts issuing first-instance decisions. The media are allowed to cover cases once they have been decided, but the regulations prohibit reports that differ in opinion from the courts—in effect banning criticism of court decisions in Guangdong. In 2005, the State Administration of Radio, Film, and Broadcasting banned television and radio stations from reporting on cases while they are still pending and prohibited local media from covering events outside their home jurisdiction.[22] This regulation mirrors a Central Propaganda Department instruction on the same topic. And SPC officials have repeatedly stated that in sensitive or high-profile cases, the courts speak with a "unified voice," with only official spokespeople talking to the media.

Judges argue that controls on media coverage are necessary to prevent biased reporting. Journalists, in turn, complain that judges are increasingly using the rhetoric of "judicial independence" to prevent media oversight of the courts. China's courts are not unique in restricting media coverage; many Western countries impose significant limitations on coverage of pending cases. But such restrictions may be particularly damaging in China, given the very limited history of transparency in the legal system and the numerous problems that continue to undermine the authority and ability of the courts. Efforts to restrict media exposure are just one example of the general attempt by the Chinese party-state to create a system of controlled transparency. Like other state actors, China's courts claim that they are open to scrutiny and thus deserving of public trust, while at the same time they are restricting and manipulating the information available to the public.

Over the past fifteen years, there has been a sharp increase in defamation litigation, with China's courts hearing 5,195 defamation cases in 2004. No official reports detail the total number of defamation cases in subsequent years, but observers note that the volume of such cases continues to be sizeable. Though some libel cases are brought against ordinary people or corporations, a significant portion of such cases are against the media. The media complain that defamation litigation is being used as a new form of control. Four trends help to explain the impact of defamation litigation on the Chinese media.

First, both anecdotal evidence and empirical studies suggest that the media lose the majority of cases brought against them. They appear to fare worst when sued by officials, party-state entities, and businesses or corporations, and are moderately more successful when sued by ordinary or famous people, although they still lose most such cases. Chinese defamation law is vague. This vagueness facilitates decisions against the media by allowing courts to find the media liable even for small errors. In addition, SPC interpretations permit courts to find against the media for using insulting language—meaning that truth is not always a defense against defamation claims.

Second, defamation litigation has become a significant means of retaliation by targets of public opinion supervision. Numerous cases are brought by officials or state or CCP entities in response to critical coverage. Plaintiffs range from officials accused of misusing funds to those linked to cover-ups of major disasters, to a prison that sued (and won emotional damages for the prison itself) following a report on a sex scandal at the prison. In a number of instances, officials who have already been subject to criminal or administrative sanctions have successfully sued for libel. Likewise, corporations—including prominent international brands such as Haier, as well as one company involved in building the Three Gorges Dam—have brought suit in response to critical reports that are designed both to retaliate against the media and to block further reporting. Most such cases are brought in plaintiffs' home courts—frequently against nonlocal media. Not surprisingly, the media lose the overwhelming majority of such cases.

Courts and judges themselves have brought a small number of defamation cases in response to critical coverage. Such cases are generally brought in a court that is superior or neighboring to the plaintiff or the home of the plaintiff judge. But a few such cases have been brought in the court that was itself the target of criticism. Again not surprisingly, courts and judges win most such cases. The practice has been widely criticized by legal and media academics in China, but judges argue that they have few other weapons with which to resist unfair media coverage.

Third, a significant number of defamation cases are brought by ordinary persons against official newspapers claiming harm from unfavorable accounts—with plaintiffs winning many such cases. Such results are counterintuitive; the traditional powerful role of the party press would suggest that ordinary people might be wary of challenging the media. Although plaintiff-friendly defamation standards help to explain such outcomes, the willingness of ordinary persons to sue the official media—and to succeed in doing so—also suggests a weakening of the media's authoritative role.

The media's susceptibility to lawsuits by both officials and ordinary persons may indicate that media, newspapers in particular, are shifting away from being powerful official institutions. Traditional media roles are now open to greater scrutiny. The media have long served as a mechanism for giving voice to public grievances. They now do so in an environment in which they face liability where such complaints prove to be false or even merely insulting.

Fourth, the growth of defamation litigation is having a significant effect on how the media operate—and is perhaps beginning to facilitate professionalism and professional identity among members of the media. Many in the media portray defamation litigation as unjust attempts to retaliate against or constrain the media. Others, however, note that the media are to blame for many such cases. Competition resulting from commercialization has increased autonomy without significant improvements in professional standards. Journalists now have incentives to push the limits of both permitted content and the facts. This was illustrated by the 2007 "fake dumplings case," when a report aired on Beijing television claiming to show dumplings stuffed with cardboard. The story turned out to be false—and the journalist responsible for it wound up in jail.

Although many awards against the media are for modest amounts, in some cases, such as those brought by corporations claiming lost profits, the financial risk of defamation litigation is significant. The threat of defamation litigation appears to be having an effect on how the media cover news, forcing journalists to think twice about the accuracy of articles before they are published. Numerous articles in journals aimed at journalists discuss the phenomenon and provide advice about how best to avoid litigation. Some publications now require potentially controversial articles to be screened by lawyers for potential liability. Most major papers have also established legal departments to deal with the wide range of legal issues they now confront.

Reporters say that publications are increasingly wary of being sued and are training them to avoid litigation. For this reason, reporters now place far greater emphasis than they did just a few years ago on maintaining notes and recordings of interviews, on corroborating information, and on checking facts before publishing critical reports. Reporters and editors say they also are more attentive to presenting both sides of a story to avoid bias, and they increasingly avoid excessively emotional reports. Journalists have also united—in conferences and on Web sites—to discuss the rising problem of defamation litigation, and to discuss strategies for combating such cases and what they perceive to be unfair legal standards and courts. The Chinese Journalists Association, working together with scholars in media and law, has also attempted to persuade the SPC to issue a new interpretation governing defamation that would provide journalists with greater protection.[23]

China's media are stuck in a changing framework, one that they can influence but not control. The media's authoritative role serves as a partial justification for strong legal protections for individuals' reputations: some in China contend that the fact that ordinary people continue to view the media as both authoritative and official justifies imposing constraints on reporting that would not be justified were the media actually free. Defamation litigation is one of the few mechanisms for challenging the authority of the press. Likewise, in a society in which criticism has traditionally been muted, unfavorable reports have particular potency—thus perhaps justifying greater limits than might be found in a democratic society. But the weakening of the media's authority also makes the media more vulnerable than in the past. One result is that the media are being forced to take steps to protect themselves, including raising their own standards for how they report on the news. The threat of litigation thus may be forcing journalists to adjust their behavior in ways that neither state regulation nor marketplace pressures have done before.

Defamation litigation reflects the courts' increasing role in judging media content. But it would be a mistake to view the growth of defamation litigation as reflecting a shift away from propaganda department control over the media. Rather, it reflects a new form of content regulation. In the past, those unhappy with the media could complain only to a propaganda department; today the media face an additional regulator of content—courts—in addition to propaganda departments. Whereas propaganda department review of content is primarily concerned with ideological correctness, courts now evaluate reports for accuracy and insulting character as well. From the perspective of many in the media, such increased scrutiny reflects a challenge to increased media autonomy.

CONCLUSION: DUELING INSTITUTIONS

Courts and the media view each other as rival institutions, each claiming to be a neutral arbiter of disputes and grievances. Each sees the other as pursuing their own interests, not as impartial decision makers or reporters. Such tensions reflect the rapid development of, and changes in, both the media and the legal system in recent years. They also reflect an important characteristic of the Chinese political system.

Over the past decade, the central party-state has attempted to curb the abuses that threaten to undermine the legitimacy of CCP rule by encouraging a range of institutions to assume roles as supervisors of misconduct and wrongdoing. Such institutions include the courts, the media, the procuratorates, the letters and visits system, people's congresses, and CCP discipline authorities. Each claims to be an appropriate forum for addressing such problems; all suffer from similar weaknesses, including local protectionism and corruption. The system appears to be designed to encourage oversight by a range of party-state actors, each with its own claim to being an unbiased and fair arbiter and investigator. One consequence is that such institutions are increasingly competing with each other for authority within the confines of CCP rule.

The range of actors with supervisory roles highlights the central party-state's efforts to create a system of controlled transparency. The growth of the commercialized media, and of investigative journalism, over the past fifteen years was largely designed to reduce the need for state subsidies to party media groups. But the tolerance and encouragement of critical reporting, though of course subject to the changing whims of propaganda authorities, reflects recognition of the need for greater transparency both to maintain legitimacy and to curb abuses. Allowing a range of state actors to voice grievances permits the state to appear responsive to public views, without encouraging nonstate actors to play too prominent a role. This institutional backdrop explains why neither press coverage of legal issues nor court retaliation against the media overstep permissible boundaries. Both are playing by the rules of the game: various state institutions provide checks on each other, and the CCP serves as the referee.

China is establishing a system of limited transparency, where some of the benefits of greater scrutiny of official action can be obtained without at the same time undermining confidence in the state or encouraging direct challenges to CCP rule. The embrace of controlled transparency explains not only the media's role but also why lawyers, individuals, and even some NGOs are being allowed to voice a widening range of grievances, both in the formal legal system and through other institutions. Yet the emphasis on controlling information about the courts demonstrates the degree to which state institutions seek some of the benefits of transparency without at the same time becoming fundamentally more open to public scrutiny.

Fear of greater openness also explains the power of populism in the legal system, and the importance of the media's claim to represent public views. In many cases, the media succeed in influencing the courts by appealing to populist views of justice—most notably in the Liu Yong case. Populist claims to justice are, of course, a common feature of most legal systems. In China, however, they have particular force. The legal system has traditionally been weak and lacking authority. Substantive justice is often privileged over procedural justice, and state concerns with maintaining stability trump all other values. CCP leaders thus intervene in the courts to appear responsive to popular views. Such intervention remains legitimate, and even encouraged, in a system in which officials and leaders are evaluated on their ability to quell and prevent discontent.

This institutional design demonstrates why media commercialization will not necessarily lead to media freedom, and why media coverage of the courts will not necessarily improve the fairness of the Chinese legal system. Newspapers, television, and radio remain arms of the state. Aggressive media seeking to maximize profit may also be serving state interests in control and oversight. Revelations of abuses in the legal system—especially those that appeal to popular demands for justice—may push the courts toward greater openness and fairness, but they may also subvert court autonomy and reinforce CCP oversight.

Recognizing that media oversight may reaffirm CCP oversight is nonetheless not an argument for restricting media coverage. Public scrutiny is raising the courts' concern with their image and with managing information. Evidence suggests that the threat of exposure is compelling courts to take more care in their cases—and thus may be having a significant positive effect on the legal system. In addition, the media have played an important role in educating the public (and even judges) about law and the legal system. An enormous volume of information about the judiciary system—much of it produced by press outlets—is now available in China. Increased knowledge appears to be having an effect: standards of popular complaint are increasingly law based, and growing numbers of individuals are using the formal legal system to protect their own interests. But there is also a risk for the courts in such increased coverage and legal awareness: fostering expectations that the legal system can be used to protect individuals risks creating greater disillusionment if such expectations are not met.

Perhaps the most important effect of media influence on the courts is to highlight the fundamental question facing the courts: how do they develop autonomy in a system that continues to encourage a range of actors to intervene in court decision making? Many in the judicial system recognize the need to resist external influence. At present, they do not appear to view greater openness and transparency as serving their own interests, because it exposes them to criticism without increasing their authority. It may be that expanded coverage will, over time, lead courts to conclude that increased transparency leads to greater public confidence and greater autonomy. But it is equally, if not more, likely that courts will conclude that the media are a threat to their autonomy and influence—not a mechanism for expanding judicial authority.

Nevertheless, recent experiences suggest that courts are adept at using claims to independence and official statements regarding the importance of the legal system to resist pressure from media. Evidence from defamation litigation likewise shows that courts are using their own power to protect themselves, and increasingly are forums for the resolution of rights-based grievances. The ability to retaliate against their critics may simply reflect power dynamics in the Chinese political system; it may also hint at a greater role for development from the ground up in China's judicial system, as courts' roles come to be defined in part by how litigants and judges act. At the very least, rising pressure from the media is forcing courts to consider how best to maximize their existing powers.

Recent experience of media influence on the courts carries lessons for the media as well as for the courts. In many respects, the media and the courts are in similar positions: they are both state institutions attempting to strengthen their autonomy within the confines of CCP oversight. Both remain subject to extensive CCP interference, and both have undergone significant change in recent years. Some of this change has been state driven. But much of the significant change is coming from within as the courts and the media seek to define and expand their positions.

One lesson of court-media relations over the past decade is that top-down attempts to balance the interests of the two institutions, or to force each to professionalize, have not worked particularly well. Courts have learned that they can protect and expand their own autonomy; members of the press have been forced to answer to the legal system as well as to the Propaganda Department. Both the courts and the media are realizing that improving their professional standards may be an important vehicle for strengthening their autonomy. This dynamic exchange is one that will help determine the future position of both of these institutions within Chinese society.

Notes

I am grateful to Chen Zi, Huang Ju, Zhang Lan, Zhang Hong, Zhou Xin, and Zhu Xinping for their research assistance for this essay.

Unless otherwise indicated, material in this article is drawn from six recent articles on the Chinese media and courts: Benjamin L. Liebman, *Innovation through Intimidation? An Empirical Account of Defamation Litigation in China*, 47 HARV. INT'L. L.J. 33 (2006); Benjamin L. Liebman, *Watchdog or Demagogue? The Media in the Chinese Legal System*, 105 COLUM. L. REV. 1 (2005); Benjamin L. Liebman and Timothy Wu, *China's Network Justice*, 8 CHICAGO J. INT'L. L. 257 (2007); Benjamin L. Liebman, *China's Courts: Restricted Reform*, 191 CHINA Q. 620 (Sept. 2007); Benjamin L. Liebman, *A Return to Populist Legality? Historical Legacies and Legal Reform*, in MAO'S INVISIBLE HAND (Elizabeth Perry and Sebastian Heilmann, eds.) (in press); and Benjamin L. Liebman, *Scandal, Sukyandaru, and Chouwen*, 106 MICH. L. REV. 1041 (2008) (reviewing Mark D. West, SECRETS, SEX AND SPECTACLE: THE RULES OF SCANDAL IN JAPAN AND THE UNITED STATES).

1. Wang Doudou and Yuan Dingbo, "Anjian yueshi meiti guanzhu faguan yueyao baochi lixing" [The more media attention given to the case, the more critical it is for the judge to maintain rationality in handling the case], *Fazhi ribao* [*Legal Daily*], 2 June 2009, http://news.sohu.com/20090603/n264302405.shtml.

2. China's procuratorates serve as a general oversight body and also serve as the prosecution in criminal cases. They are of rank equal to the courts and have the power to compel courts to rehear cases if the procuracy disagrees with court decisions.

3. For examples of coverage, see "Hangzhou biaoche zhuangsiren an—Zuixin xiaoxi" [Hangzhou drag race homicide case—Latest news], Sina.com, http://roll.news.sina.com.cn/s_fjzbc_all/1/index.shtml; Fang Yibo, "Hangzhou biaoche an zhaoshizhe yi jiaotong zhaoshi zui bei gongsu" [Perpetrator in the Hangzhou drag race case is charged and prosecuted with the crime of causing traffic casualties], *Xinhua Wang*, 3 July 2009, http://news.sina.com.cn/c/2009–07–03/191218149589.shtml.

4. In general, only Web sites linked to traditional media are permitted to generate original news content—and the total number of such sites is limited. In practice, other Web sites from time to time generate their own news content or work with traditional media to generate such content.

5. See http://xialinblog.blog.sohu.com/tag/%B5%CB%D3%F1%BD%BF/.

6. Bao Limin, "Shui gai wei xianfa xuejia 'piaoqie' fuze?—Guanyu Wuda xueshu weiyuanhui fu zhuren Zhou Yezhong jiaoshou deng shexian piaoqie de jizhe diaocha" [Who should be held responsible for plagiarism of constitutional scholars?—Journalist's investigation regarding the suspected plagiarism of scholars including professor Zhou Yezhong, vice chair of the Academic Committee of Wuhan University], *Zhongguo qingnian bao* [*China Youth Daily*], 30 November 2005.

7. He Weifang, "Zhou Yezhong jiaoshou shijian ji qita (xiuding gao)" [The Incident of Professor Zhou Yezhong and others (revised)], Beida Falü Xinxi Wang [Peking University Legal Information Web Site], n.d., http://article.chinalawinfo.com/article/user/art.

8. He Yanguang, "Guanyu Zhou Yezhong xueshu piaoqie—Gongzheng youyici chengwei ruozhe" [Zhou Yezhou academic plagiarism—Justice is again the weak party], Guantian Chashe [Guan Tian Tea House], 28 December 2005; Li Datong, "Jiu 'Bing Dian' zhoukan bei feifa tingkan de gongkai kangyi" [Public protest against the illegal termination of *Freezing Point* weekly magazine], Boxun Xinwen Wang [Bo Xun News Web Site], 25 January 2005.

9. Wang's complaint was posted by an anonymous bulletin board user at http://hi.baidu.com/%B7%E7%C8%E7%D9%E2/blog/item/24814a4356daa51a73f05dd4.html.

10. The complaint in the case was also posted online. *Wuhan Daxue faxueyuan jiaoshou Zhou Yezhong yin shexian piaoqie bei qisu* [Zhou Yezhong, a law professor of Wuhan University, was sued for plagiarism], n.d., http://chineselawyers.bokee.com/4674870.html.

11. Xu Defang, "Wang Tiancheng zhengshi qisu wuda jiaoshou Zhou Yezhong" [Wang Tiancheng formally brings lawsuit against Zhou Yezhong, a law professor of Wuhan University], *Dongfang Zaobao Wang* [*Oriental Morning Post Web*], 17 March 2006.

12. For examples, see "Guanyu cuowu kanfa 'Wang Tiancheng qisu wuda bodao Zhou Yezhong' yiwen de chuli jueding" [Decision concerning the incorrect publication of the article "Wang Tiancheng Sued Zhou Yezhong, a Doctoral Tutor of Wuhan University"], Xin Jing Bao She Shewu Guanli Weiyuanhui [Beijing News Press Affairs Administration Committee], 21 March 2006, http://post.baidu.com/f?kz=89749717.

13. "Beijingshi gaoji renmin fayuan minshi panjueshu (2006) Gaominzhongzi di 1254 hao" [(Final) civil judgment of Beijing Municipal High People's Court (2006) Gaominzhongzi, no. 1254], 20 December 2006, http://www.crd-net.org/Article/Class3/200612/20061221184342_2913.html.

14. "Zhou Yezhong shexian piaoqie zhongshen yuangao baisu (zhuan zai)" [The plaintiff loses in the lawsuit against Zhou Yezhong for plagiarism (reprinted)], 23 December 2006, http://cache.tianya.cn/publicforum/Content/No01/1/292073.shtml.

15. "Lü zongshu, jizhe diaocha: She Xianglin 'sha qi' cuo'an" [Journalist investigation: The incorrectly decided case accusing She Xianglin of "wife killing"], *Wuhan Chengbao* [*Wuhan Morning Post*], 27 July 2005, http://media.people.com.cn/GB/22114/47850/47855/3572767.html.

16. The court stated that it had reduced the sentence in light of the facts and circumstances of the case, and noted that torture could not be ruled out. The Provincial High Court Opinion is not publicly available, but the decision is summarized in the SPC's opinion.

17. Xiao Yang, "Zuigao renmin fayuan gongzuo baogao" [Work report of the Supreme People's Court], Xinhua Wang [Xinhua Agency Web Site], 19 March 2006, http://www.lianghui.org.cn/chinese/zhuanti/2006lh/1158480.htm.

18. Xue Yongxiu, "Xiao Yang: Fayuan yao zhudong xiang shehui fabu zhongda anjian xinxi" [Xiao Yang: Courts must voluntarily release information about important cases], Zhongguo Fayuan Wang [China Court Web Site], 15 January 2006, http://www.chinacourt.org/public/detail.php?id=191279.

19. Yang Weihan, "Wang Shengjun: Quanmian jiaqiang xingshi da'an yao'an shenpan gongzuo" [Speech by Wang Shengjun: Strengthening trial work in major criminal cases on all levels], Xinhua Wang [Xinhua Web Site], 30 August 2009, http://news.xinhuanet.com/legal/2009–08/30/content_11966723.htm.

20. "Zuigao fayuan yaoqiu geji fayuan jishi yingdui fumian yulun chaozuo" [The Supreme Court asks courts of all levels to timely respond to media stirring up of negative public opinion], Xinhua Wang [Xinhua Web Site], 12 May 2009, http://news.xinhuanet.com/lianzheng/2009–05/12/content_11356258.htm.

21. "Faguan weijing pizhun buke jieshou caifang" [Judges shall be forbidden from doing interviews without prior approval], *Xin Jing Bao* [*Beijing News*], 13 September 2006, http://news.thebeijingnews.com/0546/2006/0913/014@208757.htm; "[Meijie piping] fayuan sheli xinwen fayanren, meiti baodao you jinqu?" [(Media criticism) courts established press spokespeople system, do forbidden areas exist for media reports?], *Renmin Wang* [*People's Daily Online*], 24 September 2006, http://media.people.com.cn/GB/40698/4851777.html.

22. "Guangdian zongju yinfa dui guangdian yulun jiandu gongzuo de xin yaoqiu" [State Administration of Radio, Film and Television issues new requirements concerning public opinion oversight work though the media], Guangdian Zongju Wang [SARFT Web Site], 13 May 2005, http://news.xinhuanet.com/newmedia/2005–05/13/content_2952645.htm.

23. "Xinwen qinhai mingyuquan yinsiquan xin de sifa jieshi jianyi gao (tiaowen bufen)" [Proposed new judicial interpretation (provisions) concerning news media infringement of reputation rights and privacy rights], *Xinwen Jizhe* [*News Reporter*], no. 1 (2008), http://qkzz.net/magazine/1006–3277/2008/01/2263373.htm. Journalists and scholars have also for more than two decades lobbied for a media law to protect journalists.

8

What Kind of Information Does the Public Demand? Getting the News during the 2005 Anti-Japanese Protests

Daniela Stockmann

I N APRIL 2005, protests against Japan erupted in approximately forty Chinese cities. Nationalist youth criticized the Japanese government's attempt to become a permanent member of the United Nations Security Council; the government's approval of high school textbooks that they felt whitewashed Japanese war crimes during Japan's World War II occupation of China and South Korea; and Prime Minister Junichiro Koizumi's visit to the Yasukuni Shrine, which memorializes Japanese military heroes of World War II, including some convicted of war crimes. The foreign news media accused the Chinese government of mobilizing anti-Japanese sentiment through its tightly controlled mass media.[1] Chinese media scholars and propaganda officials blamed the commercialized media and Internet instead. Yet careful analysis of the way Chinese citizens actually selected and screened information from the media during the demonstrations shows that the story is more complicated than either of these interpretations. In actuality, consumer views of the relative credibility of various media sources drive their search for information, particularly during crisis situations. Commercialized and online news media can either arouse or calm down public opinion depending on the extent to which propaganda authorities restrict news reporting in these channels.

The anti-Japanese protests constitute an example of what Chinese media scholars call a "public opinion crisis." This term refers to a situation in which public opinion and the position of the state on a particular issue are in disagreement, thus endangering social stability and economic growth. During the spring of 2005 there was a discrepancy between public opinion and the position of the government on Sino-Japanese relations. During the three weeks of protests, activists demanded that the government take a strong stand against Japan while the Foreign Ministry attempted to take a softer line. Used increasingly after the 2003 severe acute respiratory syndrome (SARS) crisis, the term public opinion crisis implicitly identifies the role of the commercialized news media, the Internet, and cell phones as a catalyst for disagreement between citizens and government. Media scholars and propaganda officials claim that these new media sources provide information that differs from the position of the government, thus stimulating distrust in government and encouraging people to protest against government actions, as in the case of the anti-Japanese protests in 2005.

To calm public anger toward Japan, the Propaganda Department switched its management of the news media from relatively loose to strict control. This chapter examines how Beijingers reacted to these changes. By chance, a public opinion survey using random sampling was being conducted in Beijing both before and after press restrictions were imposed. This survey provides a unique opportunity to observe how media sources are perceived and what kind of information citizens seek out. In line with speculations that new media sources facilitate public opinion crises, I focus on differences between the Internet and newspapers as examples of new and old media sources. In contrast to these speculations, I find that the Internet, particularly online news Web sites, can aid the government in appeasing protest rather than mobilizing it, if the state is able to synchronize news content by means of press restrictions.

To analyze public demand for information, this chapter first explains how Chinese media reform has resulted in an environment in which news outlets differ in their degree of commercial liberalization. Official media are considered to have high expertise on the position of the government and rank low in terms of credibility; nonofficial or commercial media are perceived to represent public opinion and rank high in terms of credibility. These labels in turn are associated with different functions of the news media. In the remainder of the chapter I rely on a quasi-experimental research design to explain Beijingers' preferences for official and nonofficial media under ordinary circumstances, followed by an examination of people's reaction to the government's press restrictions during the 2005 anti-Japanese protests. Finally, I draw inferences from this case for how citizens, media, and the government may interact in future public opinion crises.

MEDIA REFORM AND THE STRUCTURE OF THE CHINESE MEDIA ENVIRONMENT

Economic reforms have changed the structure of the Chinese state media. Before the reforms, all media were owned and financed by the state. However, budgetary constraints forced the government to sever media subsidies as early as 1978. During the reform era, the Chinese government commercially liberalized the news media by deregulating, commercializing, and partially privatizing it.

Deregulation describes the process of diminishing intervention by the state into media organizations; the government delegates greater authority over programming, personnel, and business decisions to lower levels in the broadcast and print administrative hierarchy. Commercialization involves shifting the primary goal from serving the public (as defined by the Chinese state) toward earning profits. As part of media reform, the Chinese press was encouraged to obtain outside funding through advertising and increased sales. Today most media institutions finance themselves with advertising revenues, though some continue to receive indirect or small state subsidies. Partial privatization further promoted this profit orientation. Since the late 1990s, shares in broadcasting and print media groups have been publicly traded on the stock market and, since 2002, investment in media groups has been permitted. Although restrictions remain on the share of nonstate investment in media outlets—such a share cannot exceed 49 percent—the trend toward private ownership is clear. Today, the traditional news media differ with respect to their degree of deregulation, commercialization, and partial privatization: magazines tend to be more commercially liberalized than newspapers, and print media more commercially liberalized than broadcast media.[2]

In addition, China's media environment has also become more internationalized. With the growth of the Internet, the government has instituted policies to control access to domestic as well as foreign Web sites.[3] The government also relies on technological solutions, such as the so-called Great Chinese Firewall and built-in censorship of keywords. However, controlling the Web remains a challenge because of the large number of sites and the fragmentation of the state bureaucracy.[4] Difficulties in controlling the information circulated on the Internet give traditional media incentives to cover issues that have received significant attention online. Competition also comes from international news that is accessible to Chinese citizens, in part through the Internet. During the reform era, China opened up to such news sources as the BBC, CNN, Voice of America, and *Newsweek* magazine. Though these sources are sometimes blocked or filtered, their content cannot be directly controlled by the Chinese government. Both online and international media represent sources of information that are more autonomous from the state than the traditional domestic media. These information sources place competitive pressure on television, radio broadcasting, and print media to be bold in their reporting.

Citizens make sense of this complicated environment by distinguishing between different types of information sources, characterized by variation between media types (television, radio broadcasting, newspapers, magazines, the Internet) and within media types. Individual media sources may not always fit neatly into these categories, but these distinctions refer to general tendencies associated with commercial liberalization. For example, magazines are subject to greater private investment than newspapers, and newspapers more than television. Furthermore, less commercially liberalized newspapers are referred to as official; at the opposite end of the spectrum are the most commercially liberalized papers. Newspapers in between the two extremes are called semiofficial. Since semiofficial and commercialized papers share many similarities in the eyes of journalists, they often refer to these two types as nonofficial papers. The Internet, particularly online news Web sites, is often compared to the most commercialized papers in terms of its degree of commercial liberalization (table 8.1).

TABLE 8.1   Variation between and within Media Sources

Commercial Liberalization	Media Types (Variation Between)	Newspapers (Variation Within)
Weak	Television Radio broadcasting	Official papers
Medium	Newspapers Magazines	Semiofficial papers
Strong	Internet	Commercialized papers

Official papers include Chinese Communist Party (CCP) papers, such as the *People's Daily* or the *Beijing Daily*, and other papers under the direct supervision of state units, such as the *Legal Daily* or the *Workers' Daily*. These papers usually receive indirect subsidies through subscriptions by party and state units. In contrast, semiofficial and commercialized papers are completely financed through advertising. However, these two newspaper types differ in that commercialized papers are partially privatized, while semiofficial papers are not. Commercialized papers, such as the *Beijing Times* or the *Beijing News*, receive investment while semiofficial papers, such as the *Beijing Evening News* or the *Beijing Morning News*, do not.

While reform has brought about commercial liberalization, it would be wrong to conclude that the state has lost its ability to exercise influence over the media. All major newspapers, radio, and television stations continue to be registered under state or CCP organizations, are majority owned by them, and remain subject to institutions that exert personnel and editorial control. Through these institutional mechanisms the state still exerts considerable control over news media, especially when an issue is germane to social stability and economic growth. During public opinion crises, for example, the CCP Propaganda Department is able to quickly respond by placing phone calls, sending electronic messages, and convening meetings with senior staff of media outlets. Thus news content on a particular issue can be homogenized within one day. Even the Internet—the most autonomous news source—is not completely beyond reach. However, under regular circumstances the structure of the Chinese media environment is one in which sources have varying spaces for news reporting, though this variation remains supervised by the state.

THE FUNCTIONS OF THE NEWS MEDIA
IN CHINESE SOCIETY

State control of the media is no secret. Asked about whether media commercialization has brought about greater independence, journalists and editors commonly answer, "You know, in China all news media are owned by the state. There is no fully commercialized and private media." Despite this knowledge, Chinese citizens attach labels to the different media types introduced above. To learn about the meaning of these labels, I conducted forty-six open-ended, semistructured interviews with Chinese media experts. It turns out that labels are related to two dimensions: source expertise and source objectivity.

Interviewees were asked about their perceptions of different kinds of newspapers. Editors and journalists generally perceive that official papers are experts on the position of the government while nonofficial papers voice public opinion. In addition, media experts believe that official papers publish propaganda, and nonofficial papers what they call "real news." To media specialists, propaganda is based on subjective opinion aimed at guiding the reader in a certain direction and often omits important facts, while real news provides the audience with the complete story and includes negative aspects. Nonofficial papers play "table tennis by the edge" by constantly pushing the boundaries set by the state.

Together, expertise and objectivity create the perception of a credible source. A source that seems to know the truth but that nevertheless appears to mislead is not regarded as credible. Similarly, a source that appears sincere but unable to provide accurate information is perceived as unreliable.[5] Official media sources are considered to be experts on the position of the state and aimed at manipulating public opinion. In contrast, nonofficial media sources are seen as reporting from the perspective of the public in a less biased way. Taking into account that media credibility requires high levels of both expertise and objectivity, official sources tend to rank lower in terms of credibility than nonofficial ones.

Despite these different perceptions of media credibility, it is important to note that all of my interviewees accepted the need for propaganda for the collective benefit. The Chinese term *xuanchuan* was used in a nonpejorative way, similar to the English term *persuasion*.[6] The widespread acceptance of propaganda drew together people who had divergent and possibly incompatible positions on media control but were willing to accept it for the sake of ensuring social stability.[7]

Similarly, it would be wrong to conclude that official media sources do not serve an important function in Chinese society. Although it is common knowledge that official news organs aim to manipulate public opinion, they are useful for learning about the goals and policies of the government. This kind of information can be crucial in an authoritarian regime in which individuals tend to be vulnerable to state intervention into their private lives. During the reform era, the Chinese state has retreated from many aspects of ordinary citizens' lives, such as provision of employment or social welfare. However, it continues to be strongly involved in the economy. Chinese as well as foreign companies cannot circumvent local officials when doing business. As a result, propaganda organs that represent state opinion are by no means unimportant. On the contrary, those who expect to interact with state officials in their daily lives are more likely to use these information sources. Furthermore, the cost of obtaining official news is comparatively low for these individuals because they have access to those information sources at the workplace. As shown in more detail below, this group of people includes the Chinese political elite. Ordinary citizens will also prefer these sources when they have incentives to seek out information about the position of the government.

Yet the utility of official sources does not necessarily mean that they are perceived as credible. According to my interviews, the credibility issue is of great concern to officials in the propaganda apparatus who are worried about their ability to guide public opinion through mass media. Chinese political leaders continue to regard the news media as a necessary instrument to hold China together and push forward reform policies. Chinese communication researchers have therefore been hesitant to report public opinion data that suggests the low credibility of official media sources.[8]

Somewhat surprisingly, the nonofficial media are taking over the guiding role intended for the official media. Official media still give nonofficial media a sense of direction for news reporting, but in terms of their ability to influence public opinion, nonofficial media prevail. This point is counterintuitive as nonofficial media outlets have been regarded as troublemakers by Chinese officials rather than as useful tools to guide public opinion. Officials have become particularly concerned about the role of the nonofficial media in challenging the official line of the state and serving as catalysts of public opinion crises.[9] However, it is precisely this perceived disassociation from the government that lends credibility to the nonofficial media, improving their ability to influence public opinion. Ironically, media challenges to state control can boost the ability of the state to manipulate public opinion—provided that the state retains some control over news content and can deter media outlets from deviating too strongly from the official line.

The public opinion crisis during the anti-Japanese protest in 2005 provides a unique opportunity to examine the functions of different kinds of news media sources and the way citizens obtain information from them.

A QUASI-EXPERIMENTAL STUDY OF MEDIA USE

The following study of news media use is based on statistical analysis of the Beijing Area Studies of Beijing Residents (BAS). The BAS 2004 was conducted by the Research Center on Contemporary China at Peking University on Beijing residents exclusively. Therefore, unless otherwise noted, readership statistics in this chapter refer to Beijing residents. The survey was originally planned for late 2004 (and hence named BAS 2004), but was delayed until the spring of 2005. Sampling was done randomly, whereby the probability of selecting a sampling unit was proportional to the size of its population. Polling in the survey involved face-to-face interviewing by trained university students. The response rate for the BAS 2004 was 56.1 percent ($n = 617$).

The BAS was conducted between mid-March and mid-May 2005, allowing us to conduct a quasi-experiment. A quasi-experiment draws an analogy between a situation observed in real life and an experiment. Its main advantage is that we can observe how people behave naturally without imposing artificially created treatments and settings upon them. I employed a time-series experimental design, whereby the media consumption of similar individuals is observed over time throughout the course of conducting a survey. At some point a treatment is introduced, in this case a change in state restrictions over news media content about Japan after the first protest in Beijing. Since this method relies on nonrandom assignment to treatment and control groups, the assumption that members of treatment groups are indeed similar to each other needs to be tested. The treatment and control groups are slightly different from one another in terms of their demographic characteristics, but not much.[10]

The next section explains the broader setting of the quasi-experiment, followed by an examination of Beijingers' newspaper and Internet use under ordinary circumstances (the control group), and finally, an analysis of Beijingers' reactions to press restrictions (the treatment) during a public opinion crisis.

COURSE OF EVENTS, NEWS MEDIA CONTENT, AND ITS IMPACT ON MEDIA USE

In the months before the April 2005 anti-Japanese protests, relations between China and Japan became increasingly tense. In February, Japan and the United States for the first time explicitly stated that the Taiwan Strait issue was a concern of their security alliance, which provoked a sharp response about Japanese intervention in China's domestic affairs. The Diaoyu Islands in the East China Sea, where China and Japan had both taken steps to exploit reserves of natural gas, became a point of contention in early April when the Japanese government initiated procedures to grant Japanese firms the right to conduct test drilling. At about the same time, the United Nations was reviewing the possible promotion of Japan and other countries to permanent membership on the Security Council. When on 5 April the Japanese Ministry of Education approved new junior high school history textbooks that appeared to sanitize Japan's massacres of civilians during its occupation of China and South Korea in the 1930s and 1940s, violent attacks on Japanese businesses and protests erupted in China, Korea, and other countries.

The first protest in Beijing took place on 9 April. After a peaceful demonstration in the Zhongguancun district, several hundred protesters tried to storm the residence of the Japanese ambassador, throwing stones and bottles into the walled compound before riot police officers ended the confrontation. Meanwhile, protests continued in Shanghai and other cities until the government made it clear that it would not tolerate any additional protests. In Beijing, a further protest march was effectively prevented on 17 April when the police presence at a meeting point intimidated protesters. This protest would have coincided with a meeting between Chinese Foreign Minister Li Zhaoxing and his Japanese counterpart Nobutaka Machimura as part of the Seventh Asia-Europe Meeting.

Before the first demonstration, editors and journalists in Beijing reported feeling unconstrained in their coverage of Japan. After the first demonstration in Beijing took place on 9 April, however, space for news reporting closed. The Propaganda Department prohibited coverage of the protests and in order to subdue them instructed the media to keep news reporting close to the government line. The media were asked to publicize calls by the Foreign Ministry for people to express their feelings in a "calm, rational, and orderly manner in accordance with the law" and to let the government handle the crisis through diplomatic means.[11]

Newspaper reporting in the following weeks was homogenized. Editors kept coverage on Sino-Japanese relations close to the line held by Xinhua News Agency, whose reports were aimed at calming public anger. Changes in the choice and tone of headlines illustrate this point. In the five days prior to the imposition of press restrictions on 10 April, the main headlines on the online news Web site Sina.com were related to the Japanese history textbook, including such headlines as "Support Publicizing the List of Names of Japanese People Who Selfishly Revised the History Textbook" (7 April) and "Regarding the History Textbook Issue, Japan Falsely Accuses the Chinese Side of Instigating Anti-Japanese Sentiment" (8 April). Starting on 10 April, Japan disappeared from the main headline and individual news reports were toned down. By 14 April, news reports were titled "Japanese Foreign Minister Will Visit on April 17 to Suggest Investigating History Together" and "(Chinese) Foreign Ministry Spokesman Denies That Chinese Foreign Students in Japan Have Been Killed." Concerning the protests, an article detailing a press conference by the Beijing Public Security Bureau appeared. The report publicized information regarding regulations on demonstrations: although citizens had a right to demonstrate, protesters had to register with the government in order for the protest march to be legal. Furthermore, the report informed citizens not to participate in illegal demonstrations and to trust that the government would handle the issue to the benefit of the entire population. In another report on a Foreign Ministry press conference, it was made clear that the central government was against boycotting Japanese goods.[12]

Restrictions of news content related to Japan continued throughout April and May for two main reasons. First, spring has traditionally been a time during which students have organized protest marches, such as on the anniversary of the 4 May 1919 movement. Second, the government hosted two important visitors from Taiwan in late April and early May: Lien Chan, the leader of the Nationalist Kuomintang Party, visited the

FIGURE 8.1. Timeline of Events in Beijing.

mainland for about a week in late April. This was the first time a Taiwanese political leader had paid an official visit since the Nationalists retreated to Taiwan in 1949. Immediately afterward, James Soong, the leader of the People's First Party in Taiwan, arrived for a nine-day visit. Reporting on Japan continued to be tightly controlled during the two politicians' visits.

Figure 8.1 summarizes the above events. The change in media management from loose to tightened state control constitutes the treatment of our quasi-experiment. The BAS was conducted between mid-March and mid-May, thus allowing us to investigate media use during two periods. Before the first anti-Japanese demonstration in Beijing, state control over the news media was normal. Therefore, respondents who were interviewed during this first period are placed into the control group. This allows for observation of people's news media consumption behavior during periods of relatively unconstrained reporting. Those people who were interviewed after 9 April, when news content on Japan uniformly hewed to the government's line, are assigned to the treatment group. This allows for observation of people's news media consumption when media content is tightly controlled and synchronized. During this period the more lenient stance of the Chinese government propagated through the media conflicted with people's demand for more negative news stories.

How do people's choices to consume media news change when provided with information by the mass media that conflicts with their beliefs? Much evidence in social psychology and communications indicates that people will attempt to reduce dissonance between their personal negative views and the less negative tone in news reporting. This can be achieved by selectively seeking information consistent with their beliefs or by avoiding information that contradicts their beliefs. These reactions have been found to be most pronounced at moderate levels of dissonance—as in the case at hand, when news content and a person's beliefs only moderately differed.[13] We would therefore expect that Beijingers would be less likely to use media sources once news content on Japan was synchronized, in order to avoid information that is inconsistent with their beliefs. This effect should be stronger the more negatively a person feels about Japan.

Due to the public's perceptions of various media types, we would also expect it to avoid the official media more than nonofficial media. If citizens believe that nonofficial media sources divert from the official line and report from the perspective of "ordinary people," they will choose nonofficial media over official media when their own opinion conflicts with the position of the state. This expectation is confirmed by research in psychology that finds that source credibility and search for information consistent with a person's beliefs usually travel together. People seek supporting information in their attempt to select the best information, particularly when dissonance increases.[14] The reverse should also be true. When denied the choice of a news product that is consistent with a person's opinion, the person should prefer the news product that she finds most credible in her attempt to seek supporting information. In the case of the anti-Japanese protests, we therefore expect that Beijingers would show a preference for nonofficial media and avoid official media. The relative credibility of these media sources should have important implications for what information people use during crisis situations.

To test whether these expectations hold true, I compared BAS respondents' self-reported use of newspapers and online news Web sites. Consistent with my previous explanation of media labels, I regard newspapers as an official media type and online news Web sites as a nonofficial media type. To establish a baseline for comparison, I now turn to an examination of patterns of newspaper and Internet use under ordinary circumstances (the control group).

PATTERNS OF NEWSPAPER AND INTERNET USE

Not much is known about patterns of Chinese media consumption. I therefore first provide some background information about general patterns of newspaper and Internet consumption in urban China. Subsequently, I turn to the individual-level analysis, which will provide a more nuanced understanding of who is reading the news in the newspaper and online.

Newspapers are one of the most popular news media sources in urban areas, ranking second after television. In Beijing, about 80 percent of residents read newspapers. Since reading requires literacy, those who do not read any newspapers tend to have lower education levels. Those who do not read newspapers also indicate that they do not have the time to read newspapers and that they already feel sufficiently informed by electronic media, such as television or radio broadcasting.[15]

In contrast to American and European readers, Chinese read newspapers in the late afternoon or evening, spending, on average, forty-two minutes a day reading newspapers. Only a minority of Chinese readers subscribe to newspapers. Instead, they usually read newspapers at work or purchase them at a newspaper stand. This allows Chinese readers to switch frequently between newspapers and to read a great variety of them. According to the BAS, average readers peruse two newspapers, but some report reading as many as ten different papers. People have a clear preference for nonofficial papers, such as the *Beijing Evening News* or the *Beijing Times*. Only about 36 percent of readers choose to read official papers, such as the *People's Daily*; the rest pick only semiofficial or commmercialized papers.

The Web is a less popular information source than newspapers. According to China Internet Network Information Center (CNNIC), less than 30 percent of Chinese citizens had access to the Internet in 2009. However, the number is growing at a rapid pace. In 2008 the number of Internet users grew by 41.9 percent. According to reports by CNNIC, urban Chinese citizens indicate that their own lack of skills and access to facilities constitute the two main reasons for not surfing the Web. Access requires a computer, which still comes at a large expense for most. As a result, the proportion of the population who are Internet users is still low relative to developed countries. However, reading the news is the second most frequently used online service, according to CNNIC. The BAS indicates that 17.5 percent of residents went online to read the news. Though the majority of Internet users have access at home, about 20 percent also use other ways to go online. CNNIC reports that there are two important alternative means to go online: accessing the Web at work and using Internet cafés.

The BAS data shows that there is a significant overlap between newspaper readers and online news consumers: 87.9 percent of those who read the news online also read newspapers on a regular basis. By comparison, only 19 percent of newspaper readers also report reading the news online. One reason for this overlap between readers and Netizens is that news reports printed in newspapers and articles published on news Web sites are often identical. This requires further explanation of where Chinese online news consumers get the news.

Despite their comparatively greater ability to read English, those who read the news online rely almost exclusively on domestic news Web sites.[16] In the BAS sample of 617 Beijingers, only two reported accessing English-language Web sites; only one reported accessing Web sites based in Hong Kong, Macao, or Taiwan. Contrary to frequently heard speculation about citizens' preferences for sources outside the direct supervision of the Propaganda Department, Netizens stay inside the Great Firewall—at least when it comes to getting the news.[17]

For those who read the news online, there remain two options when choosing what kind of Web site to access. The most popular choice is to use news Web sites that are not directly run by other news entities, such as Sina.com. Editors at those Web sites select articles that have previously been published by news agencies or newspapers. They are generally not allowed to write their own news content.[18] Articles that are reprinted online tend to originate from nonofficial papers. According to the BAS survey data, most consumers prefer this option.

The second kind of news Web sites are sponsored by official news media organizations, such as Xinhua Net, which belongs to the Xinhua News Agency, or the People's Daily Net, which belongs to the *People's Daily*. Among BAS respondents, 18.5 percent of users read the news at this second kind of news Web site. Most newspapers in Beijing also have online editions. According to my interviewees, online editions of traditional media outlets are given more space for news reporting and are thus similar in news content to nonofficial papers. As a result, online editions of newspapers—even official ones, such as the People's Daily Online—tend to be similar in style to the most freewheeling newspapers.[19]

Obviously, reading the news online is much different from reading a hard copy version of the news. For example, some online news Web sites give readers the option to comment on articles, thus allowing for greater interaction between readers and journalists. However, the substance of news articles is strikingly similar between online news Web sites and nonofficial papers. Not surprisingly then, if online news consumers decide to read a hard copy version, they prefer nonofficial papers. In the BAS sample, readers who get the news online are more likely than readers who do not surf the Web to read nonofficial papers.

Patterns of Newspaper and Internet Use at the Micro Level

To simplify my explanations, I have so far talked about Beijingers as if they form a homogenous group—obviously they do not. In this section I therefore identify three kinds of media users, henceforth called Old Wang, Comrade Shu, and Little Zhao. These profiles for the typical consumers of official and nonofficial media sources are empirically drawn based on pre-dicted probabilities to read the news online versus in the newspaper among BAS respondents (see table 8.2).[20] Individual-level differences

TABLE 8.2 Patterns of Media Use in Beijing

Dependent Variable Independent Variable	Newspaper Consumption Coefficient (s.e.)	Online News Consumption Coefficient (s.e.)
Cadre	1.035^{**}	-0.031
	(0.423)	(0.234)
Travel	-0.557^{*}	0.953^{***}
	(0.286)	(0.274)
English	-1.179	7.779^{***}
	(1.148)	(1.365)
English squared	1.723	-9.633^{***}
	(2.021)	(2.742)
Years of education	2.923^{***}	3.718^{***}
	(0.647)	(1.120)
Income	0.449^{*}	0.960^{**}
	(0.270)	(0.379)
Constant	-1.766^{***}	-5.297^{***}
	(0.516)	(0.942)
N	610	604
Pseudo R^2	0.08	0.26

Source: Beijing Area Studies of Beijing Residents, 2004.
Table displays probit coefficients before transformation into the cumulative normal distribution.
All variables were recoded running from 0 to 1, whereby 1 represents the highest value.
Results are based on the whole sample to increase observations for Internet use. However, results do not change much once the analysis is limited to only those respondents interviewed before April 10. $^{***}z < 0.01$; $^{**}z < 0.05$; $^{*}z < 0.1$.

between these three kinds of people will reveal not only who places what kinds of demands on the news media, but also who is likely to be mobilized by the mass media.

Old Wang is an average Beijinger. He earns about RMB 2,200 per month and has received about eleven years of education, the equivalent to a Chinese high school degree. Old Wang usually buys newspapers at a nearby newspaper stand rather than reading the news online. He is 81 percent likely to read newspapers, but only 10 percent likely to surf the Internet.[21]

Comrade Shu and Little Zhao both differ from Old Wang in ways that make them more likely to use specific media types. Comrade Shu is a regular cadre (official) working for a party or government unit, has received about three more years of education, and earns a monthly salary about 2.5 times higher than Old Wang's (RMB 5,450). Party or government units usually subscribe to official newspapers because officials need to remain abreast of political decisions made at higher and lower levels of government. Since Comrade Shu is conveniently supplied with newspapers at his workplace, he is 98 percent likely to read newspapers; he is also 22 percent likely to read the news online. Comrade Shu is thus 17 percent more likely than Old Wang to read newspapers and 12 percent more likely to get news online.

Finally, Little Zhao is part of a small Western-oriented group of citizens. Little Zhao's monthly salary is about as high as Comrade Shu's (RMB 5,700) and he is about as highly educated as the cadre (fourteen years of education). What distinguishes Little Zhao from the other two is his interest in Western industrialized nations. The contrast is most striking with Old Wang, who has never traveled to North America or Europe and who speaks little English after having studied it for three years in school. Little Zhao has traveled to these countries and has studied English for about six years. This characteristic makes him only 69 percent likely to read newspapers, but 68 percent likely to read the news online; this is 58 percent more likely than Old Wang, whose likelihood is only 10 percent. As mentioned above, Little Zhao's foreign language ability and orientation toward Western nations does not necessarily lead him to search for international news media on the Web. On the contrary, he primarily surfs Chinese-language news Web sites. Somewhat surprisingly, his Western orientation and knowledge about countries other than China does not make him more tolerant. In fact, Little Zhao has just as much nationalist and anti-Japanese sentiment as Comrade Shu and Old Wang.

CITIZENS' REACTIONS TO PRESS RESTRICTIONS ON NEWS CONTENT

Let us now examine how Beijingers' behavior with respect to news media selection changes during a public opinion crisis. Detailed statistical results are included in the online appendix available at www.danie stockmann.net.

Figure 8.2 shows the estimated effects of press restrictions on newspaper and Internet use of our average Beijinger, Old Wang, as his feelings toward Japan become more negative. Sentiment toward Japan, displayed on the x-axis, has been recoded from the original feeling thermometer into a 0 to 1 scale, whereby higher values represent colder feelings toward Japan. The y-axis indicates the likelihood of the average person in Beijing to use newspapers or online news Web sites.

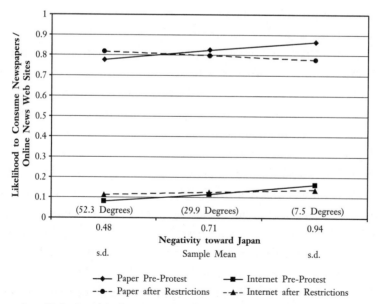

FIGURE 8.2. Relationship between Sentiment toward Japan and Media Use among Average Beijingers before and after Press Restrictions. *Source:* Beijing Area Studies of Beijing Residents, 2004.

Let us first take a closer look at the situation before press restrictions were issued, as indicated by the solid lines in figure 8.2. As Old Wang's feelings toward Japan become more negative, he appears more likely to use both media sources. The trendlines for reading newspapers and reading the news online in figure 8.2 both indicate a positive relationship between more negative sentiment toward Japan and seeking information from the media. As the Chinese news media were reporting about Japan in a relatively negative way during this period, this makes sense: the colder Old Wang's feelings toward Japan become, the more likely he is to read these negative articles. However, when he has warmer feelings toward Japan, he tends to abstain from reading news media articles that contradict his beliefs.

When press restrictions pull news media reporting in a more positive direction, however, Old Wang's choice to read newspapers and surf news Web sites changes. This situation is illustrated by the dashed lines in figure 8.2. We observe the strongest reaction when it comes to newspapers. As Old Wang's feelings become colder, he is less likely to read newspapers. Negativity toward Japan and newspaper use becomes negatively related. With respect to using online news Web sites, we also observe a reaction, but this reaction is less pronounced (and statistically not significant). Old Wang is still more likely to read the news online as he feels colder toward Japan, but the relationship is weaker: for example, when he holds strongly negative feelings toward Japan (about 8 degrees), he is 14 percent likely to read the news online before the protests. After press restrictions are imposed, he is still 12 percent likely to access news Web sites—press restrictions make only 2 percentage points of difference. Comparatively, press restrictions make Old Wang 9 percentage points less likely to read newspapers while he holds equally negative feelings toward Japan.

The other two media users mentioned earlier, Comrade Shu and Little Zhao, are not much different from Old Wang with respect to the relationship between sentiment toward Japan and newspapers and online news consumption. They share the same basic pattern. However, Comrade Shu always remains more likely than others to read newspapers and Little Zhao continues to be more likely than the other two to read the news online.

How can we explain the fact that usage of online news is less affected by press restrictions during public opinion crises than newspapers? Due to the strict enforcement of press restrictions with respect to news about Japan, the primary explanation cannot be news content. First, the Propaganda

Department was very sensitive to reporting on this particular issue and successfully communicated the importance of press restrictions to editors in Beijing. Even the act of mentioning protest action was immediately condemned. Second, news Web sites generally reprint newspaper articles. Only sites of official media publications are allowed to create their own articles. As a result, state control over newspapers indirectly affects online news content. The Internet may set the news agenda by being the first place for breaking news, but when the authorities order newspapers to censor sensitive issues during a period of crisis, online news content follows. The tone of news reporting does not differ significantly between the most commercialized papers and the online news Web sites that reprint those articles.

If news content is not the main explanation, what is it about newspapers that drove Beijingers away from using them? The answer is related to perceptions of media outlets rather than the substance of news content. When news content was homogenized during the 2005 public opinion crisis, media users searched for the information that they perceived to be most credible. As press restrictions were imposed, all media types, official and nonofficial, lost credibility, but newspapers lost more credibility than news Web sites because they were considered to be closer to the state.

This conclusion is further strengthened when comparing consumption of different newspaper types. Readers moved away from official papers as their negativity toward Japan increased after press restrictions were imposed. However, the consumption of nonofficial papers, in particular commercialized papers, was less affected by press restrictions. This similarity between Beijingers' media consumption behavior concerning variation between and within media types underlines that the effects we observe after the "treatment" were induced by variation in media labels rather than media content.

Overall, the empirical findings presented in this chapter demonstrate that public perceptions of media outlets matter a great deal in China, especially when a person's beliefs strongly diverge from the official line of the state. Ordinary citizens demand information sources that they perceive as credible, that tell the whole story, and that report about issues from a perspective with which they can identify. Yet despite their lower levels of credibility, official sources remain useful to individuals who need to know about the position of the government for their work. Hence, cadres like Comrade Shu had a greater likelihood of reading newspapers than others did.

LIMITATIONS AND IMPLICATIONS
FOR CITIZEN ACTIVISM

All evidence presented in this chapter has come from Beijing, which is in many ways different from other parts of China. Beijing not only is the site of the central government, but also hosts visits of foreign leaders. As we have seen, these special characteristics affect the dynamic between the state, the media, and citizens during public opinion crises. When important visitors are expected in Beijing, the central and municipal governments tighten controls over media content to prevent any embarrassing protests. But visitors connected to the issue that touched off the public opinion crisis can also spark citizen activism. Tension between the government and citizens may be stronger in China's capital than in other regions during public opinion crises, especially when the issue involves international relations.

In addition, Beijing is located in the more developed coastal region where the media are more commercially liberalized and internationalized than in the less developed interior. Beijing, along with Shanghai and Guangzhou, is at the forefront of media commercialization. Western-oriented citizens like Little Zhao make up the primary audience of China's nonofficial media sources and may be most highly concentrated in these three cities.

In urban areas characterized by lower levels of economic development, the Web and commercialized papers play a less important role. In these cities, media audiences consist of two rather than three groups and are similar to Old Wang and Comrade Shu in their media consumption. For example, citizens in Chongqing can distinguish between official and semiofficial papers. However, the city lacks the third, commercialized newspaper type.[22] Furthermore, only about 21 percent of Chongqingers had Internet access in 2008, according to CNNIC, compared to 60 percent in Beijing, 60 percent in Shanghai, and 48 percent in Guangdong Province. As a consequence, the Web and commercialized papers likely play a less important role in most Chinese cities.

In the countryside, this difference is even greater. Since most newspapers do not deliver to rural areas and Internet access is uncommon, villagers primarily watch television or listen to the radio. In rural areas, news choice is limited to official media sources.[23] In the cities, broadcasting media are also popular, but citizens have more choice as to which media type they would like to use. Therefore, villagers are more dependent on official media sources compared to people living in the cities.

Overall, as we move away from the more developed eastern provinces toward the less developed western interior people are surrounded by less commercially liberalized media to get the news. As we move from the cities to the countryside people become more dependent on broadcasting as opposed to newspapers and the Internet as sources of information. What implications do these different media environments have for the relationship between the media and citizens?

My previous research suggests that access to more or fewer media sources affects patterns of consumption, but not necessarily the credibility of various types of media. Compared to Beijing, Chongqingers read more semiofficial papers, simply because commercialized papers do not exist. However, semiofficial papers are still perceived to be more credible than official papers. When they have less choice between media types, consumers tend to use more official media sources, but still perceive nonofficial media sources as more credible.[24] Therefore, greater dependency on official media may lead to high consumption rates of these sources but does not necessarily imply that citizens in the countryside and the western interior of China also believe what they read. According to data from the World Value Survey 2007, Chinese living in more commercially liberalized provinces tended to perceive newspapers and television as somewhat more trustworthy than the central government, the party, and the National People's Congress. Those living in less commercially liberalized provinces, by comparison, did not perceive any difference at all between these media and political institutions.[25] Such a credibility gap has implications for who the Chinese state can reach and persuade by means of the news media in crisis situations. Lack of media credibility poses problems for the government in its management of political crises because citizens who are searching for information but do not believe what is written in the news rely on rumors. There are numerous examples of this phenomenon. In 2005, rumors spread that Chinese students in Japan had been killed in reaction to high levels of tension between China and Japan. The Foreign Ministry had to make a statement to negate the rumors.[26] During the 2003 SARS crisis, people overestimated how far the disease had spread. Even after the government had made public the official number of SARS patients, citizens became panicked because they believed that the government underreported the numbers in an effort to maintain social stability.[27]

However, commercialized and online news media have helped to address this problem by improving the credibility of information sources. Despite little difference in the substance of news reporting between media types, Beijingers had a clear preference for nonofficial news sources during public opinion crises. When a person's opinion strongly conflicted with messages published in newspapers, citizens were more likely to read the news online than in newspapers, just as they preferred reading non-official papers over official ones. If the state can walk the fine line between allowing some variation between information sources and maintaining restrictions on the content of reporting, then market mechanisms can be beneficial to the state. Not only can commercially liberalized media sources help the state to reach citizens, but they can also help the state shape their views.[28]

The extent to which the government can or cannot influence citizens' views through the mass media has implications for citizen activism. That manipulation of people's beliefs directly translates into political behavior is commonly assumed by politicians in China. However, this assumption has been disputed by social science research. In political science, political attitudes are generally viewed as less important in fostering political action than other factors, such as socioeconomic status and political mobilization.[29]

In recent years, however, there has been a revival of the argument that political views can make a difference.[30] Two studies in particular seem relevant for cases of public opinion crises. First, strongly held beliefs have been found to play a key role in political action. In a study of two cities in the United States, Burns, Kinder, and Ortiz found that Americans who held strong beliefs or convictions about an issue were more likely to become politically active.[31] If we apply this logic to the case of the anti-Japanese protests, those citizens who held the most negative views about Japan would also have been more likely to engage in protest. These citizens were alienated by official media and therefore were more likely to obtain information from nonofficial media. In other words, an outraged nationalist is more likely to believe the *Southern Weekly* or news reports published on Sina.com than those published in the *People's Daily*. Thus, it is likely that nonofficial media have a greater potential to influence political behavior during a public opinion crisis. This logic also underlies worries by Chinese officials that the commercialized media and the Web mobilize citizen activism and thus endanger social stability.

Of course, the Chinese public does not care only about international issues. In the case of the anti-Japanese protests, the issue at stake did not directly affect most citizens' lives. Urban residents in China care much more about issues related to their personal livelihoods than foreign affairs. According to a 1999 national public opinion survey using a random sample of Chinese citizens conducted by political scientist Wenfang Tang, about 32 percent cared strongly about China's status in the world. However, respondents reported caring much more strongly about other issues; 100 percent considered health important, 59 percent wealth, 59 percent housing, 46 percent family life, and 41 percent income and job opportunities.[32] Accordingly, a major health-related crisis similar to SARS or an economic crisis could create even more activists than the anti-Japanese protests in 2005, when demonstrations took place in about forty cities.[33] In this case, observers would be well advised to watch how the nonofficial media report on domestic issues that people care intensely about because such information is most likely to be consumed by citizens and influence their political beliefs.

What kind of news content should observers look for? A second argument recently developed in research on political participation suggests that political protest is best characterized as a coordination problem between citizens.[34] A coordination problem occurs when a person's participation in an action is contingent on others participating as well. Communication transmitted through the mass media can establish common knowledge between potential activists and either mobilize or prevent them from turning to overt action. In the anti-Japanese protests in 2005, the state at first refrained from sending out any signals about its position on the protests. Press restrictions on news related to Japan were not issued before 9 April. During the first week of April, the absence of government restrictions created the impression that the government was at least not against the protests and thus gave signals to potential political activists that mobilization was permissible.

However, after 9 April the Foreign Ministry and Public Security Bureau sent out messages through the mass media that indicated the absence of government support for further protest marches. Warnings were publicized in newspapers and through the Internet and cell phone messages reminding citizens that demonstrations needed approval by the Public Security Bureau and that because further demonstrations had not received such approval, they would be considered illegal. Via such communications, the government successfully deterred participants from engaging in further protest action. Just as the absence of warnings or limitations on reporting signal toleration and mobilize potential activists, warnings and limitations have the opposite effect.

CONCLUSION

This chapter shows how citizens actively engage with information sources under authoritarianism and how Chinese citizens prefer and trust media outlets they can identify with. In light of these findings it is not surprising that Chinese audiences viewed American and European media coverage of the Tibetan protests in the months before the 2008 Beijing Olympics as biased against China. At the time, criticism of the foreign media was expressed on the Internet and in slogans shouted during protests against Tibetan independence. When reporting on China, foreign media primarily cater to their own domestic audiences and not to the Chinese audience. Therefore, even Chinese citizens who speak English and are oriented toward the West primarily read and believe domestic media sources.

Yet ordinary citizens are not easily manipulated by the state; they filter government messages when an issue is important to them and may even abstain from consulting media as a source of information if their own opinion strongly conflicts with the position of the state. The commercial look of domestic media sources creates the perception of a media outlet that represents the public as opposed to the state and thus aids the government in guiding public opinion to favor its policies.

How the dynamics between the state, news media, and citizens will play out in future public opinion crises will depend on the conflict and the signals the state sends via the mass media to potential protesters. Because of their high credibility, commercialized papers and online news media are going to play a key role in convincing citizens to either march in the streets or stay at home during the next public opinion crisis.

Notes

This chapter is part of the author's book project examining the impact of media commercialization on news content and public opinion in China, tentatively titled *Propaganda for Sale.* If references are not provided, sources on specific events and research findings are cited in Daniela Stockmann, "Who Believes Propaganda? Media Effects during the Anti-Japanese Protests in Beijing," *China Quarterly*, Vol. 202, 2010, pp. 269–289. For providing me with the opportunity to collaborate with ongoing research projects and sharing data, I would like to thank Shen Mingming and Iain Johnston. I am grateful for research support for conducting fieldwork in China provided by the Harvard-Yenching Institute and the Center for Chinese Studies at the University of Michigan. Many thanks as well to Ken Lieberthal, Mary Gallagher, Don Kinder, Mark Tessler, Ted Brader, Nick Valentino, Chen Changfeng, Zhang Jie, Susan Shirk, and Steve Oliver for helpful comments and suggestions on earlier drafts.

1. For an example, see Joseph Kahn, "In Rare Legal Protest, Chinese Seek Boycott of Japan Goods," *New York Times*, 9 April 2005.

2. Joseph Man Chan, "Commercialization without Independence: Trends and Developments of Media Commercialization in China," in Joseph Cheng (Ed.), *China Review 1993* (Hong Kong: Hong Kong University, 1993), pp. 25.1–25.21; Yuezhi Zhao, *Media, Market, and Democracy in China: Between the Party Line and the Bottom Line* (Urbana: University of Illinois Press, 1998).

3. Regulations restrict pornography, gambling, and publication of "counterrev-olutionary" materials, ask Internet content providers to monitor Web site content, and require users to register when opening an account. Certain foreign Web sites are blocked. See, for example, Eric Harwit and Duncan Clark, "Shaping the Internet in China: Evolution of Political Control over Network Internet Infrastructure and Content," *Asian Survey*, Vol. 41, no. 3, 2001, pp. 377–408.

4. The Internet developed as part of the telecommunications bureaucratic structure rather than the propaganda apparatus. In 1998 the Ministry of Information Industry was put in charge of coordinating Internet policy. See Eric Harwit and Duncan Clark, "Shaping the Internet in China." For a summary of the recent discussion on Chinese internet control see Jens Damm, "The Internet and the Fragmentation of Chinese Society," *Critical Asian Studies*, Vol. 39, no. 2, 2007, pp. 273–294, and Bingchun Meng, "Moving Beyond Democratization: A Thought Piece on the Chinese Internet Research Agenda, *International Journal of Communication* [Online], Vol. 4, 2010. Available: http://ijoc.org/ojs/index.php/ijoc/article/view/755/425.

5. See Alice Eagly, Wendy Wood, and Shelly Chaiken, "Causal Inferences about Communicators and Their Effects on Opinion Change," *Journal of Personality and Social Psychology*, Vol. 36, no. 4, 1978, pp. 424–435.

6. *Xuanchuan* is defined as "using various symbols to communicate a certain concept in order to influence people's thought and their actions." Chen, "Yong Shishi Shuo Hua Shi Xuanchuan Fangfa Er Bu Shi Xinwen Xiezuo Guilu" [Using Facts to Write News Is a Propaganda Method and Not a Rule to Write News Reports], *Renmin Wang* [*People's Daily Online*], 27 June 2003, http://www.people.com.cn/ (accessed 21 July 2010).

7. See Kevin Latham, "Nothing but the Truth: News Media, Power and Hegemony in South China," *China Quarterly*, Vol. 163, 2000, pp. 650–651.

8. Based on personal conversations with Chinese media scholars.

9. Numerous examples of media personnel dismissals illustrate this point. Most of the time, editors are dismissed due to news reporting supposedly provoking instability. Most of these dismissed editors were working for nonofficial media, such as *Southern Weekly* in 2003 or the *Beijing News* in 2006.

10. Further details are available in the online appendix at www.daniestockmann.net.

11. See "Japan Told to Face Up the Past," *China Daily*, 13 April 2005. Similar announcements followed on April 19 (see *New York Times*, 20, 21, 23 April).

12. All reports are available online at http://news.sina.com.cn. In general, the protest marches themselves were not reported. At the most, demonstrations were mentioned in reports as on Phoenix television on 11 April, http://www.phoenixtv.com/ (accessed 31 May 2007).

13. See Leon Festinger, *A Theory of Cognitive Dissonance* (Evanston, IL: Row, 1957). For a detailed explanation of how preconditions for cognitive dissonance are met in this case, see Daniela Stockmann, "Propaganda for Sale: The Impact of Newspaper Commercialization on News Content and Public Opinion in China" (PhD diss., University of Michigan at Ann Arbor, Department of Political Science, 2007).

14. See Aaron Lowin, "Further Evidence for an Approach-Avoidance Interpretation of Selective Exposure," *Journal of Experimental Social Psychology*, Vol. 5, no. 3, 1969, pp. 265–271; Peter Fischer, Eva Jonas, Dieter Frey, and Stefan Schulz-Hardt, "Selective Exposure to Information: The Impact of Information Limits," *European Journal of Social Psychology*, Vol. 35, 2005, pp. 469–492.

15. See BAAJ (Beijing Xinwen Xuehui, Beijing Academic Association of Journalism), *Beijing Duzhe, Tingzhong, Guanzhong Diaocha [Survey of Beijing Newspaper, Radio, and Television Audience]* (Beijing: Worker Press, 1984); Guoming Yu, *Chuanmei Jingzhengli: Chanye Jiazhi Anli Yu Moshi [Competitiveness between Media Outlets: Connecting Cases and Patterns to Assess the Value of the Industry]* (Beijing: Hua Dan Press, 2004).

16. On average, Internet users in Beijing had studied English for 5.7 years. By comparison, Beijingers have studied it only 2.6 years, on average. (BAS 2004).

17. For scholarly articles that imply these arguments, see, for example, Geoffry Taubman, "A Not-So World Wide Web: The Internet, China, and the Challenges to Nondemocratic Rule," *Political Communication*, Vol. 15, no. 2, 1998, pp. 255–272.

18. See "Provisions on the Administration of Internet News and Information Services," http://www.chinaitlaw.org (accessed 31 May 2007).

19. This claim differs from that of He and Zhu since their study did not take into account differences in types of news Web sites. See Zhou He and Jian-hua Zhu, "The Ecology of Online Newspapers: The Case of China," *Media, Culture and Society*, Vol. 24, 2002, pp. 121–137.

20. Studying English was squared to account for the nonlinear relationship between the independent and dependent variable. For details on question wording, coding, and robustness test results, see the online appendix at www.daniestockmann.net.

21. Percentages were calculated based on the sum of the constant term, coefficients, and independent variables at average levels of the sample, and finally transforming the results into the cumulative normal distribution.

22. For a closer investigation of this argument see Stockmann, "Propaganda for Sale."

23. See, for example, Xiaohong Fang, *Dazhong Chuanmei Yu Nogncun [Mass Media and the Countryside]* (Beijing: Zhonghua Shuju, 2002).

24. Greater access to media sources and commercial liberalization both affect media consumption, but in opposite directions. Therefore, official media are not always less popular than nonofficial media. Even official media sources are able to increase

consumption rates when they are highly commercialized. For a closer investigation of this argument, see Stockmann, "Propaganda for Sale."

25. The World Values Survey has been conducted in over ninety countries between 1981 and 2007. In China, the 2007 survey was carried out by the Research Center of Contemporary China (RCCC) of Peking University. Sampling was done randomly according to probability proportional to size (PPS). Detailed regression results, controlling for the percentage of rural citizens and Han Chinese in the region, regional administrative status, and regional level of economic development, are included in table A6 in the online appendix. Note that people living in villages and townships also tend to perceive newspapers and television as more trustworthy than those living in larger cities. This difference may be a result of lower education levels in rural compared to urban areas.

26. See "Foreign Ministry Spokesman Negates That Chinese Foreign Students in Japan Have Been Killed," published by Sina.com, 14 April 2005.

27. Guoming Yu, *Biange Chuanmei: Jiexi Zhongguo Chuanmei Zhuanxing Wenti* [*Reforming the Media: Analyzing the Chinese Media's Pattern of Transformation*] (Beijing: Hua Dan ChubanShe, 2005).

28. The same logic does not necessarily apply to all other media types. Broadcasting media remain powerful propaganda organs in China. Features associated with TV and possibly radio lend broadcasting media the potential for considerable influence, even if citizens believe that broadcasting media are less commercialized than print media and the Internet. See Daniela Stockmann and Mary E. Gallagher, "Remote Control: How the Media Sustains Authoritarian Rule in China," *Comparative Political Studies* (in press).

29. See Steven J. Rosenstone and John Mark Hansen, *Mobilization, Participation, and Democracy in America* (New York: Macmillan, 1993); Sidney Verba, Kay Lehman Schlozman, and Henry Brady, *Voice and Equality: Civic Voluntarism in American Politics* (Cambridge, MA: Harvard University Press, 1995).

30. See Donald Green and Jonathan Cowden, "Who Protests: Self-Interest and White Opposition to Busing," *Journal of Politics*, Vol. 54, 1992, pp. 471–496; Morris Fiorina, "Parties, Participation, and Representation in America: Old Theories Face New Realities," in Ira Katznelson and Helen Milner (Eds.), *Political Science: The State of the Discipline* (New York: APSA, Norton, 2002), pp. 511–541.

31. Nancy Burns, Donald R. Kinder, and Anna Maria Ortiz, "Conviction and Its Consequences," paper presented at the annual meeting of the American Political Science Association, Boston, 2002.

32. Wenfang Tang, *Public Opinion and Political Change in China* (Stanford, CA: Stanford University Press, 2005).

33. See Jessica Weiss, "Powerful Patriots: Nationalism, Diplomacy, and the Strategic Logic of Anti-Foreign Protest" (PhD diss., University of California at San Diego, Department of Political Science, 2008).

34. Dennis Chong, *Collective Action and the Civil Rights Movement* (Chicago: University of Chicago Press, 1991); Michael Suk-Young Chwe, *Rational Ritual: Culture, Coordination, and Common Knowledge* (Princeton, NJ: Princeton University Press, 2001). A coordination problem is distinct from the free-rider problem. For more on free-rider problems, see Mancur Olson, *The Logic of Collective Action: Public Goods and the Theory of Groups* (Cambridge, MA: Harvard University Press, 1971).

9

The Rise of Online Public Opinion and Its Political Impact

Xiao Qiang

B EGINNING IN MARCH 2007, freelance columnist Lian Yue posted a series of articles on his Weblog warning the people in his hometown of Xiamen that a paraxylene (PX) chemical factory being built in the city could have a disastrous environmental impact. Lian Yue called on his fellow residents to speak out against the proposed plant. On 29 March, he wrote, "Don't be afraid. Please just talk to your friends, family and colleagues about this event. They might still be in the dark."

Fujian Province and Xiamen city authorities vigorously deleted anti-PX factory messages on any servers within their jurisdiction, but Lian Yue's Weblog remained intact because it was hosted on a server in another province. Word of the PX plant subsequently spread throughout Xiamen via e-mail, instant messaging, and SMS on mobile phones. On 1 and 2 June, in defiance of warnings from local authorities, several thousand citizens showed up "to walk" in protest in front of city hall. Participants reported the protest live with their cell phones, which directly transmitted photos and text to their Weblogs.

Six months later, following two rare public hearings on the matter, Xiamen authorities decided to relocate the lucrative project. The official

Xinhua News Agency praised the turnaround as indicating "a change in the weight given to the views of ordinary Chinese in recent years."[1] The outspoken *Southern People's Weekly* magazine elected "Xiamen citizens" as the "people of the year," and Lian Yue won *Deutsche Welle*'s Weblog Award as the best Chinese blogger of 2007.

The Xiamen story marks the rise of a remarkable new force in China's contemporary social and political life: public opinion communicated through online forums and Weblogs together with liberal elements in the traditional media are setting the public agenda. According to the annual blue book on social development published in January 2008 by the Chinese Academy of Social Sciences, over 50 million Chinese read Weblogs regularly. This makes Weblogs "an important channel for people to voice their opinions about important events."

The year 2007 was particularly remarkable in this regard. Xiao Shu, a well-known commentator in China's influential *Southern Weekend* newspaper, called 2007 "the first year of public events (*Gonggong Shijian Yuannian*)."[2] Here "public events" refers to events that the Internet helped to push into the official media, despite resistance from censors. By pushing these events into the official media, the Internet effectively set the agenda for subsequent public discourse. Prominent examples include the protests in Xiamen against the PX chemical plant; an exposé of slave labor in brick kilns; and the Chongqing "nail house" case where homeowners won public acclaim for asserting their property rights against developers. All of these stories were spread on the Internet first, where they generated such public interest and debate that censors and the official media had little option but to report on them.

I begin by discussing the explosive growth of Internet access and use among the Chinese populace and moves on to introduce the tools and methods with which authorities attempt to control content and the flow of information. I then go on to detail the emerging dynamics of the cat and mouse game being played by Netizens and censors, offering a series of poignant cases where the Internet has provided channels to circumvent information bans issued by censors. Finally, I assess the claim that the Internet is simply being used as a safety valve for the airing of public discontent and argues that the expansion of the Internet and Web-based media are changing the rules of the game between society and state. Authorities are increasingly taking note and responding to public opinion expressed on the Web. I conclude by arguing that these trends are likely to continue in the future, with Web-based public opinion formation playing an important role in the future development of Chinese society.

THE RISE OF THE INTERNET

Since the introduction of the Internet in China, the Chinese Communist Party (CCP) and Chinese government have shown ambivalence toward its effects as a new force in Chinese society: on the one hand, the party-state considers the adoption and expansion of both the Internet and information and communication technologies as essential parts of the country's economic development, and has actively (and successfully) supported e-commerce and e-government projects. By the end of 2009, the number of Internet users in the country had skyrocketed to 384 million, gaining 53 million new users in just six months, according to the government-run China Internet Network Information Center (CNNIC).[3]

According to CNNIC's 2010 statistics, Chinese Internet users are disproportionately young: over 60 percent of them are under age twenty-five and 70.6 percent are under age thirty. The Internet population is also relatively well educated, with more than 40 percent holding college or university degrees. Their education level contributes to the degree to which they participate in public affairs online.[4]

The rise of blogging, instant messaging, and social networking services such as QQ, and search engine and RSS aggregation tools such as Baidu (baidu.com) and Zhuaxia (zhuaxia.com), have given Chinese Internet users, or Netizens, an unprecedented capacity for communication. Internet bulletin board systems (BBS) play a particularly important role in Chinese Internet life. According to research data from the beginning of 2008, 80 percent of Chinese Web sites are running their own BBS and the total aggregate daily page views are over 1 billion, with 10 million posts published every day. By the end of 2007, China had more than 11.73 million BBS users. BBS is the primary way that Chinese Netizens access and transmit information online to a large number of people, almost as effectively as mass media. For example, the Hainan-based Tianya Club (tianya.cn) has 33.4 million total registered accounts and 100,000–500,000 users online at any one time. The online community has 200,000 daily online users, hundreds of thousands of new posts, and millions of commentaries per day. The entire Tianya online community has more than 6 million registered users. Another online forum,

Mop (mop.com), which is very popular among university students, is believed to be even larger, with more than 50 million visits per day. These popular Internet portals and smaller virtual communities allow users to discuss current events by posting comments on bulletin boards. Even when the subject is politically taboo or sensitive, many participants, using the cover of anonymity or coded euphemisms, can express themselves in far bolder language and views than would be permitted in official media.

At the same time, blogging activities have also exploded. Like BBS, blogging also has a very low entry cost—anyone with Internet access can open a Weblog on a hosting service. According to CNNIC, by the end of 2009, the number of blog users reached 221 million. The proportion of active blog users also continued to grow, with the number of users who updated their blog within six months rising to 145 million, an increase of 37.9 percent from just six months before.[5]

While most posts are personal in nature, an increasing number of bloggers are writing about public affairs and becoming opinion leaders in their local communities. Weblogs usually allow room for readers' comments, and because they often contain numerous links to other Weblogs and sites, they each act as a unit in a dynamic community. Together they form an interconnected whole—the "blogosphere." While the popular online communities (BBS) often become the locus of the formation and crystallization of public opinion, the redundancy of clusters and links in the blogosphere constructs a networked information environment that makes absolute top-down control of content nearly impossible.

In addition to BBS and Weblogs, chat rooms and instant messaging services such as QQ and MSN are also extremely popular channels for communication. QQ has 270 million active accounts. A research report by Analysys International on China's instant messaging market reveals that in the third quarter of 2007, active accounts of Chinese users numbered 388 million, with QQ being the most popular, and the highest number of users online at the same time reached 19.5 million.[6] These instant messaging services play a crucial role in connecting Internet users, facilitating information communication and coordinating actions through social networks. Finally, new photo and video sharing sites such as Youku and Tudou are the fastest growing online applications. The richness of images, video, and sound online has created a powerful media space where millions of users can themselves generate, distribute, and consume content.

ONLINE CENSORSHIP

The role of the Internet as a communications tool is especially meaningful in China, where citizens previously had little to no opportunity for unconstrained public self-expression or access to free and uncensored information. Furthermore, these newfound freedoms have developed in spite of stringent government efforts to control the medium. Three Chinese characters may best describe the dynamic between authorities and Netizens in Chinese cyberspace: *feng* ("block" or censorship); *shai* ("place under the sun" or reveal), and *huo* ("fire" or information cascade).

Ever since the People's Republic of China was established in 1949, information control has been an essential component of the CCP's governing strategy. The CCP has a monopoly on political power and has exerted firm control over all mass media, from newspapers and magazines to television channels and radio stations, making them mouthpieces of the party line. As Lu Yuegang, a reform-minded, senior investigative journalist and the former deputy director of the news center at *China Youth Daily* once wrote, the CCP "must depend on two weapons: guns and pens. . . . The logic behind this philosophy is not only to control the pen but to have this control backed by the gun."[7]

Since the Internet first entered China in September 1987, the government has used a multilayered strategy to control online content and monitor online activities at every level of Internet service. Authorities at various levels employ a complex web of regulations, surveillance, imprisonment, propaganda, and the blockade of hundreds of thousands of international Web sites at the national gateway level, known as the Great Firewall.

Several political bodies are in charge of Internet content, including most prominently the CCP central Propaganda Department, which ensures that media and cultural content follows the official line as mandated by the CCP, and the State Council Information Office (SCIO), which oversees all Web sites, both official and independent, that publish and post news, including the official sites of news organizations as well as independent sites that post news content. Municipal, provincial, or county-level offices of the Propaganda Department and SCIO are responsible for overseeing all media, including Web sites, published or hosted within their jurisdiction. Central propaganda officials frequently issue censorship directives to their local counterparts, who have some leeway to implement them as they see fit. Local officials also go beyond the center's instructions to issue their own censorship directives, and to fine, threaten, or close down media outlets that report information they do not wish be made public.[8]

Officials use a number of tactics to control online content, including keyword filtering through which posts on politically sensitive topics can be automatically censored. A list obtained by the China Internet Project in Berkeley found that over 1,000 words, including *dictatorship*, *truth*, and *riot police*, are automatically banned in China's online forums. Banned content, including lists of filtered keywords, is not made explicit by censors. The government's primary strategy for shaping content is to hold Internet service providers and access providers responsible for the behavior of their customers, so business operators have little choice but to proactively censor content on their sites. For example, regulations posted by the Guangdong Provincial Communications Administration state, "The system operator will be responsible for the contents of his/her area, using technical means as well as human evaluation to filter, select, and monitor. If there should be any content in a BBS area that is against the regulations, the related supervisory department will hold the BBS as well as the individual operator responsible."[9]

Business owners therefore use a combination of their own judgment and direct instructions from propaganda officials to determine what content to ban. In an anonymous interview with this author, a senior manager at one of China's largest Internet portals acknowledged receiving instructions from either SCIO or other provincial-level propaganda officials at least three times a day.

Additionally, human monitors are employed by both Web sites and the government to manually read and censor content. Tens of thousands of Web sites hosted overseas are also blocked at the level of the nine national gateways that connect the Chinese Internet to the global network.[10] Web sites hosted inside China can be warned or shut down if they violate rules of acceptable content; and individual Internet users who post or distribute information deemed harmful by authorities have been threatened, intimidated, or thrown in jail, most often on national security charges such as "subversion."

When Hu Jintao spoke to the Politburo of the Central Committee of the CCP on 23 January 2007, he called on government authorities to improve the technologies, content controls, and network security that are used to monitor the Internet, saying, "Whether we can cope with the Internet is a matter that affects the development of socialist culture, the security of information, and the stability of the state."[11] During the run-up to the People's CCP National Congress in September 2007, authorities shut down numerous Internet data centers, each of which houses servers that host hundreds or thousands of Web sites.

The year 2007 also saw the debut of two animated cartoon figures, Jingjing and Chacha (from *jingcha*, the Chinese word for police), who pop up on Internet users' screens on various Web sites. This includes Sina.com, China's largest news portal, and Tianya.cn, one of China's largest online communities. These images provide links to the Internet police section of the Public Security Web site, where readers can click to report any illegal information they see. A Shenzhen police officer explained the use of Jingjing and Chacha to *China Youth Daily*: "The Internet police have existed for a long time. This time we publish the image of Internet Police in the form of a cartoon, to let all Internet users know that the Internet is not a place beyond the law. The Internet Police will maintain order in all online behavior. The main function of Jingjing and Chacha is to intimidate, not to answer questions."[12]

Throughout 2008, Internet control was increasingly tightened because of government attempts to present a harmonious image to the world during the Olympics. Since the beginning of 2009, the Chinese government has further systematically escalated control over the Internet. For example:

> On 5 January, the SCIO, Ministry of Industry and Information Technology, Ministry of Public Security, Ministry of Culture, and three other ministries and agencies jointly launched an antivulgarity campaign aimed at all search engines, Web hosting services, and online communities.[13] *Antivulgarity* is defined broadly to include not just pornography, but also dirty words, slang expressions, and images that are socially and politically unacceptable. The interpretation of what is vulgar varies among different government agencies. According to official Chinese media reports, thousands of Web sites were closed as part of this campaign.
>
> In the run-up to the twentieth anniversary of the 4 June massacre at Tiananmen Square, massive numbers of Web sites were temporarily closed down in the name of "technical maintenance." Prominent foreign Web 2.0 services outside of China, such as Twitter, Flickr, Wikipedia, Bing, Hotmail, and Facebook, were all blocked during this period.

In June, the Ministry of Information Technology introduced plans to mandate the preinstallation of filtering software, called Green Dam Youth Escort, on all computers manufactured and sold in China by 1 July. Following public protest, these plans were later cancelled.

In the aftermath of violent riots in Urumqi, Xinjiang, on 5 July, Twitter was blocked in China and domestic microblogging sites were closed down throughout the country. Except for a few official sites, the Internet remained shut down in Xinjiang Province until May 2010.

All together, these events clearly demonstrate the determination of the Chinese government to maintain dominance in cyberspace.

DIGITAL RESISTANCE

Even with the censors' constant presence, the ephemeral, anonymous, and networked nature of Internet communication limits their impact. Moreover, a number of factors make the censors' work particularly daunting. The first is that the Internet is a many-to-many communication platform that has very low barriers to entry (and risks of use) for anyone who has an Internet connection to access and produce information. Second is the network topology itself. When we look at a Weblog or a BBS as an isolated publication form, it is easy to apply traditional methods of content control: putting the publisher of those forms under some kind of editorial control or self-censorship is not difficult. But when one deals with the blogosphere and the whole Internet with its redundant connections, millions of overlapping clusters, self-organized communities, and new nodes growing in an explosive fashion, total control is nearly impossible.

Internet scholar Yochai Benkler wrote, "In authoritarian countries, it is also the absence of single or manageable small set of points of control that is placing the greatest pressure on the capacity of the regimes to control their public sphere, and thereby to simplify the problem of controlling the action of the population."[14] In the case of China, the government's Internet control system mainly aims to censor content that openly defies or attacks the CCP's rule, or contradicts the government's official line on historically taboo subjects, such as the 1989 Tiananmen Square crackdown or Beijing's relationship with Tibet. The most important aim of censorship is to prevent large-scale distribution of information that may lead to collective action, especially offline actions such as mass demonstrations or signature campaigns.

However, the results of censorship efforts are mixed at best. The government's pervasive and intrusive censorship system has generated resentment among Chinese Netizens, inspiring new forms of social resistance and demands for greater freedom of information and expression. As a result, the Internet has became a quasi-public space where the CCP's dominance is being exposed, ridiculed, and criticized, often in the form of political satire, jokes, songs, popular poetry, code words, mockery, and euphemisms. There are clear parallels between this sort of behavior and the "hidden transcripts" described by political scientist James Scott in studying how power distorts communications in societies where punishment is uncertain, arbitrary, and depends on constant surveillance.[15]

Chinese society has long been full of such coded communication, usually whispered in private. However, such information is no longer only transmitted secretly behind the backs of the powerful, but is publicly communicated and distributed, and occasionally aggregated in the networked space. For example, since censorship is carried out under the official slogan of "constructing a harmonious society," Netizens have begun to refer to the censoring of Internet content as "being harmonized." Furthermore, the word "to harmonize" in Chinese (*hexie*) is a homonym of the word for "river crab." In folk language, *crab* also refers to bullies who exercise power violently. Thus the image of a crab has become a new satirical, politically charged icon for the Netizens who are fed up with government censorship and who now call themselves the River Crab Society. Photos of a malicious crab travel through the blogosphere as a silent protest under the virtual noses of the new cyberpolice officers. Even on the most vigorously self-censored Chinese search engine, Baidu.com, a search of the phrase "River Crab Society" will result in over 5,830,000 posts or articles.

"INFORMATION WANTS TO BE FREE"

The nebulous nature of the Internet in turn leads to *shai* ("put under the sun" or reveal). In general, the Internet allows a huge amount of information not easily accessible elsewhere in China to be revealed. Those who can get online are exposed to diverse and numerous sources of information and have unprecedented opportunities to communicate and express themselves on social, political, and personal issues. As Stewart Brand has characterized it, "information wants to be free."[16] Simultaneously, the interaction between information and communication technology and the traditional media creates a dynamic that is challenging the boundaries of the existing censorship system and thereby the official media as well.

On BBS, the blogosphere, and video and photo sharing services, Netizens have launched endless so-called *shai* activities: For "*shai* salaries," people put their own or others' salary amounts online to compare and comment on; for "*shai* vacations," users show their vacation photos and experiences; and "*shai* corruption," "*shai* bosses," and "*shai* riches" are ways that Netizens use the Internet to publish information and opinions that otherwise would go unpublished.

The *feng* and *shai* processes are constantly at odds with each other. When information is censored at a high level, it can often still find its way through cracks in the online system to spread among Netizens. Overseas Web sites and news media also play a critical role by publishing information censored in China, which is then often redistributed inside China by a small but active group of tech-savvy "information brokers" who know how to circumvent the Great Firewall. Even if such news does not make it into the official media, it still has an incremental impact—as more and more people become aware of it, it reshapes their perceptions of social reality. While most of the major overseas news Web sites that provide Chinese-language services—including the BBC, Radio Free Asia (RFA), and Hong Kong– or Taiwan-based newspapers—are blocked by the Great Firewall, the content of these publications often still enters China and is then spread through bulletin boards, mass e-mails to individual inboxes, and other online channels. These publications, including dissident newsletters, Voice of America news updates, and overseas Chinese-language news alerts, can reach Chinese readers despite the government's use of advanced filtering technology.

The last character, *huo* ("fire" or information cascade), describes the phenomenon when news reports, comments, photos, or videos resonate among Netizens and spread through cyberspace like wildfire. The original piece of information may appear in a BBS or Weblog post, or an article from local media, and can generate thousands of subsequent BBS comments and posts on the same or related subjects. Driven by dense clusters of users who find the subject interesting or engaging, the spread of such information outpaces the control of censors.

Politically, this *huo* process is important. An analogy is water pouring through a hole in a dam: if the speed and volume of the water is great enough, any attempt to staunch the flow will be in vain. When sensitive information appears on Weblogs or BBS, Netizens quickly republish and distribute it such that it would be wasteful for government censors to attempt to stop its spread, as it has already become public knowledge. This is especially potent when a story has images or videos, which can be quickly transmitted and understood. Thus, before many commercial Web sites receive and implement instructions from the office of the Propaganda Department, which has jurisdiction, sensitive information can already be spread on the Web and blogosphere widely enough to become public knowledge, thereby seriously eroding the impact of censorship. When such a *huo* phenomenon occurs, the Internet plays the role of a massive distribution platform that denies the government agenda-setting power.

The *huo* process is especially potent when information about a localized phenomenon resonates with a broader audience and spreads beyond the limited jurisdiction of local officials, sometimes even making it into the national media. When information about a local event such as corruption, protests, environmental damage, or other politically sensitive topics is exposed, local authorities implicated in causing the problem frequently crack down on news Web sites hosted within their jurisdiction that report such news. But when such news finds its way to a Web site beyond their jurisdiction, these officials cannot directly suppress the spread of such information. Furthermore, officials outside of their jurisdiction are less likely to have the same incentives to censor such information. Depending on the potency, sensitivity, and relevance of a particular story, central authorities may likewise not choose to impose an online news blackout on a story about a local phenomenon.

This gap in control between local authorities as well as between local and central authorities can provide a space for Netizens to transmit information. As previously noted, in the case of the Xiamen anti-PX movement, one of the most vocal advocates for the issue was the blogger Lian Yue, whose Weblog was not hosted within Fujian Province. Because officials outside Fujian, including the central government, did not share the local government's interest in censoring news about the PX plant, Lian Yue was able to continue his Weblog posting and even get coverage in newspapers published outside Fujian. Lian Yue's Weblog posts also reflected opinions advocated by a local Chinese People's Political Consultative Conference (CPPCC) member, Zhao Yufen, who led a proposal to terminate the construction project. The proposal was cosigned by 105 CPPCC members, and was named the top proposal at the 2007 CPPCC meeting. Although local Fujian officials had a stake in silencing voices against the project, their interests were not shared at parallel and higher administrative levels, which allowed the information to get out.

The *huo* phenomenon also plays a critical role in the interplay between Internet expression and changes in the traditional media. A large number of Chinese journalists are themselves bloggers. They live a double life, working for the state-controlled media during the day and blogging or participating in BBS forums at night. When covering sensitive stories in China—like natural disasters, major industrial accidents, or official corruption cases—print reporters must follow the lead of official sources before conducting interviews and publishing their findings. But journalists now can evade these guidelines by distributing and collecting information online, making it more difficult for censors to silence sensitive stories. The fact that much of such information becomes *huo* on the Internet gives traditional media a legitimate reason to cover it. Some official media follow developments that break on the Web. For example, *Southern Weekend* has an editorial section called Net Eye (Wang Yan) in which reporters monitor the Internet, pick up interesting tips and materials, and then publish them in print.

EXAMPLES OF THE INTERNET'S ROLE IN DRIVING PUBLIC OPINION EVENTS

Defending Rights: Chongqing Nail House

A property dispute that erupted in Chongqing in 2007 provides a window into how the processes of *feng*, *shai*, and *huo* work. On 26 February 2007, a Netizen from Chongqing posted a photograph of a two-story house, sticking up all alone like a giant nail in the middle of a construction site. Within days, all major BBS posted this photo along with questions and commentaries from Netizens. The house, whose owners refused to relocate to make way for a new development, was soon named by Netizens "China's Most Incredible Nail House."

Because the image was quite poignant and touched upon the common problems of urban construction, property rights, and forced evictions, the official media soon jumped on the story. The homeowners were also successful and articulate entrepreneurs, who welcomed media exposure of their situation and quickly gained celebrity for their stand. Moreover, the story happened to break just as the National People's Congress was passing a new property rights law that purported to protect individual homeowners. The official media therefore framed the story as a sample case of the spirit of the new law, describing the situation as a middle-class couple standing against a powerful alliance of local officials and property developers.

The story soon became popular on China's Internet. Sina.com, China's largest Internet portal, offered a monetary reward for digital images and videos that captured developments in the story. Mop.com, one of the most popular online forums, ran a real-time monitoring page. When a local court ruled that the couple would have to vacate their house or be forcibly removed, the husband hung a huge red banner reading "defending human rights according the law [sic]" in front of the cameras. His actions gained empathy from a public frustrated by their feelings of powerlessness in the face of business and government interests, and generated significant online support. Facing heated public opinion, the local court delayed enforcing the eviction notice so that days after the deadline, the house remained standing.

After the couple disobeyed the court order and refused to move, the central government issued orders to limit reporting. When journalists for official media outlets were no longer allowed to report the story, many Netizens assumed the reporters' role, using digital cameras and cell phones to follow the fate of the house and keep the story alive. Despite the reporting ban, many print and broadcast media outlets continued to run commentaries and discussions on this case, exploring its relationship to the new property law. Under continuing public pressure, the developer finally settled the case and compensated the couple for their property, which was eventually destroyed. The case vividly illustrates the pressure faced by local officials when millions of individuals come together through the Internet, especially when the official media also come on board.

Hunting Down Injustice: Shanxi Brick Kilns

Often government control over a story is a not black-and-white issue, as there can be official reasons to acknowledge some elements of a story while censoring others. A good example of this dynamic is the exposé of the widespread use of slave labor in brick kilns in Shanxi Province. The story started when a group of fathers from Henan Province ventured to Shanxi Province to rescue their children, who had been abducted and illegally forced to work as slaves. After rescuing around forty of an estimated two thousand children, the fathers' efforts were obstructed by the local police, who, it was later discovered, were in alliance with the kiln owners. After obtaining no response from the local government, the fathers published a moving open letter on 7 June 2007 on Tianya Club, one of the most-viewed Chinese online forums. The letter spread through the Chinese blogosphere and ignited national outrage. Reports in the official media followed, and soon top party officials, including General Secretary Hu Jintao and Premier Wen Jiabao, publicly expressed their concern over the issue.

After the top leadership weighed in on the case, local and central Chinese media outlets began reporting waves of horrifying stories about the brick kilns. The Internet further circulated the media reports, bloggers' comments and analysis, and photos of missing children, leading the public to begin asking more and more critical questions about how this could happen in modern China. Investigations into the case soon revealed that local CCP officials and police were profiting from the kidnapping and slavery operation. Facing public questions over the story, the Internet Bureau of the State Council Information Office (also called the CCP External Communication Office) sent out the following notice to all its subordinate offices and to the main news Web portals on 15 June 2007:

> Regarding the Shanxi "illegal brick kilns" event, all Web sites should reinforce positive propaganda, put more emphasis on the forceful measures that the central and local governments have already taken, and close the comment function in the related news reports. The management of the interactive communication tools, such as online forums, blogs, and instant messages, should also be strengthened. Harmful information that uses this event to attack the party and the government should be deleted as soon as possible. All local external communication offices should enhance their instruction, supervision and inspection, and concretely implement the related management measures.[17]

While trying to keep online public opinion under control, the central government also took action against kiln owners and officials who had been implicated in the event, sending 35,000 police officers to raid 7,500 kiln sites and penalizing ninety-five local officials. The state also turned the incident into a positive public relations ploy, displaying their response to the specific crimes that had been committed, while suppressing other sharper critics and persistent investigations into related societal issues.

While the cases above demonstrate the weaknesses in official Internet censorship, we should not forget that the government is still able to exert near-total control over information distributed online in particularly sensitive cases where officials make it a priority. In November 2007, 10,000 people demonstrated in front of local government offices in Shenyang, Liaoning Province, against a pyramid scheme in which up to a million people, mostly poor or unemployed workers, had invested their life savings but received nothing when the company went bankrupt. The story was potentially explosive not only because of the mass protests that it inspired but also because the company involved, Yilishen, had ties with powerful officials, including Bo Xilai, the former governor of Liaoning Province and then minister of commerce (Bo currently is Party Secretary of Chongqing). The central government quickly imposed a complete blackout on reporting the incident. For a period, news about the scheme and subsequent protests could not be found through searches on the Chinese Internet. Once the foreign media began covering the case, however, those news reports found their way back into online forums, but were censored before they could be distributed widely enough to reach the mainstream of Internet users.

Nonetheless, the examples of the Chongqing nail house and the Shanxi brick kilns, as well as the anti-PX protests in Xiamen, point to early signs of a changing dynamic: first, these stories initially broke online and were later carried by the traditional media. In this process, bloggers such as Lian Yue played a distinct role as online agenda setters. Nevertheless, thousands, and sometimes hundreds of thousands, of public-minded bloggers and some journalists also played a critical role in amplifying these messages. Second, despite government censorship efforts, the sheer speed and number of messages and Internet posts made it impossible for censors to stay ahead of the game. The timing gap between the information cascade and top-down censorship instructions was critical, as was the gap in control between central and local authorities. In all of these cases, this gap allowed local events to become national news and make it into the centrally controlled media. Once sensitive stories are carried by the official media, the Internet amplifies and keeps stories alive, creating an event that the government cannot ignore or suppress. Yet the Yilishen story also shows us that when it is a political priority, the central government still has the means and the will to exert almost complete control over information online.

CREATING A PUBLIC DIALOGUE

Since traditional media outlets still remain under control of the CCP, even the more progressive and outspoken publications such as *Southern Metropolis Daily* or *Southern Weekend* possess only very limited space to push the envelope on political reporting. When mass protests, health epidemics, official corruption cases, or other public events occur, the Internet is now the first place people go to find the latest news and to share experiences and opinions. For the first time, citizens are able to participate in public dialogue about issues of crucial importance to the future of their lives and their country.

An interesting study by Xinhua Net in early 2008 reveals what kind of topics are most popular in the three most influential online communities—Strong Country Forum (bbs.people.com.cn), Tianya Club (www.tianya.cn), and Kaidi (club2.cat898.com).[18] Xinhua's report studied the most popular posts in all three online communities, not including the posts that had been deleted by monitors. In addition to the Xiamen PX protests, Chongqing nail house, and Shanxi brick kiln stories, Xinhua Net's study also found that other "sensitive social events" were popular, including those relating to governance, police violence, environmental protection, public health, judicial reform, and natural disasters. The study also suggested that Netizens' consciousness of rights is rising as expressions such as "right to know," "right to express," and "right to monitor [the government]" are often used in connection with those large online public events. Furthermore, participants cited the credibility and responsiveness of different levels of government as well as issues of public morality and the crisis of values in society as concerns.

As Beijing-based Internet expert Hu Yong has written: "Since ordinary people now have the means to express themselves, 'public opinion' has finally emerged in Chinese society. Since China never had mechanisms to accurately detect and reflect public opinion, blogs and BBS have become an effective route to form and communicate such public opinions of the society."[19]

One of the direct impacts of this new information landscape is that negative reports and criticism of local officials, especially relating to corruption, social justice, or people's daily experiences, are now being exposed and nationally distributed though the Internet, and can resonate broadly in society. Sometimes such a process is also tolerated or deliberately used by central authorities to keep lower officials in check and to allow the public to let off steam before it erupts in an uncontrollable manner such as public protests. Such Internet-generated public opinion can be the sole channel to provide crucial feedback for government decision makers.

Online oversight has an especially large impact on local officials such as county-level CCP secretaries, who are in charge of administrative, legal, law enforcement, and propaganda agencies, and as such have the ability to control information within their jurisdictions. As we saw with the Xiamen PX protests, the Shanxi brick kilns, and the Chongqing nail house, once local officials lose control and information spreads beyond their jurisdiction, it can force them to change their policies by making them accountable to public opinion. Recently, a local propaganda official expressed his anger to a journalist by saying "it was so much better when there was no Internet."[20]

In addition to impacting local politics, Internet-driven public events have played an important role by highlighting issues that start as local concerns but have broader implications for Chinese society. For individuals who are advocating political reform and social change, the Internet and the more reform-minded traditional media give them an outlet to focus public attention on topics that were previously taboo. For example, after the conclusion of the Chongqing nail house event, some reform-minded media outlets raised more fundamental questions brought up by this event. The *Southern Metropolis Daily* published an editorial that read:

> From the view of civil rights, reclamation, demolition and relocation ... are problems related to the protection of private property. From the perspective of the execution of the government power, these issues raise a constitutional problem of whether the power of a government is checked. For the first time, the Property Law defines the limits of private property protection. But without a real checks-and-balances system, the law can't harness today's public authority in China. . . . It will be too narrow to interpret various public opinions on the Property Law just about the protection of private property. The public's widespread anxiety on unchecked government power is inherently implied in both the nail house event in Chongqing. The current authorities put emphasis on governing according to laws and building a modern government ruled by laws. However, governing according to laws is not a problem of administrative procedure under the current rhetoric. First of all, it's a problem of defining the limits of government power. How big a government's power is and whether the power is checked is something that can never be taken for granted on the enunciation of institutions. What

China currently lacks is this fundamental institutional arrangement and checks and balances on power.[21]

CITIZEN MOBILIZATION

Often, the next step after public dialogue is collective mobilization and organization over issues of common concern. This is an area where Internet-based public opinion has the potential to make a powerful impact on Chinese society and politics. While authorities stifle civil society and independent social organizations, various grassroots groups that depart from the official line with regard to such social issues as protecting the environment, women's rights, and homosexuality rely on the Internet to organize and distribute information. The expanded space for discussion of public affairs facilitated by the Internet has thus created and fostered a space for civil society to push the boundaries of associative and communicative freedoms.

The Xiamen anti-PX protests are now considered a milestone. One protester told a foreign reporter covering the story that at last, people "can be heard." The city government, in return, listened to public opinion and adjusted its decision accordingly. This was a first in China and is a very encouraging sign. The state-run Xinhua News Agency concluded, "The suspended controversial Xiamen city PX plant probably will not become a landmark wherever it finally stands, but it may have helped lay a cornerstone that boosts ordinary Chinese people's participation in policy making."[22]

Xinhua's article needs to be interpreted with caution, however, since the ruling CCP has not shown any sign of giving up its monopoly on political power, and therefore is still highly sensitive to the increasing political impact of the Internet. The Xiamen protests are still seen as an exception, rather than the rule. However, only two months after the Xiamen PX issue was settled, a similar protest, apparently inspired by Xiamen's success, was launched in Shanghai against the construction of a Maglev high-speed railroad through a residential district.

Online mobilization and protests have also made an impact beyond China's border, becoming a significant factor influencing China's international image and diplomacy. In November 2009, to commemorate the twentieth anniversary of the fall of the Berlin Wall, the city created a virtual Berlin Twitter Wall where individuals could post their thoughts on the occasion through use of a

Twitter hashtag "#FOTW." The site's introduction further invited participants to "let us know which walls still have to come down to make our world a better place!" In response, Chinese comments blasting the Great Firewall and Internet censorship dominated the virtual Berlin Wall for weeks. Chinese bloggers also waged a "Tear Down This Firewall" campaign prior to American President Barack Obama's first visit to China in November 2009. Largely due to such efforts, President Obama addressed the issue of online freedom of speech on the Internet at a town hall meeting with students in Shanghai.

Not all online mobilization is spontaneous and anonymous like the campaign against the Great Firewall. Influential bloggers may also mobilize a movement by acting as spokespersons for certain issues or giving personal authentication to messages that resonate within the larger public, or articulating what others could not say in the face of political censorship. Twenty-eight-year-old bestselling author, race car driver, and blogger Han Han is such a figure in Chinese cyberspace. Han is one of the most outspoken critics of government censorship, and his blog posts are often deleted by censors. Nevertheless, his main blog received over 300 million hits between 2006 and 2009. In April 2010, *Time* magazine listed Han Han on its Web site as a candidate for the one hundred "most globally influential people." Han Han subsequently wrote a blog post asking the Chinese government "to treat art, literature and the news media better, to not impose too many restrictions and censorship, and to not use the power of the government or the name of the State to block or slander any artist or journalist." His post generated over 25,000 comments from his readers and was viewed by more than 1.2 million people. The article has also been widely reposted online; in May 2010, a Google search found more than 45,000 links reposting all or part of the essay. Despite official efforts to use the Great Firewall to block Chinese Netizens from voting for Han Han on the *Time* website, Han Han came in #2 in the final tally, showing the mobilization power his writing generates.

A SAFETY VALVE OR CHANGING THE RULES
OF THE GAME?

Government officials have started to recognize that the Internet has produced an irreversible trend toward a more transparent society, a more participative citizenry, and an increasing power of online public opinion. Some officials advocate the need for political reform to adapt to these forces.

A rather telling observation of the political impact of Internet-driven events comes from a researcher at the Central Party School. In a long article published in 2007 in the official press, the director of the Research Department of the Central Party School, Xin Di, listed five concrete examples to show the "incremental progress" taking place in China's political system.[23] Interestingly, four of the five examples he mentioned were not top-down political reform efforts; rather, they were related to the reactions of the CCP and government to Internet-driven public events. Although genuine political reform did not appear on the leadership's agenda at the Seventeenth CCP National Congress in 2007, some lower officials recognize the important role of the Internet as a catalyst for political changes in Chinese society.

From the perspective of these more forward-looking officials, the government should selectively tolerate or even welcome Internet expression as a barometer of public opinion. Permitting such expression allows the CCP and government to cheaply collect information about society, to be more responsive to citizens' concerns, and to provide a safety valve that releases public anger. As with the Shanxi brick kiln case, the Internet can also help hold local officials more accountable—to central authorities, as well as to the public. The role of the Internet in promoting political change may also be felt when the interests and agendas of different government agencies or administrative levels do not align. In such a case, public opinion may help bolster one side over another.

An analysis of the impact of the Internet on public opinion published by the Chinese Academy of Social Sciences in December 2009 describes the dual methods the government uses to cope with the growing challenge of online activism.[24] The authors identify a "new opinion class" that consists of "Netizens who are concerned with news and current affairs and express their opinions online . . . [and who] can gather consensus, transform emotions, induce action and influence society within a very short period of time. . . . In a series of sudden events, the new opinion class demonstrated their enormous energy to incite public opinion." To manage this phenomenon, "the government both intensified Internet control, in order to manage overly-radical expressions, and accelerated its reaction to Internet public opinion."[25]

For those inside and outside of the government who wish to see deeper and more fundamental political change, rising public participation online is an indicator that the rules of the political game in China may have started to change. Xiao Shu, a commentator for *Southern Weekend* magazine, has written about this process:

The process is . . . to discover public events, follow public events, publicize the truth of those public events, and the logic behind and value within those events; for the public to discuss, form a consensus in the society, and then change the current rules of the game according to such consensus. . . .

Through SARS reporting we have established a new principle, which is that information must be public when there are matters of public security in such a crisis. Through the Chongqing Nail House event we are also changing the current rules of the game of building and evictions. Through Xiamen PX we are also changing a rule of the game, this time is to establish the following principle: before major public projects undergo construction, all people who would be affected by such a project must be consulted, and their permission granted.[26]

CONCLUSION

The CCP's censorship of both traditional media and the Internet is certain to continue. However, the rise of online public opinion shows that the CCP and government can no longer maintain absolute control of the mass media and information. The Internet is already one of the most influential media spaces in Chinese society—no less so than traditional forms of print or broadcast media. Beneath the surface of the constantly increasing and intensifying control measures is a rising level of public information and awareness in Chinese society. Furthermore, through online social networks and virtual communities, the Chinese Internet has become a substantial communications platform across which to aggregate information and coordinate collective actions.

The conflicting forces of *feng* (censorship), *shai* (reveal), and *huo* (information cascade) will continue to interact with each other. The result is an emerging pattern of public opinion and citizen participation that represents a power shift in Chinese society. As news events, from the Chongqing nail house to environmental protests in Xiamen to slave labor in the Shanxi brick kilns, covered in this chapter vividly demonstrate, the Internet allows citizens to propagate, comment on, and promote certain topics (albeit limited) from a local platform to the national stage. Moreover, these "public events" now play a role in promoting human rights, freedom of expression, rule of law, and government accountability. An entire generation of online public agenda setters has emerged during online public events to become influential opinion leaders. They will no doubt be playing an important role in China's future.

Furthermore, some of China's more outspoken media outlets such as *Southern Metropolis Daily* or *Southern Weekend* are also actively expressing much more liberal political ideas and pushing the envelope whenever they have a chance. Prior to the spread of the Internet, such reform-minded discourse was vulnerable in the face of the CCP's propaganda. Now, however, as more liberal elements within the established media converge with independent, grassroots voices online, they are creating a substantial force that appears to be slowly eroding the CCP's ideological and social control.

China is becoming an increasingly transparent and mobile society with more pluralistic values. The Internet has become a training ground for citizen participation in public affairs: it creates a more informed and engaged public and increases the public's demands on government. The CCP's authoritarian regime is learning to be more responsive and adaptive in this new environment. Events such as the Shanxi brick kilns, Chongqing nail house, and Xiamen PX cases have produced real change on the ground. We are starting to see new compromise, negotiation, and rule-changing behaviors in the regime's response to this challenge, indicating the possibility of more open and accountable governance with greater citizen participation. From this perspective, the Internet is in fact catalyzing social and political transition.

Notes

1. Xinhua Net, http://www.hxzg.net/society/2009/0420/133.html.
2. *Nanfang Zhoumo* [*Southern Weekend*], 26 December 2007.
3. China Internet Network Information Center, *25th Statistical Report on the Development of China's Internet* (January 2010), http://www.cnnic.net.cn/uploadfiles/pdf/2010/1/15/101600.pdf.
4. Ibid. Since July 2007, CNNIC has counted as "Internet users" anyone over six years old, who visited the Internet from any terminal including mobile phones, at least once within six months. Before July 2007, an Internet user was defined as anyone who spent at least one hour per week online. This change in the definition has impacted the demographic characteristics of Internet users. More low-income users, such as migrant workers and the rural population who use mobile phones instead of personal computers as their main communication interface, are now being included into the CNNIC's user base. In CNNIC's 2007 survey, over 70 percent of users were under age thirty, and 40

percent had college degrees. China Internet Network Information Center, *20th Statistical Report on the Development of China's Internet,* June 2007.

5. China Internet Network Information Center, *25th Statistical Report.*

6. Analysys International Market Analysis of Instant Messaging Services in China, 22 November 2007; Hua Jun Information, "More Than 50 Million QQ Users Online at the Same Time," 9 February 2009.

7. "A Bold New Voice—Lu Yuegang's Extraordinary Open Letter to Authorities," *China Digital Times,* 20 July 2004.

8. U.S.-China Economic and Security Review Commission, Hearing on Access to Information in the People's Republic of China. Testimony by Xiao Qiang, 31 July 2007.

9. U.S.-China Economic and Security Review Commission, Hearing on China's State Control Mechanisms and Methods, testimony by Xiao Qiang, 14 April 2005.

10. Jonathan Zittrain and Benjamin Edelman, "Empirical Analysis of Internet Filtering in China," working paper, Berkman Center for Internet and Society, Harvard Law School, 2003, http://cyber.law.harvard.edu/filtering/china/.

11. "Hu Jintao Asks Chinese Officials to Better Cope with Internet," *People's Daily,* 24 January 2007.

12. "Starting from September 1, New Virtual Cops Will 'Cruise' All Thirteen Internet Portals in Beijing," *Beijing News,* 22 August 2007.

13. The other agencies are the State Administration for Industry and Commerce (SAIC), State Administration of Radio, Film and Television (SARFT), and General Administration of Press and Publication (GAPP).

14. Yochai Benkler, *The Wealth of Networks* (New Haven: Yale University Press, 2006), p. 180.

15. James C. Scott, *Hidden Transcripts* (New Haven: Yale University Press, 1990).

16. Stewart Brand, *Whole Earth Review,* May 1985, p. 49.

17. China Digital Times, http://chinadigitaltimes.net/2007/06/a-notice-from-the-central-government-to-censor-news-related-to-shanxi-brick-kilns-event/.

18. "Study Report of Online Public Opinions in 2007," *Xinhua Net,* 5 February 2008.

19. Hu Yong, "Blogs in China," China Media Project Case Study (on file at the Journalism and Media Studies Centre, University of Hong Kong), 4 August 2005.

20. Southern News Net report, January 30 2008, http://news.qq.com/a/20080130/000639.htm.

21. *Southern Metropolis Daily,* 3 April 2007.

22. "Common Chinese Have More Say in Policy-Making," *Xinhua Net,* 3 January 2008.

23. "Political Civilization in Details," Xinhua News Agency, 4 February 2008.

24. Shan Xuegang, Hu Jiangchun, and Zhu Huaxin, "People's Net," 22 December, 2009, http://yq.people.com.cn/htmlArt/Art392.htm.

25. The "2010 Society Blue Paper," published by the Chinese Academy of Social Sciences on 22 December, 2009, contained a paper titled, "2009 China Internet Public Opinion Analysis Report," written by analysts Zhu Huaxin, Shan Xuegang, and Hu Jiangchun; Shan, Hu, and Zhu, "People's Net."

26. Xiao Shu, "New Media in the Times of Gaming," *Nanfang Wang* [*Southern Net*], 15 June 2007.

10

Changing Media,
Changing Foreign Policy

Susan L. Shirk

THE COMMERCIALIZATION OF the media and the emergence of the Internet have revolutionized the way Chinese leaders and the public interact in the foreign policymaking process. Public opinion has become an important influence on the process. Commercial media outlets compete with one another for audiences by appealing to the tastes of these audiences. Editors decide which news events to cover based on their judgments about which topics will attract audiences. In today's China, that means publication of a lot of stories about Japan, Taiwan, and the United States, all topics that stimulate Chinese popular nationalism. Tibet has emerged as another hot-button issue in the aftermath of the violent protests that preceded the 2008 Olympic Games. The press given to these topics makes them domestic political issues—potential focal points for elite disagreement and triggers for mass protests. Public response to reporting on these topics increasingly influences the way Chinese Communist Party (CCP) leaders and government diplomats conduct foreign policy.

Most foreign policy issues in China receive little media attention and are handled by professional diplomats in the Foreign Ministry. However, even relatively minor events involving China's relations with Japan, Taiwan, or the United States can become big news and evoke a strong nationalistic response. Relations with these governments must therefore be handled carefully by politicians in the highest organ of the CCP, the Politburo Standing Committee. Because of the Internet and complementary technologies such as cell phones, it is nearly impossible for government censors to screen out news from Japan, Taiwan, or the United States that might elicit a public response. When common knowledge of such news is established, officials are forced to respond, no matter how trivial the issue. Foreign policymakers feel especially constrained by nationalist public opinion when it comes to Sino-Japanese relations; media commercialization and the Internet have helped make the Sino-Japanese relationship China's most emotionally charged international issue.

Reporting on international affairs, while guided by CCP propaganda officials, has become more open to interpretation than in the past.[1] Local newspapers are supposed to base all their international news coverage on reports from the official Xinhua News Agency, which as of 2009 had over one hundred foreign bureaus. However, this rule is often violated by the commercial media. Lacking their own foreign correspondents, commercial papers often rely on plagiarized translations of foreign news reports or on interviews or forums among locally based experts to provide content that puts their own stamp on the story.

Like editors everywhere, Chinese editors seek to attract audiences by dramatizing international news events, exaggerating threats, and emphasizing conflict over cooperation. As one Chinese scholar observes, "Chinese readers interested in foreign affairs will find more threat, conspiracy, hostility and conflict around their country from newspapers, though the official line is that China enjoys the best period in its relations with neighboring countries. . . . Good news is no news—it doesn't sell."[2] In a parallel statement, a television producer I interviewed pointed out, "News shows get more viewers in a crisis, so the media likes crises the best."

Yet journalists have to dramatize international affairs for their audiences without challenging the current government line. A *Global Times* editor I interviewed put it this way: "We always have two whips on us. The Propaganda Department gives us the policy, and then we have to satisfy the market." The interaction of these two drivers—the market and CCP control—has produced mass media that stir up nationalist sentiments that feed back into the foreign policy process in a kind of echo chamber. When government decision makers read the media, they come away with an impression that nationalist ardor is sweeping the country.[3] This perception of an intensely nationalist public opinion influences their foreign policy choices.

The top priority of China's leaders is the preservation of CCP rule; they are haunted by the fear that their days in power are numbered. Their worst nightmare is a nationwide movement of discontented groups united against the regime by the shared fervor of nationalism. Chinese history gives them good reason to worry. Mass movements that accused leaders of failing to defend the nation against foreign aggression brought down the Qing Dynasty in 1911 and the Republic of China in 1949. China's current leaders make foreign policy with a close eye to nationalist criticism in the media and on the Web because they are intent on avoiding a similar fate.

THE DEMAND FOR INTERNATIONAL NEWS

International news is a big draw for the commercial media. A survey conducted by sixteen television networks found that people's main motive for watching television was "to know about current affairs inside and outside China."[4] Newspaper editors say that their market research indicates that international news is second in popularity only to sports. Many commercial tabloids, such as Shanghai's *Xinmin Evening News*, have expanded their international news from two pages to four or more.

The demand for international news is reflected in the fact that *Reference News* (*Cankao Xiaoxi*), published by the Xinhua News Agency, is the most popular nationally circulated newspaper, selling over 3 million copies per day. Originally consisting entirely of Xinhua's translations of foreign news reports prepared for distribution among officials, *Reference News* has begun to include original content.[5] Xinhua editors proudly claim that *Reference News* is the fifth largest newspaper in the world.

GLOBAL TIMES

Global Times (*Huanqiu Shibao*) is the publication that best illustrates the way China's commercialized but politically guided media mobilize public opinion on foreign policy and then feed it back into the foreign policymaking process. The CCP's flagship newspaper, *People's Daily*, founded *Global Times* in 1992. A nationally circulated and highly profitable newspaper devoted entirely to international news, *Global Times* has privileged access to the *People's Daily's* foreign correspondents and the political protection of the CCP leadership. It is a tabloid, but an authoritative one. As a *Global Times* editor I interviewed said dismissively, *Reference News* is just a digest of foreign news reports, whereas *Global Times* represents "the Chinese view of international affairs." He continued, "We try to represent the national interest. We don't want to make problems for China's foreign policy. The American press considers itself a watchdog of the government, but in China the press has a more cooperative spirit toward the government."

Global Times began tentatively, publishing once a week and covering mostly "soft" international news topics such as Princess Diana's death, the wedding of the late Palestinian leader, Yasser Arafat, the Japanese royal family, Chinese film stars in Hollywood, World Cup football, and the Olympics. During the 1995–1996 tension in the Taiwan Strait following President Lee Teng-hui's visit to the United States, *Global Times* ran only one front-page story on the confrontation. The paper positively covered President Clinton's visit to China in June 1998, but devoted more ink to his scandalous behavior with Monica Lewinsky than to the visit.[6]

Beginning in 1999 with sympathetic stories on Yugoslavia's resistance to bombing by NATO and the United States, the newspaper began to feature harder news from a bold, nationalist angle. The trend accelerated after the accidental bombing by an American bomber under NATO command of the Chinese embassy in Belgrade in May 1999.[7]

Since that time, about half of the newspaper's front-page stories deal with the United States. As a *Global Times* editor said in an interview, "People care most about China's national security and U.S.-China relations. . . . You have to have a front page that will make people want to buy the paper." Furthermore, "A good way to attract readers is to have an exciting cover story on the U.S., Japan, or Taiwan, or if possible, two or more." Another *Global Times* editor acknowledged, "Our reporting is very critical of Japan on the history issue. We react with a story whenever the Japanese right wing says or does something that shows its support of militarism."

Global Times' nationalist slant is driven largely by commercial considerations. Beginning in 2000, *Global Times* began to publish biweekly; in 2004, three times a week; in 2005, five times a week. In 2009 it started an online English edition, which takes a more neutral tone toward the West and Japan than the print version. *Global Times* is one of the most profitable publications in China. Half of its profits come from a circulation of about 2 million and half from advertising. It sells for RMB 1.2 and earns RMB .20–.30 for every copy sold. Per unit, this is a substantially higher margin than other publications. According to independent market research commissioned by the paper to impress advertisers, most of its readers are well-educated, upper-income young urbanites. *People's Daily* journalists are keen to publish pieces in *Global Times* because the paper pays more generously than other publications. Additionally, *Global Times* editors receive bonuses based on a percentage of the profits the paper earns for the *People's Daily*.

Other newspapers, such as *World News Journal*, have tried to break into this lucrative market for lively international news. However, to date none have proven a match for *Global Times*.[8] One promising contender founded in 2002 by the Nanfang newspaper group in Guangdong, *Twenty-first Century World Herald*, was shut down a year later for publishing an interview with Mao Zedong's elderly secretary and for other sensitive domestic news reports.[9]

Chinese academics disparage *Global Times* for sensationalizing international news and pandering to ultranationalist views. The State Council Information Office (SCIO) and some journalists worry that its sensational stories give foreign readers a bad impression of Chinese foreign policy. Sensitive to the criticism from abroad and from Chinese academics that *Global Times* promulgates xenophobic nationalism, its editors adamantly insist they promote "patriotism" (*aiguozhuyi*), not "nationalism" (*minzuzhuyi*).

To reach audiences that are put off by parochial nationalism and desire a more moderate approach, the newspaper frequently publishes debates between foreign policy experts. *Global Times* has also pioneered the practice of publishing interviews and dialogues with foreigners, including diplomats from the U.S. embassy in Beijing and academic experts.[10] In 2004 the newspaper published a dialogue between this author and America expert Wang Jisi on public opinion and foreign policy in China and the United States.

Unlike their counterparts in Guangdong newspapers, *Global Times* editors have never been fired. The difference, according to *Global Times* journalists and editors, is that they have close relations with the CCP Propaganda Department and know what it wants. In addition, if they have a query, they can call to get direct guidance from the *People's Daily* chief editor, who is a Central Committee member.

Regardless, the editors of *Global Times* rarely need instructions because, they say, "our thinking and the government's thinking are unified. We want China to develop well, to have stability, and to be integrated in the world, and that's what the government wants. We always think about whether or not something is good for China." For example, during the 2005 student demonstrations against Japan, *Global Times* decided on its own not to report the protests even before a ban was imposed because, as one editor said, "When foreigners see the pictures of violent demonstrations in China, it gives a bad impression and is not good for China. Also, if we did report the demonstrations, people would do it again . . . there would be five million people in Tiananmen Square." As this editor stated in our interview, "If we did report it, it would be good for us, but not good for the country. We didn't need the government to tell us that. We have our political responsibility."

Readers, recognizing the tight relationship of *Global Times* with the powers that be, say that reading the newspaper is a good way to get the "undertones" of Chinese foreign policy. Because reporting is also lively and informative—a marked departure from the sterile *People's Daily* style—it has proven to be a very influential medium for the CCP to guide the public. At the same time, the newspaper is read by Chinese decision makers as an expression of what the public is thinking. Whenever a foreign policy official tells me that he or she feels under pressure from nationalist public opinion, I ask, "How do you know what public opinion actually is?" "That's easy," the official says. "I read *Global Times* and the Internet."

TELEVISION

The vast majority of the Chinese public, including the 60 percent who live in the countryside, acquire their news from television. The official network, China Central Television (CCTV), is still considered the most authoritative network and the best place for advertisers to win consumer recognition and trust for their products.[11] CCTV carries commercial advertising on all its channels and competes as best it can with local cable networks. Most television stations are still required to broadcast the CCTV nightly news at 7 P.M.

However, CCTV lags behind the local cable networks and Hong Kong–based Phoenix Television when it comes to timely reporting of international crises. During the terrorist attacks on New York City and

Washington, DC, on 11 September 2001, the nationally popular Hunan and Chongqing cable networks ran live Cable News Network (CNN) reports, and satellite networks broadcast the Phoenix coverage.[12] CCTV went silent for three hours until it ran a brief report on the late night news. Viewers later griped on the Internet about the delay in CCTV coverage. Presumably CCTV had to get clearance from the political authorities before broadcasting the footage. One Chinese media expert explained that CCTV had driven the audience away by being overcautious in its reporting.[13]

The commercial importance of timely reporting on international news is underlined by the success of Phoenix Television. The station was founded in 1996 as a joint venture between Rupert Murdoch's Star TV and several Chinese investors, including the Bank of China. Without up-to-date statistics, it is impossible to know exactly how many viewers on the mainland watch Phoenix TV by satellite. The network's own Web site still cites 147 million viewers from a 1999 survey.[14] By now, its market share could have reached close to 50 percent in China's largest cities; many apartment complexes provide it to residents and its slick international-style news shows play nonstop in the Beijing University student cafeteria.

Phoenix Television got its big break in the aftermath of the 1999 U.S. bombing of the Chinese embassy in Belgrade. The network's timely and patriotic reporting over seven days drew large audiences and turned its anchor people into celebrities.[15] During the 9/11 terrorist attacks on the United States, Phoenix Television reported round the clock and played and replayed the footage of the planes crashing into the Trade Center towers. Network newscasters compared the events to scenes in popular American disaster movies like *Pearl Harbor* and *Air Force One*.[16]

Phoenix Television can be considered the television equivalent of *Global Times*—splashy, nationalistic, and highly believable because it sounds nothing like old-style propaganda. Moreover, Phoenix Television is protected by its ties with the CCP. The network, which is based in Hong Kong and attracts audiences there and in Taiwan as well as on the mainland, is more daring in covering Taiwan-related issues than *Global Times*: it even carried the inauguration address of Taiwanese President Chen Shui-bian.[17] In May 2008, the new president of Taiwan, Ma Ying-jeou, used an interview on Phoenix to extend an olive branch to the PRC.

Facing competition from Phoenix, CCTV tried to win back audiences and advertisers through its reporting on the 2003 invasion of Iraq by the

United States and Britain. Its coverage was so extensive that one Chinese academic told me he joked to his friends, "I didn't realize that it was a Chinese war."[18] CCTV established its own twenty-four-hour news channel in May 2003. Yet sophisticated urban audiences still disdain CCTV because its news coverage remains comparatively sluggish and hamstrung by tight censorship. If they watch international news on CCTV at all, they prefer the English-language channel or the channel designed for overseas Chinese audiences because they are more lively and reliable than the news reports on CCTV's domestic channels.

When CCTV reflexively cut away from President Barak Obama's inaugural speech after he uttered the word "communism," it exposed CCTV censorship, and the CCP's sense of its own political vulnerability, to millions of viewers. President Obama had not made specific mention of China. Nevertheless, the CCTV broadcast and the translation of the speech on the major Chinese Web sites deleted the reference to communism as well as a sentence on corruption and dissent[19] Chinese bloggers ridiculed the deletions and posted the full unexpurgated version. Perhaps to avoid a replay of such criticism, the Chinese leadership decided not to allow President Obama's November 2009 town hall meeting with students in Shanghai to be televised live outside of Shanghai.

Public contempt for CCTV peaked in February 2009 when its news programs buried the big story that the CCTV's own Lunar New Year fireworks had set fire to and destroyed a skyscraper that is part of the new CCTV complex. Photos and videos of the towering inferno taken by citizens standing on the sidewalk spread immediately over the Internet, but the CCTV news report featured the wildfires in Australia that had started several days earlier, not the fire in its own building.

INTERNET AND WEB-BASED MEDIA

The Internet has accelerated and multiplied the Chinese public's access to information about events outside the country. Since China was first connected to the Internet in 1995, the number of users has exploded. Only 10 percent of Chinese adults had even heard of the Internet in 1997. Two years later, 2 percent had accessed the Internet.[20] By the end of 2009, the number had increased to almost 384 million, one-third of the population. Two-thirds of Netizens are under thirty, the age group that is considered most likely to engage in antiforeign nationalist protest.[21]

Hungry for news and not satisfied with the information they get from newspapers and television alone, the Chinese public goes online to obtain news. A higher proportion of Chinese Netizens (80.1 percent) access news online than U.S. Internet users do (71 percent).[22] Reading news is second only to listening to music as the reason Netizens give for going online.[23] The latest trend, especially among young people, is to have news alerts automatically sent to their cell phones. Only a small minority (10 percent in 2005) of Chinese Internet users access international media sources directly; most international news is channeled through Chinese Web sites.[24]

CCP propaganda officials have exerted a massive effort to maintain control over the content of Internet news and communications. They have devised ingenious technologies to block certain Web sites considered subversive and to prevent access to information on subversive topics by filtering searches according to keywords. International technology companies like Google, Yahoo, and Cisco have to comply with these restrictions if they want to continue doing business in China. China's determined effort to use technological methods to restrict access to information has attracted sharp international criticism, especially after Google carried through on its January 2010 threat to stop operating its search business in China unless the electronic fetters were removed. The SCIO tells large news Web sites what they cannot say and what they should say, and every chat room, BBS, and Weblog platform has a manager who is held responsible for deleting postings on topics that have been or might be banned. The CCP also uses paid employees and volunteers to help police the Internet and to post comments that make it appear as if the tide of opinion favors the CCP's line. No one knows how large the censorship corps actually is, but the CCP appears to be willing to spend whatever it takes not to lose the information battle.

Nevertheless, as Xiao Qiang observes in chapter 9, Internet communication is just too fast, too decentralized, and too internationalized for the censors to block breaking news before it reaches the online public. Keeping the Chinese people ignorant of a speech by Taiwan's president, Japan's prime minister, or the U.S. secretary of defense is no longer possible. Information usually appears online first. In the short time between the posting of a news story and its deletion by monitors following the instructions of the propaganda authorities, news stories can spread far and wide. News Web sites post stories from the international press much more rapidly than do print and television sources, which first have to clear reports with their editors. On 1 April 2001, a Chinese Netizen posted a story from the Associated Press reporting that an American EP-3 reconnaissance plane and a Chinese fighter jet had collided off China's southern coast, setting off an uproar in the chat rooms. The official Xinhua News Agency did not announce the accident for another two hours. Further underlining the delays imposed on reporting by traditional media, the story didn't hit the *People's Daily* front page until three days after it occurred.

Because of its speed and comprehensiveness, the Internet sets the international news agenda and forces officials, as well as the print and television media, to react. In the old days citizens were ignorant of international news or learned about it days later in a form already shaped by the policymakers. But today, much foreign policy is made on the fly by Foreign Ministry officials reacting to fast-breaking news that citizens have learned about over the Internet. For example, when in February 2009 Japanese Prime Minister Taro Aso asserted for the first time that the Diaoyu Islands, claimed by both China and Japan, were Japanese territory protected under the U.S.-Japan Security Treaty, the online furor compelled the Chinese Foreign Ministry spokesman to issue a stern warning: "Any words and deeds that bring the Diaoyu Islands into the scope of the Japan-US Mutual Cooperation and Security Treaty are absolutely unacceptable to the Chinese people."[25]

Another distinguishing feature of the Web is its interactivity; it is sometimes called a "read-write" medium. Web users express their reactions to news events in chat rooms, BBSs, and Weblogs and link up with other citizens with similar views. Online discussions become virtual collective action, and, most worrisome from the standpoint of Chinese leaders, Web-based protests can mobilize people to join actual protests in the streets. Urban young people—who constitute the largest proportion of Web users—represent the greatest risk.

So long as the protest remains online, China's leaders consider it comparatively harmless. As one Chinese student said in an interview, "The Internet is an outlet for people to express themselves. If you didn't have it, you would have extreme action instead. It is a way to relieve tension, but also can arouse feelings of a large group of people and put pressure on the government to do something. Then people feel they have really done something so it reduces the necessity to protest." The government tolerates online collective action as a safety valve and may view it as a useful mechanism for enhancing its leverage in international negotiations.[26] Petitions regarding domestic political reform, such as Charter '08, a democratic manifesto signed by hundreds of Chinese intellectuals, are quickly suppressed, but petitions against Japan or the French chain store Carrefour remain on major news sites for long periods of time, in a clear sign to the public that the government approves of them.

In an example from 2003, a Web site operated by Lu Yunfei, a Beijing computer engineer, collected more than 80,000 signatures on a petition opposing the selection of Japanese technology for the bullet train linking Shanghai and Beijing. The site's address, www.1931–9-18.org, commemorates the date the Japanese army began occupying northeast China. In a separate example—on the 18 September 2003 anniversary of that date—an orgy at a Guangdong resort hotel involving approximately four hundred Japanese tourists and five hundred Chinese prostitutes sparked an outraged reaction on the bulletin boards of major Internet news Web sites such as Sina.com and Sohu.com. During the same period, seven Web sites obtained over 1 million signatures for a petition demanding that Japan apologize for and compensate victims poisoned by World War II–era chemical weapons unearthed in northern China. One man died and more than forty were injured when metal canisters containing mustard gas were unearthed at a construction site in Qiqihar.

The potential of the Internet to mobilize antiforeign nationalist protests was realized in April 2005 when hundreds of thousands of students demonstrated against Japan in approximately forty cities for three weeks. Demonstrators pelted the Japanese embassy and ambassador's residence with bottles, tiles, stones, and eggs. In Beijing, Shanghai, and other cities, students trashed shops displaying Japanese-made electronic products, Toyota automobiles, and Japanese banks and restaurants.

In the months preceding the protests, as chapter 8 describes, young Chinese people interpreted media and Web content as a signal that the CCP would tolerate patriotic, anti-Japanese collective action. Censorship of Web content is more obvious than censorship of the print media or television. It gives the public subtle cues about policy preferences of CCP leaders, and reveals how nervous and insecure they are. Any story or petition that remains online gives readers a signal that it has been tacitly approved by the political authorities.

That is why young Web users construed as a green light to protest an online petition—initiated by Chinese living abroad but prominently displayed on mainland Web sites and signed by more than 40 million people— that urged the Chinese government not to support Japan's application to become a permanent member of the United Nations Security Council until it properly acknowledged its historical crimes. People in offices and facto- ries rounded up signatures with no hint of disapproval from CCP authori- ties.[27] In a 24 March briefing, the Foreign Ministry spokesman replied to a journalist's question about the petition by saying, "I don't regard it as 'anti- Japan' sentiments; on the contrary I think this is a request for Japan to adopt a right and responsible attitude on some history issues." At the same time, the print media reported extensively on the distortions in recent revisions of history textbooks in Japan and on protests in South Korea against these textbooks.[28] The *People's Daily* pointed out the irony of Japan's desire to join the Security Council to represent the people of Asia while millions of Asians were signaling their lack of trust in Japan by signing the petition.[29]

CENSORSHIP AND SPIN

Foreign policymakers are not always in a reactive mode. The government and the CCP retain substantial ability to dictate the political content of the media even in the context of market competition. The CCP Propaganda Department and its provincial branches are responsible for guiding the content of print media and television. The SCIO oversees the content of news Web sites; as print media have expanded their online presence, the clout of the censors has grown along with them. Journalists have told me in interviews that the censorship of Web-based news content used to be more lax than that of print, but now control of Web site content is more stringent than that of print media.[30]

In the aftermath of two dangerous crises with the United States—the 1999 Belgrade embassy bombing and the 2001 plane collision—the censors banned all press criticism of the president of the United States and directed the media to tone down their negative rhetoric toward the United States. This top-down directive effectively changed the tenor of the public discourse on U.S. relations: the number of mentions in *People's Daily* of "hegemonism" and "multipolarity," polemical terms directed against the United States, was high during the 1990s, and rose during 1999, the year in which relations were strained by the American bombing of the Chinese embassy in Belgrade, but diminished in following years and remains very low today.[31]

Every journalist and think-tank expert can cite at least one situation in which the Propaganda Department has quashed a planned news story or television show concerning international events. Right before the Japanese prime minister's scheduled visit to the fall 2001 Asia-Pacific Economic Cooperation summit in Shanghai, a television panel of experts discussing a meeting between President Bush and Premier Koizumi was canceled in order to play down criticism of Japan. According to a CCTV producer, the Propaganda Department controlled the framing of stories after the 2000 collision between the Chinese fighter jet and the U.S. EP-3 spy plane off the coast of the southern island of Hainan. "People don't like it," he said. "They want to make money, make attractive and interesting shows. People worry about ratings because the companies that buy commercials watch to see which stations and shows have more viewers." One academic expert who appeared on a CCTV talk show a few days after the collision to discuss the event found that all the participants were handed a list of issues the panel was supposed to address so they could decide who would talk about what. When asked who had prepared the points, he was told "the Party center."

CCP control of media content tightens up during certain politically significant times of the year, such as the anniversary of the 4 June 1989 Tiananmen Square demonstrations and the annual meeting of China's legislature, the National People's Congress (NPC). CCP leaders also forbid the media from raising issues that could arouse public emotions against the United States before or after summit meetings with the U.S. president or other high-level meetings. For example, the media were silent and there was no public reaction in 2001 when the Pentagon issued the Nuclear Posture Review, which discussed building new weapons. As one think-tank expert noted in an interview, this was because "Jiang Zemin laid down the line that nothing should disrupt positive momentum in relations with the U.S. since his visit to see Bush." The media resumed their critical stance toward U.S. actions during 2009 when popular nationalism appeared to surge in reaction to America's failures and China's successes related to the global financial crisis.

In March 2005, when the North Korean government for the first time declared that it had produced nuclear bombs, Beijing signaled its disapproval by lifting the blanket ban on reporting on North Korea and allowing the media—but not *People's Daily*—to publish stories about the dangers of a nuclear North Korea. Media criticism of North Korea was permitted to burst forth again after Pyongyang actually tested a nuclear bomb in October 2006, a clear indication that Beijing was building popular support for a tough response to the test.

As for Taiwan, the CCP has modulated its reactions to Taiwanese prov-ocations over the past decade. Since 1999, China has restrained its rhetoric toward Taiwan, especially during Taiwanese election campaigns. And today, as Beijing attempts to ingratiate itself with the Taiwanese population to improve cross-Strait ties, almost all criticism of Taiwan and its leaders has disappeared from the mainland media. In early 2010, however, Beijing allowed the press to lambast the Obama administration for continuing arms sales to Taiwan.

In addition to outright censorship, the Chinese government has learned to shape news content by using increasingly sophisticated press manage-ment methods. In 1990, the SCIO was created to improve China's overseas image (its responsibility for Web-based news content was added later). As China's international public relations department, the SCIO manages rela-tions with the foreign press corps, oversees China's international radio service, and tries to spin events in China in a positive light for international audiences. The head of the SCIO during 1998 to 2005, Zhao Qizheng, was a Shanghai cosmopolitan whose understanding of public relations was highly valued by China's leaders. During the Jiang Zemin era, Zhao and his colleagues helped prep President Jiang for foreign trips and coached the president before foreign press appearances.

In the late 1990s, the SCIO recognized that the impassioned anti-Japa-nese and anti-American rhetoric in China's domestic media was aggravating the country's foreign relations. In a 2000 speech at Tsinghua University, U.S. Secretary of Defense William Cohen complained about the way the Chi-nese media were slanted against the United States. The Japanese also had complained about the virulent anti-Japanese tone of the Chinese Web and commercial media. Zhao Qizheng and his associates began summoning the foreign news editors of the major domestic media to brief them on interna-tional issues and to urge them to use less loaded language in their reports on Japan and the United States. (It should be noted that the Propaganda Department was unhappy about the SCIO usurping its role of supervising the content of the domestic media.)

The SCIO was in the forefront of encouraging government officials to shape the way news stories are reported by providing firsthand information to journalists and the public. The agency assisted government ministries and the People's Liberation Army in creating the new post of press spokesman and training them to conduct regular press briefings. Every ministry also established its own Web site, following the philosophy that by providing more information, the government increases its credibility with the public and reduces its vulnerability to criticism. As one Chinese commentator said, "Public opinion is like a giant container. If you put more information into it publicly, there will be less room left for others to question or launch attacks on you."[32] The Ministry of Foreign Affairs makes active use of its Web site and discussion forum. China's ambassadors to India and to Afghanistan and even the foreign minister himself have participated in online question-and-answer sessions.

BLOWBACK: HOW OFFICIALS GET INFORMATION ABOUT PUBLIC OPINION ON INTERNATIONAL ISSUES

Although there is no hard evidence on how reporting by the news media affects public opinion, the effect of reporting on the policy formation process is evident. China's foreign policymakers pay close attention to the media and believe that the contents of *Global Times* and other tabloids genuinely reflect what the Chinese public thinks. For the same reason, they also pay close attention to what is said on news Web sites, discussion forums, online bulletin boards, and Weblogs.

The commercialization of the media and growth of the Internet have produced a new information loop: the media create nationwide common knowledge about international and local news items; stimulate responses to these news items—usually simply emotional but in some cases mobilizing collective action like petitions or demonstrations; and communicate Chinese public opinion back to the foreign policymakers.

When all Chinese media were official propaganda organs, the leaders found them useless for ascertaining elite or popular reaction to their policies. Their best option for obtaining information on public opinion was to read the uncontrolled newspapers published in Hong Kong. I witnessed firsthand this reliance on the Hong Kong media when as a U.S. State Department official I traveled with Premier Zhu Rongji during his visit to the United States in 1999. President Clinton had disappointed Zhu by deciding at the last minute not to sign the almost fully negotiated agreement on China's accession to the World Trade Organization until after the visit was concluded. Zhu and his entourage were worried about the domestic reaction in China to this humiliation. They spent much of their time on the plane reading and worrying over the Hong Kong press reports. Nowadays top officials take the temperature of public reaction more from the mainland commercial media and the Web than from Hong Kong newspapers.

Before the advent of the commercial media and the Web, Chinese politicians and officials also relied on an elaborate bureaucratic system of internal reporting (*neican*) to obtain information about Chinese public opinion. Local bureaus of Xinhua News Agency and *People's Daily*, along with provincial and municipal party newspapers and television stations, reported to CCP leaders. Individual journalists in these organizations were assigned a quota of internal reports their bureau was required to produce and received substantial financial rewards if their reports were considered significant enough to reach top CCP leaders.[33] Education officials also were required to report on student opinions. Furthermore, Foreign Ministry officials traveled outside the capital to give speeches and sample mass opinion just as American diplomats do.

Today, although internal reporting still continues, officials get more of their information about public opinion directly from the popular media and the Web and rely less on information mediated through the bureaucracies who previously had acted as their ears. In February 2009, before Wen Jiabao held an online question-and-answer session with Netizens, China.gov and Xinhua.net commented on the influence of the Internet on China's political life: "The Internet has become an important tool for all levels of government officials in China to stay in touch with public opinions. The old ways of listening to briefings, reading documents, and visiting local areas have been increasingly challenged. In the meantime, more and more people in the country are using the Internet to express their opinions and participate in public and political issues. . . . The top leadership in China has started to pay unprecedented attention to public opinions on the Internet since last year."[34]

Summaries of Web-based news and discussions are prepared by the SCIO and the Information Department of the Foreign Ministry, as well as by the secretaries of high-ranking officials. Directly obtained information is particularly vivid and believable, and therefore is likely to have a sharper impact on decision makers than bureaucratically collected information. Officials claim that they go online themselves to sample public opinion. As early as the 2003 SARS crisis, President Hu Jintao and Premier Wen Jiabao said publicly that they had gone online to find out what people were saying. The official English-language newspaper *China Daily* observed, "Cyberspace has, to some extent, gradually evolved into a valuable place to gauge public opinion. Obviously, the public has one more channel to interact with the government. . . . [W]e have seen cases of public opinion expressed in cyberspace being taken into consideration by the government."[35]

In June 2008, President Hu Jintao visited the headquarters of *People's Daily* and chatted with ordinary citizens on People's Daily.com. "Although I am too busy to browse the Internet every day, I try to spend some time on the Web. . . . The Strong China Forum of People's Daily Online is one of the Websites I often visit," Hu said. The Strong China Forum, as People's Daily.com explained, was established in 1999 for citizens to express their anger about the U.S. bombing of the Chinese embassy in Belgrade, Yugoslavia. Hu went on to say that he reads domestic and international news on the Web, and also uses it to learn about Netizens' opinion and get their advice.[36]

Based on the feedback they get from the commercial media and the Web, Chinese foreign policymakers form the impression that nationalist views are intensifying and spreading. Foreign Ministry officials repeatedly relate the story of how ordinary citizens mail them calcium pills to urge them to show more backbone in standing up to the United States. Although this story may be apocryphal and a bureaucratic myth to counteract the standard American negotiating ploy of talking about pressures from Congress, it also reflects the new reality of making foreign policy with one eye on Chinese public opinion.

Officials should be aware that the information they obtain from the Web is skewed toward extreme nationalistic views. Posting one's opinions online carries some danger of being flagged by the CCP as a potential troublemaker, so people concerned about their own careers are cautious about doing so. In China, as in the West, the people who express their ideas on the Web are usually those with more extreme points of view. Why do officials then pay so much attention to online opinion when they know it is unrepresentative of the population as a whole? One explanation may lie in the nature of politics in authoritarian countries. Politicians in democracies rely on elections and on polls of scientifically selected representative samples because they need to know what the average voter thinks in order to win elections. But the political survival of politicians in authoritarian countries depends not on elections, but on being attentive to the people who feel so strongly about something that they might come out on the streets to protest. The individuals taking the risk of fulminating online are the ones most likely to take the greater risk of participating in or organizing mass protests.[37]

REACTING TO ANTI-JAPANESE PUBLIC OPINION

During the 1990s, President Jiang Zemin initiated the Patriotic Education Campaign to cultivate Chinese nationalism with a strong anti-Japanese flavor. Nationalism appeared to be a good way to foster popular identification with the CCP at a time when belief in socialist ideology was waning. Nationalist themes struck a chord in a country seeking to revive itself as a major power after over a century of humiliating weakness vis-à-vis foreign powers. Therefore the interests of the commercial media in taking a nationalist slant in their international news reporting were largely supported and reinforced by the CCP Propaganda Department. However, by the end of the 1990s, public opinion toward Japan had become so negative that it was constraining policymakers and becoming a possible domestic threat to CCP legitimacy. If the Chinese public perceived the government as weak for not standing up to Japan, they might turn against it and bring it down in a manner similar to the nationalist movements that toppled the Qing Dynasty and the Republican government.

As noted above, Sino-Japanese relations are the foreign policy area where public opinion has the greatest impact. According to Foreign Ministry officials, no matter how minor, every incident concerning Japan that might be construed as insulting to Chinese national honor requires, at a minimum, condemnation by Foreign Ministry spokesmen at the regular ministry press briefings.

Web sites posting stories related to Japan attract significantly more hits than Web sites posting other news, and anti-Japanese online petitions are focal points for organizing collective action. The English-language newspaper *China Daily* blamed jingoistic coverage in the media for drumming up nationalist emotions; it reported that open hostility among Chinese, especially the young, toward Japan "is apparent in barbed newspaper and television coverage and conversations with citizens."[38]

Diplomats who handle Sino-Japanese relations in the Asia Department of the Foreign Ministry read the bitter online attacks on Japan and its World War II–era involvement in China.[39] Then they rush out their statements and actions toward Japan to stay ahead of domestic online criticism. Take the example of a 2003 accident in the northeastern city of Qiqihar in which uncovering World War II–era Japanese chemical weapons injured more than forty construction workers and killed one. Foreign Ministry officials knew that they had to deliver a strong protest to the Japanese ambassador and quickly post it on the ministry's Web site to preempt a firestorm of Internet criticism. They also recognized that they had to seek an apology and compensation from the Japanese to appease public opinion. In a similar situation, China's refusal to invite former Japanese Prime Minister Koizumi for a state visit after he visited the Yasukuni Shrine was based on the sense among Chinese leaders that they would be lynched on the Web if they did allow the visits. For five years after Koizumi's trip to the controversial shrine (which houses memorials to Japanese World War II dead, including convicted war criminals), no high-level visits from Japanese leaders were permitted.

According to one think-tank expert, shortly before Jiang Zemin visited Japan in 1998, Foreign Minister Tang Jiaxuan made a statement about Japanese aggression being past history and China needing to look forward in its relationship with Japan. Upon hearing Tang's statement, members of the public vehemently criticized the Foreign Minister on the Web. The very next day while attending a seminar at a private bookstore, the expert reported hearing people strongly attacking Tang based on what they had learned on the Web. According to the expert, this experience provided the impetus for the Foreign Ministry to establish its own Web site to communicate directly with the Chinese public. The effect of this controversy on Jiang Zemin's actual visit is hard to determine. Nonetheless, when in Japan, Jiang did make numerous and highly publicized demands for a written apology for wartime atrocities that played well with the Chinese public while antagonizing the Japanese.

According to interviews with Chinese foreign policy experts, when President Hu Jintao and Premier Wen Jiabao assumed office in 2002, they had plans to try to restore friendly relations with Japan. But two articles published in the influential journal *Strategy and Management* (*Zhanlue Yu Guanli*) that criticized anti-Japanese xenophobia and advocated a more mature and confident approach to Sino-Japanese relations sparked such a vicious reaction on the Web that Hu and Wen backed down.[40]

The March 2005 petition demanding that the Chinese government block Japan's bid to join the United Nations Security Council, publicized by links on the main pages of China's major news Web sites, was followed a week later by Beijing's official announcement that it would not support UN Secretary General Kofi Annan's timetable for the General Assembly to decide on the expansion of Security Council membership, effectively postponing a decision indefinitely. After students began demonstrating against Japan in April 2005, Wen Jiabao firmly declared his opposition to Japanese membership in the Security Council.

Following the anti-Japanese protests in 2005, the Chinese and Japanese governments turned their efforts to stabilizing relations. Politicians in both countries had come to realize that playing to their nationalist publics was not as risk-free as it once might have appeared. Nationalist protests were domestically destabilizing in China. In addition, Japanese and Chinese vessels were rubbing shoulders in the contested energy-rich waters of the East China Sea; an accident could set off a crisis that would be hard to manage because of inflamed opinion in both countries. When Prime Minister Koizumi left office, the Chinese negotiated an informal agreement with his successor, Shinzo Abe, that he would not visit the Yasukuni Shrine in order to open the way for a diplomatic rapprochement. Successors to Abe have so far upheld Abe's commitment.

The CCP Propaganda Department was directed to orchestrate less hostile rhetoric about Japan in the media during Prime Minister Abe's "ice-breaking" October 2006 visit to Beijing.[41] In advance of the visit, word went out to all media outlets to do nothing that would "spoil the harmony." Yet sustaining this level of control over the content of commercial media with strong market incentives to run stories that appeal to popular emotion against Japan is not easy.

Chinese leaders continue to tread carefully in diplomacy with Japan because they remain highly sensitive to anti-Japanese public opinion in the media and on the Web. Before President Hu Jintao visited Japan in May 2008, the two sides had reached a compromise on joint development of the gas fields in the East China Sea. But according to Japanese and Chinese Foreign Ministry officials, China insisted on deferring the announcement of the agreement until after the visit—when the Chinese public would be paying less attention and would be less likely to criticize the government for conceding too much to make the visit successful. The joint statement issued at the time of the visit said nothing more than that the two sides wanted to turn the East China Sea into a sea of "peace, cooperation, and friendship."[42] The agreement itself was rolled out in a very low-key announcement on the Foreign Ministry Web site a month later. Negotiations on implementing the agreement have moved slowly since spring 2008 because both governments feel constrained by public opinion.

Chinese officials, in interviews, say that they have been reluctant to negotiate on the basis of the general agreement because it has been characterized inaccurately by the Japanese media as involving big concessions on the part of Beijing—a characterization that has been passed on by the Chinese media to the Chinese public.

This gingerly approach to Japan was evident during the May 2008 earthquake in Sichuan Province. Press reports and photographs of the sixty-member team of Japanese rescue workers who were the first foreign contingent to reach the devastation played well. But negative online reaction to the very idea of having a Japanese military jet land on Chinese soil led the two governments to cancel plans for Japan to fly in earthquake aid.[43]

Online criticism in response to Prime Minister Taro Aso's statement in February 2009 that the disputed Senkaku Islands in the East China Sea were Japanese territory protected by Japan's military alliance with the United States may have been the reason that China requested that Aso postpone a visit to China originally planned for March 2009.[44] The invitation was postponed just two weeks after Premier Wen Jiabao had publicly extended it during the Japanese foreign minister's visit to Beijing. When Aso finally visited at the end of April 2009, the media were tightly controlled to put a positive spin on the visit.

TIBET BECOMES THE NEW HOT BUTTON

Until recently, the issue of Tibet did not loom large in China's media or popular consciousness. When they reported on Tibet at all, Chinese media described a positive story of lifting a region out of backwardness and improving the lives of its people. Tibet got a bit more attention during 2007 when television news stories glorified the opening of a beautiful new train, complete with oxygen supply for high altitudes, linking Tibet with the rest of China. Yet editors still did not consider Tibet an exciting story for attracting readers.

All that changed in March 2008 when a demonstration by Tibetan monks and laypeople in Lhasa turned into a violent riot against Han Chinese shopkeepers. This event quickly drew the attention of the Chinese public and sparked a firestorm of nationalist emotions. The official Chinese media initially suppressed news of the event. Xinhua issued a terse report and the authorities imposed a news blackout on other media coverage. But eyewitness accounts by foreign tourists and Lhasa residents, including photographs and videos of monks beating Chinese merchants, spread instantaneously via the Internet. On Web sites like Strong Nation Forum the reactions were furious. People expressed outrage that the ungrateful Tibetans had turned against their Han Chinese benefactors. They blamed the Dalai Lama and other murky foreign backers for instigating the violence. Moreover, they urged their government not to be so cowardly and to punish the Tibetan demonstrators, even by execution.[45]

The government authorities responded by allowing video of the riots to be broadcast on CCTV and by publicly attacking the Dalai Lama. Premier Wen Jiabao, in his annual news conference following the meeting of the NPC, said there was "ample fact and plenty of evidence proving this incident was organized, premeditated, masterminded, and incited by the Dalai clique" to sabotage the Olympics.[46] The local media in the Tibet Autonomous Region vilified the Dalai Lama with harsh rhetoric (e.g., "a wolf in monk's clothing") of the sort not heard since the Cultural Revolution. Eager to capitalize on the clash, national media spewed out stories. *Global Times* published one hundred stories mentioning the Dalai Lama during 2008, compared to only forty-two articles mentioning him during the entire decade between 1998 and 2007.

The media publicity stoked the public's anger. When a freshman from China tried to intercede to prevent a clash between pro– and anti–Dalai Lama students on the Duke University campus, she became the target of an online mob of Chinese vigilantes who posted her photograph with the words "traitor to China" emblazoned on her forehead, revealed the home address of her parents, and forced her to flee her dorm room to protect herself.[47]

The public opinion furor ratcheted up when Chinese Netizens criticized the Western media for biased coverage of the Lhasa events and established an anti-CNN Web site. CNN became the target because it supposedly cropped a photograph to remove Tibetans throwing stones at a Chinese tank, and subsequently an intemperate CNN commentator, Jack Rafferty, described the Chinese as "a bunch of goons and thugs."[48] Videos of the disruption of the Olympic torch parade in Paris by demonstrators who supported the Tibetan cause further fanned the nationalist flames. Online rumors that the French chain store Carrefour had funded the Dalai Lama and anger over the Paris demonstrations motivated some angry youth to use phone text messages to mobilize protests outside Carrefour stores in five Chinese cities and to call for a Carrefour boycott. Large protests by overseas Chinese in Paris, Los Angeles, and other cities kept up the nationalist drumbeat.

The Chinese government took up these attacks on the Western media in its public statements. The Foreign Ministry spokesman critiqued the "irresponsible and unethical reports that infuriated our people to voice voluntarily their condemnation and criticism. . . . The Lhasa incident is . . . a mirror to see the true face of some people out there. It is also a textbook of bad examples, and it helps our people discern clearly the essence of the much-vaunted 'justice' and 'objectiveness' by some western media."[49] When I asked a senior Foreign Ministry official whether it made sense for the Chinese government to slam Western journalists just a few months before they were due to arrive to cover the Olympics, he replied, "We had to. The people on the Internet weren't just criticizing the bias of the Western media; they were criticizing us [the Chinese government] for allowing it." The Chinese government felt forced to take a tough stand to defend itself from online criticism that they feared might turn into something even more politically threatening.

The public uproar has driven the Chinese government to elevate the Tibet issue in its diplomacy with the United States, Europe, and other countries. It now puts the Tibet issue on the same plane as the Taiwan issue, that is, as a "core issue of Chinese sovereignty." Chinese diplomats have been instructed to complain about Tibet in every meeting and lean on foreign officials not to meet with the Dalai Lama or otherwise support the cause of Tibetan independence. By taking a harder line on Tibet, Chinese leaders maintain their popularity at home but put new obstacles in the way of achieving other objectives in their relations with the United States, Europe, and other countries.

THE MEDIA AND FOREIGN POLICY

Although the CCP exerts great efforts to control the content of newspapers, television, and Web sites—and by and large succeeds in doing so—the commercialization of the media has nevertheless changed the context for foreign policymaking. As they compete for audiences, editors and journalists seek to provide the most exciting news they can from home and abroad, pushing right up to, and occasionally beyond, the limits set by the censors. Information about international events travels rapidly and widely over the Web before monitors can remove it. The print media try to compete with the news Web sites by producing timely information from abroad as well. And the new CNN-style twenty-four-hour news broadcast by Phoenix Television has driven CCTV to provide its own round-the-clock news cycle.

The availability of information about international events has helped create a public acutely aware of world events and of how the Chinese government responds to them. The CCP can no longer keep people ignorant of statements from Japanese or Taiwanese politicians, no matter how inflammatory to mainland sensibilities they are. Officials in the Foreign Ministry and CCP leaders react publicly to international news because the Chinese public is now aware and interested. Leaders feel under pressure from the public to take strong stances, especially in dealing with Japan, Taiwan, and the United States—the three international relationships that are the objects of fascination to the Chinese public.

At times, the blowback from the media onto the policy process can trap policymakers in a corner from which is difficult to escape—which is essentially what happened during the five years after Japanese Prime Minister Koizumi visited the Yasukuni Shrine. Media blowback can also send policy dangerously offtrack during a crisis when the leaders' perception of an outraged public may drive the leaders to make public threats they feel they cannot back down from without losing their own popular support. Yet despite the information explosion produced by the commercialization of the media and growth of the Internet, the CCP retains its ability to manage the contents of the media. More important, it has used this ability to give itself greater latitude to pursue pragmatic foreign policy, even regarding domestic hot-button issues, as can be seen in the recent efforts to improve relations with Taiwan and Japan.

Notes

1. Fan Shiming, "Popular, but Not That Positive: Changing Chinese Media and Its Effect on Public Opinion of International Affairs," *Review of Asian and Pacific Studies*, no. 29 (July 2005): p. 68.

2. Ibid.

3. The media's actual effect on public opinion is impossible to determine given a lack of empirical research. Two earlier studies of media effects were conducted when the media were under monopoly Communist Party control. Zhao Xinshu, Zhu Jian-Hua, Li Hairong, and Glen L. Bleske, "Media Effects under a Monopoly: The Case of Beijing in Economic Reform," *International Journal of Public Opinion Research*, Vol. 6, no. 2 (1994): pp. 95–117; Chen Xueyi and Shi Tianjian, "Media Effects on Political Confidence and Trust in the People's Republic of China in the Post-Tiananmen Period," *East Asia: An International Quarterly*, no. 19 (Fall 2001): pp. 84–118. A 2005 sample survey of citizens in five cities that examined their attitudes toward the United States found that 62 percent said that their impressions of the United States were shaped mainly by the media; but the survey did not study how people's use of various kinds of media affected their views. The survey was a joint effort by the Institute of American Studies, Chinese Academy of Social Sciences, and *Global Times* (*Global Times*, 2 March 2005). The one sample survey that studied Chinese views of Japan and the United States over time, Alastair Iain Johnston's Beijing Area Survey, did not include questions on media use. See Alastair Iain Johnston, "Chinese Middle Class Attitudes Towards International Affairs: Nascent Liberalization?" *China Quarterly*, no. 179 (September 2004): pp. 603–628.

4. This finding, from 1998, contrasted with the finding of a similar 1992 survey that readers watched television mainly for entertainment. Luo Jianhua, *Beijing Youth Daily*, 14 October 1998, quoted in Zhao Bin, "Mouthpiece or Money-Spinner? The Double Life of Chinese Television in the Late 1990s," *International Journal of Cultural Studies*, Vol. 2, no. 3 (1999): pp. 291–305.

5. Its circulation was 25 million in 1982, but fell to 8 million by 1993 because of the emergence of other sources of international news and a relaxation of mandatory subscriptions for important official publications. Daniel C. Lynch, *After the Propaganda State* (Stanford: Stanford University Press, 1999): p. 133. The 3 million figure is from an interview with Xinhua editors in 2009.

6. The paper's treatment of Clinton was not unsympathetic. For example, its front-page headline on 15 November 1998 was "Sexual Affairs and National Affairs Are Two Different Things. The President and Ordinary People Are All Human Beings."

7. It is little wonder the Chinese public believed that NATO's bombing of the Chinese embassy in Belgrade was intentional: Based on what they read in *Global Times*, they must have inferred that China was covertly assisting the Yugoslav government.

8. The other internationally focused newspapers taking aim at *Global Times* are in Beijing: *World Guardian Herald* [*Guoji xianqu daobao*], run by *Reference News* under Xinhua News Agency; *World News* [*Shijie xinwen bao*], run by China Radio International; and *Youth Reference* [*Qingnian cankao*], run by *China Youth Daily*. According to the *Global Times* editors, the only serious competitive threat is the large-circulation *Reference News*, the only newspaper in China that is allowed to directly translate foreign press reports, although others sometimes will do so.

9. Journalistic circles buzzed with speculation that *Global Times* may have used its political clout to eliminate a potential rival.

10. The idea of having debates on controversial issues, and sometimes including foreign experts in them, was first proposed to *Global Times* by Tsinghua University international relations expert Yan Xuetong, who now organizes these forums for the newspaper. Yan Xuetong is also a well-known media commentator because of his sharp sound bites on international power politics.

11. "China's Media: Please Adjust Your Seat," *The Economist*, 18 November 2004.

12. CNN is directly available in China only in international hotels and government offices; some individuals rented hotel rooms for several days to watch the CNN coverage of the 11 September 2001 terrorist attacks.

13. Associated Press, 15 September 2001.

14. http://06miss.phoenixtv.com/phoenixtv/77412215665197056/20070604/908207. shtml (accessed 24 August 2009).

15. "Anchor Celebrities: CCTV and Phoenix TV," *Sanlian Shenghuo Zhoukan* [*Sanlian Life Week*], 12 April 2004.

16. Peter Hessler, "Straight to Video," *The New Yorker*, 15 October 2001.

17. Mark Landler, "Entrepreneur Walking a Fine Line at a News Channel for China," *New York Times*, 8 January 2001.

18. Market competition also inspired many newspapers that previously had never sent correspondents abroad to send them to Iraq. The journalists were furious when the Chinese government ordered them to leave Iraq to protect their safety when the invasion began, forcing them to report it from the sidelines in Jordan.

19. What the president said was, "Recall that earlier generations faced down communism and fascism not just with missiles and tanks, but with sturdy alliances and enduring convictions. . . . [And] to those who cling to power through corruption and deceit and the silencing of dissent, know that you are on the wrong side of history, but that we will extend a hand if you are willing to unclench your fist." Reuters, 20 January 2009.

20. "Netizens Change China's Political Landscape," Xinhua News Agency, 28 February 2009, http://news.xinhuanet.com/english/2009–02/28/content_10917341. htm.

21. China Internet Network Information Center, "25th Statistical Survey Report on Internet Development, 2010," http://www.cnnic.net.cn/uploadfiles/pdf/2010/1/15/101600.pdf.

22. Ibid.

23. The other reasons Netizens give for why they go online: (3) use a search engine; (4) use instant messaging; (5) play games; (6) watch videos; (7) blog. Ibid.

24. Gallup, "Internet Use: Beyond the Great Firewall of China," February 2005, http://www.gallup.com/poll/14776/Internet-Use-Behind-The-Great-Firewall-China. aspx.

25. "China Lodges Stern Representation to Japan over Japanese PM's Remarks on Diaoyu Islands," Xinhua News Agency, 26 February 2009, http://news.xinhuanet.com/english/2009–02/26/content_10904293.htm.

26. On the utility of actual protests as a form of audience costs that enhances China's leverage in international negotiations with democracies, see Jessica C. Weiss, "Powerful Patriots: Nationalism, Diplomacy and the Strategic Logic of Anti-Foreign Protest" (PhD diss., University of California at San Diego, Department of Political Science, 2008).

27. "China Raises Stakes in Dispute with Japan," *International Herald Tribune*, 12 April 2005.

28. For example, "Japan Hurts Self and Others by Cooking History Books," *Xin Jing Bao* [*Beijing News*], 6 April 2005, http://comment.thebeijing news.com/0728/2005/04–06/005@014900.htm; "Distorted History Textbook Unacceptable," Xinhua, 31 March

2005; "Lies in Ink Can Never Cover Up Facts in Blood," Xinhua, 5 April 2005; "Republic of Korea Public Protest Against Distorted Japanese History Textbook," People's Daily Online, 6 April 2005.

29. "Commentary: Can It Be One's Own Wishful Thinking?" People's Daily Online, 14 April 2005, http://english.peopledaily.com.cn/200504/14/eng20050414_181090.html.

30. For example, see comment by Zhang Ping in "Liu Jianqiang, Zhang Ping, Wang Lixiong: On the Impact of New Media," *China Digital Times*, comments posted on 20 April 2009, http://chinadigitaltimes.net/2009/04/liu-jianqiang-zhang-ping-wang-lixiong-on-the-impact-of-new-media/.

31. *People's Daily* electronic version and People's Daily Online (www.people.com.cn).

32. Hu Baijing, deputy director for the Institute of Public Communication, People's University, quoted in *News China*, 5 March 2009, p. 8.

33. As of a few years ago, Xinhua journalists were paid RMB 5,000 if their internal report was selected for the daily briefing of Politburo members and RMB 10,000 for Politburo Standing Committee members. If a Standing Committee member responded to the report, they got RMB 20,000.

34. "China's Wen Makes Internet Debut," Agence France Presse, posted on China Digital Times, 28 February 2009, http://chinadigitaltimes.net/2009/02/chinas-wen-makes-Internet-debut/.

35. "Booming Economy Props Up Increase in Internet Users," *China Daily*, 21 January 2005.

36. "President Hu Jintao Inspects People's Daily: First Live Online Chat with Netizens," People's Daily Online, http://english.peopledaily.com.cn/90001/90782/6435851.html.

37. Susan L. Shirk, *China Fragile Superpower* (New York: Oxford University Press, 2007), pp. 102–103.

38. "Open Hostility Toward Japan Prevalent Among Chinese," *China Daily*, 27 February 2005.

39. Zhang Kunsheng, "Unconventional Visit: Memorandum of Li Zhaoxing's Visit to Japan and South Korea," *Guancha Yu Sikao* [*Observe and Think*], 1 September 2003.

40. See Ma Licheng, "New Thinking on Relations with Japan, Worries by People in China and Japan," *Strategy and Management*, Vol. 55, no. 6 (2002): pp. 41–47; and Shi Yinhong, "China-Japan Rapproachment and the 'Diplomatic Revolution,'" *Strategy and Management*, Vol. 57, no. 2 (2003): pp. 71–75.

41. According to a review of comments posted on www.sina.com.cn and www.people.com.cn.

42. James Manicom, "Hu-Fukuda Summit: The East China Sea Dispute," *China Brief (The Jamestown Foundation)*, Vol. 8, Issue 12, 6 June 2008, http://www.jamestown.org/programs/chinabrief/single/?tx_ttnews%5Btt_news%5D=4968&tx_ttnews%5BbackPid%5D=168&no_cache=1.

43. Jeremy Page, "Warship's Visit Signals Japan-China Breakthrough," Times Online, 25 June 2008, http://www.timesonline.co.uk/tol/news/world/asia/article4204432.ece.

44. Mainichi Daily News Online, 17 March 2009, http://mdn.mainichi.jp/mdnnews/.

45. Jim Yardley, "Chinese Nationalism Fuels Tibet Crackdown," *New York Times*, 31 March 2008, http://www.nytimes.com/2008/03/31/world/asia/31china.html?pagewanted=print.

46. "Premier: Ample Facts Drove Dalai's Role in Lhasa Riot, Door to Dialogue Still Open," Xinhua News Agency, 18 March 2008, http://news.xinhuanet.com/english/2008–03/18/content_7813012.htm.

47. Shaila Dewan, "Chinese Student in U.S. Is Caught in Confrontation," *New York Times*, 17 April 2008, http://www.nytimes.com/2008/04/17/us/17student.html?pagewanted=1&_r=1&sq=china%20tibet%20Duke&st=cse&scp=1.

48. "Jack Cafferty CNN Insulted Chinese People by Racism Words," YouTube, video posted on 10 April 2008, http://www.youtube.com/watch?v=2j2bvOq3fLA. CNN also mistakenly used photographs of Nepali and Indian police dragging away Tibetan protesters there to illustrate stories about repression by the Chinese authorities in Tibet itself.

49. "Who Is Really Behind the Tibet Riots?" Spirit of the Night Blog, translated by China Digital Times, http://chinadigitaltimes.net/2008/03/who-is-really-behind-the-tibet-riots/.

Acknowledgments

This volume emerged from a conference organized by the University of California Institute on Global Conflict and Cooperation and supported by the McCormick Tribune Foundation. I worked on it during a wonderful sabbatical year as the Arthur Ross Fellow at the U.S.-China Center of the Asia Society, New York City. I am very grateful to John LeJeune and Steven Oliver, PhD students in Political Science at University of California, San Diego, for their assistance in editing the chapters, and to Peng Zeng, Li Yuhui, and Josephine Hua Pan, for their research assistance.

Contributors

David Bandurski is a China analyst at the China Media Project, a research program of the Journalism and Media Studies Centre at the University of Hong Kong. He has also been a regular contributor to a number of publications, including the *Wall Street Journal* and the *Far Eastern Economic Review*, where he won Human Rights Press awards in 2006 and 2007 for his coverage of media censorship in China.

Tai Ming Cheung is an associate research scientist at the University of California Institute on Global Conflict and Cooperation, located at the University of California, San Diego. He received his PhD from the War Studies Department, Kings College, London University. He is a longtime analyst of Chinese defense and national security affairs and the author of several books on these topics. His latest book is *Fortifying China: The Struggle to Build a Modern Defense Economy*.

Hu Shuli is the editor in chief of Caixin Media and the former editor in chief of *Caijing* magazine. Before joining the staff of *Caijing*, Ms. Hu was an assistant editor, reporter, and international editor at the *Worker's Daily*, China's second largest newspaper. She joined *China Business Times* in 1992 as international editor and became chief reporter in 1995. She is the author of several books, including *New Financial Time, Reform Bears No Romance*, and *The Scenes Behind American Newspapers*. *Foreign Policy* magazine named Ms. Hu as one of the top 100 public intellectuals in the world in 2009.

Benjamin L. Liebman is Professor of Law and the Director of the Center for Chinese Legal Studies at Columbia Law School. His current research focuses on the role of the media in the Chinese legal system and on the evolution of China's courts and legal profession. Professor Liebman's recent publications include "Toward Competitive Supervision? The Media and the Courts," *China Quarterly* (forthcoming 2011) and "Reputational Sanctions in China's Securities Markets" (with Curtis J. Milhaupt), *Columbia Law Review* (2008). Prior to joining the Columbia faculty in 2002, Professor Liebman was an associate in the London and Beijing offices of Sullivan & Cromwell. He also previously served as a law clerk to Justice David Souter and to Judge Sandra Lynch of the First Circuit.

Miao Di is Professor of Television Arts at the Chinese University of Communications. He serves as an adviser to Hubei Television Station, Dalian Television Station, and other television organizations and is the author of many books, including *Reading Television* and *The Philosophy of Television Art.*

Qian Gang is director of the China Media Project, a research program of the Journalism and Media Studies Centre at the University of Hong Kong. Formerly managing editor of *Southern Weekend*, one of China's most progressive newspapers, he was removed in 2001 for a series of hard-hitting reports. The author of *The Great Tangshan Earthquake*, Mr. Qian is also one of China's foremost writers of reportage literature.

Susan L. Shirk is director of the University of California Institute on Global Conflict and Cooperation and Ho Miu Lam Professor at the School of International Relations and Pacific Studies, University of California, San Diego. During 1997 to 2000 she served as Deputy Assistant Secretary of State in the Office of East Asia and Pacific Affairs. Her most recent book is *China: Fragile Superpower.*

Daniela Stockmann is Assistant Professor of Political Science at Leiden University in the Netherlands. Prior to arriving in Leiden in 2007 she received a PhD in Political Science from the University of Michigan, Ann Arbor, and an MA in Chinese Studies from the School of Oriental and African Studies. Her research has been published in *China Quarterly* and the *Chinese Journal of Communication,* among others. She is currently completing a book manuscript tentatively titled *Propaganda for Sale: How Media Commercialization Sustains Authoritarian Rule in China.*

Xiao Qiang is an adjunct professor at the Graduate School of Journalism, University of California at Berkeley, and the founder and editor in chief of *China Digital Times*, a bilingual news Web site. He also runs the Counter-Power Lab at the School of Information, UC Berkeley. A theoretical physicist by training, Xiao Qiang studied at the University of Science and Technology of China and entered the PhD program (1986–1989) in Astrophysics at the University of Notre Dame. He became a full-time human rights activist after the Tiananmen Massacre in 1989. Mr. Xiao was the executive director of the New York–based NGO Human Rights in China (from 1991 to 2002), and he received the MacArthur Fellowship in 2001.

Zhan Jiang is a professor in the Department of International Journalism and Communication, Beijing Foreign Studies University, and the former Dean of the School of Journalism and Communication, China Youth University for Political Sciences. He is a very well-known media reformer and is frequently quoted in the Western media. He was a reporter and weekend edition editor of the *Yangzhou Daily News* (Yangzhou City, Jiangsu Province) from 1976 to 1985 and has written several books, including *Theories of Wartime Journalism, Journalism and Courage*, and *Watchdog Journalism and Global Democracy*.

Index

Note: Page numbers in *italics* indicate illustrations and tables.

Central Party School, 221

Central Propaganda Department, 61, 98, 123–24, 156–57, 165. *See also* propaganda

Century Weekly, 13

chat rooms, 205, 233

chemical spills, 20, 122–26

chemical weapons, 235, 242–43

Chen Feng, 62–63

Chengdu Commercial Daily, 53

Cheng Yawen, 35n26

Chen Shui-bian, 231

Chen Xiwen, 124

Chen Yizhong, 64, 66, 70

Chen Yu-hao, 66

Cheung, Tai Ming, 31–32

Chi Haotian, 131

China Business, 67–69, 78

China Business Times (CBT), 81–82, 139–40

China Central Television (CCTV)

  and advertising, 93–94, 94–95

  CCTV News, 105–8

  and classification of television stations, 92

  and commercialization of the news media, 41

  and court journalism, 154, 161

  and foreign policy, 230–32

  and government control of media, 8, 237

  and government transparency, 24–25

  and leadership politics, 31

  and military journalism, 135

  and monitoring of local officials, 20

  news programming, 105–8

  and public opinion, 108

  and *Super Girl,* 101–2

  and television journalism, 110–11

  and the Tibet issue, 246

  and twenty-four-hour news, 248

  viewership of, 99

  and watchdog role of the media, 109

China Chemical Industry News, 67

China.com, 139

China Computerworld, 40

China Daily, 240, 242

China Defense News (CDN), 135

China Development Institute, 121

China Digital Times, 13

China Economic Times, 63, 65

China Environmental Cultural Promotion Association (CECPA), 118–19

China.gov, 240

China Internet Network Information Center (CNNIC), 187, 194, 204, 205

China Internet Project, 207

China Law Society, 152

China Media Project, 56

China Military Online (CMO), 135, 140

China National Petroleum Company (SINOPEC), 121

China National Radio, 105

China News Service, 42–43

China Newsweekly, 43

China Ordnance Industry Enterprise Group (COIEG), 138

China Reform, 13

China Securities Journal, 78

China Securities News, 82

China Securities Regulatory Commission (CSRC), 79–80

China Television Service Company, 93

China Youth, 24

China Youth Daily

  and agenda-setting power of the media, 65

  and court journalism, 153, 156

  and Internet censorship, 206, 208

  and military journalism, 139

  and professionalization of the media, 58

  and the Songhua River incident, 123

  and Sun Zhigang story, 63

  and the Xiamen PX project, 67

China Youth Journal, 10
China Youth League, 58
Chinese Academy of Social Sciences,
63–64, 86, 203, 221
Chinese Air Force, 137
Chinese Communist Party (CCP). See
also propaganda
and agenda-setting power, 39
and anti-Japanese sentiment, 235
and the business media, 83
and censorship, 32–33, 39, 233, 241
and citizen mobilization, 219
and citizen news, 104–5
and civil-military relations, 130
and commercialization of the media,
40–43
and control of commercial media, 39
and court journalism, 29, 151, 152,
161–62, 169–70, 172
and credibility of the media, 23,
47–49
and cross-regional reporting, 21–22
and defamation cases, 166
and foreign policy, 3, 225–26, 226–27,
237–38, 247–48
and Global Times, 228
and growth of Chinese media, 116
and information management, 3, 32
and internal reports, 161, 240
and the Internet, 3, 13–14, 55, 205,
206–7, 207–8, 233, 237
and leadership politics, 29–31
and licensing of media, 12
and loss of media control, 222–23
and military journalism, 31–32, 129, 132
and monitoring of local officials,
19–22
and nationalism, 242
and Phoenix Television, 231
and political reform, 221
and privatization of media, 1–2
and professionalization of
journalism, 57–59, 71
and protest coverage, 26
and public opinion, 39, 56, 217–19, 240
relationship to Chinese
government, vii
and resistance to government
controls, 209
and Shanxi Brick Kilns case, 215
and television media, 91, 92, 96–97,
101, 106–7
and Tiananmen Square protests, 16,
39, 71–72n4
and transparency, 25, 32–33
and the Xiamen PX project, 68
Chinese Diaspora, 138
Chinese Embassy bombing, 35n27
Chinese Journalists Association, 168
Chinese Lawyer, 152
Chinese New Year Gala Show, 99
Chinese People's Political Consultative
Conference (CPPCC), 66–68,
118, 212
A Chinese Restaurant, 98–99
Chongqing, 194–95
Chongqing Nail House event, 213–14,
222, 223
Chongqing Party, 22
Chongqing Satellite TV, 108
Chutian Metropolis Daily, 41, 63
Chwe, Michael Suk-Young, 6
circulation figures, 41–42, 42, 229
Cisco, 233
citizen news, 104–5
Civil Affairs Bureau, 63
civil-military relations, 130–32
civil rights, 116
civil society, 61, 117, 119, 125–26, 130, 219
Clinton, Bill, 228, 239
Clinton, Hillary, 3
Clouds Chasing the Moon, 102
CNN (Cable News Network), 178, 231,
246, 248
coastal areas, 120
coded communication, 210

Mao Zedong, 14, 30, 34n20, 37n55
market economics
    and the business media, 79–81, 87
    and commercialization of media,
        38–39
    and court journalism, 168, 170
    and entertainment news, 102
    and environmental journalism, 115
mass media, 7–8. *See also specific media
        types*
Ma Ying-jeou, 231
media blackouts, 18, 21–22, 212, 216, 246
Media Control in China (He), 4
melamine-tainted milk scandal, 18
Meng Fei, 103
Mengniu Yogurt, 100
Metropolitan Channel, 103
Miao Di, 11, 20
microblogging, 209. *See also* blogging
Midnight News, 108
migrant workers, 151, 159–60
Military Digest, 137
military journalism
    audience of, 140–41
    and civilian media coverage, 139–40
    and civil-military relations, 130–32
    and commercialization, 134–36, 136–39
    comparative perspective on, 143–45
    and nationalism, 128–30, 142
    and public opinion, 136, 141–43,
        144–45
    and the reform era, 132–33
military media, 31–32, 37n55
Military Observation Post, 139
military power, 16–17. *See also* People's
    Liberation Army (PLA)
Military Reporting, 135–36
Military World Pictorial, 137
mining accidents, 49–53
Ministry of Culture, 208
Ministry of Environmental Protection
    (MEP), 120
Ministry of Finance (MOF), 93, 94

Ministry of Health, 120
Ministry of Industry and Information
    Technology, 208
Ministry of Information Industry, 40,
    199n4
Ministry of Information Technology,
    209
Ministry of Justice, 152
Ministry of National Defense, 142
Ministry of Public Security, 208
Ministry of Science and Technology,
    120
Ministry of State Security, 23
mobile phones, 2, 6, 202, 214, 226, 233
mobility of Chinese population, 223
mobilization, 196, 217–19, 219–20. *See also*
    activism
modernization, economic, 1
Modern Navy, 137
Modern Weaponry, 137
monopolies, 14–15
Mop.com, 204–5, 214
muckraking, 10, 12. *See also* investigative
    journalism
Mulvenon, James, 132
municipal authorities, 20–21
municipal television, 92
Murdoch, Rupert, 116, 231
Myanmar, 143

Nanfang Chuang, 31
Nanfang Daily, 10, 40–42
Nanjing, 9, 10
National Auditing Bureau, 101
National Day, 128–29
National Development Planning
    Commission, 125
nationalism
    and anti-Japanese sentiment, 175,
        242–45
    and foreign policy, 225–27, 229, 235,
        237, 241
    and military journalism, 128–30, 142

Radio Free Asia (RFA), 211
Rafferty, Jack, 246
Rand Corporation, 132
ratings, 103
Rational Ritual (Chwe), 6
Reading Time, 95–96
read/write culture, 59–62
reality television programs, 100–102
reconnaissance plane incident, 234,
    236, 237
Red Guard, 37n55
Reference News, 227, 228
reform
    and advertising, 177
    and business media, 81–82
    economic reforms, 81–82, 108–9,
        177–79
    and environmental journalism,
        115–19
    and function of Chinese news media,
        181
    impact on Chinese media, 177–79
    media reforms, 8–11
    and military journalism, 132–33
    political reforms, 220–22
    and television, 8–9, *179*
regional propaganda bureaus, vii
Regulations on Open Government
    Information, 24
Regulations on Political Work, 145
repatriation system, 18, 62–66,
    159–60
*Report on Development of China's Media
    Industry*, 55
Republic of China, 28, 227, 242
Research Center on Contemporary
    China, 182
resource competition, 183, 244
River Crab Society, 210
RSS aggregation tools, 204
rule of law, 222
rural areas, 11, 96, 120, 194–95, 201n25,
    223n4

Sanqin Metropolitan Daily, 70
Schelling, Thomas, 6–7
school collapse disaster, 24
Science and Technology Daily, 139
Scott, James, 210
search engines, 3–4, 204, 208, 210. *See
    also* Google
Securities Times, 82
Seed Law, 158
semiofficial media, 178, *179*, 195
Senkaku Islands, 245
sensationalism, 44, 87, 104–5
September 11 terrorist attacks, 108,
    230–31
severe acute respiratory syndrome
    (SARS)
    and commercialization of the media,
        63–64
    and media censorship, 157
    and media credibility, 23, 195–96
    and political activism, 197
    and public opinion, 176, 240
    and public security policy, 222
    and television news, 107–8
    and watchdog role of the media,
        84–85
Shaanxi Daily, 70
shai, 206, 210–11, 213, 222
Shandong satellite TV station, 95
Shanghai, 35n27, 194
Shanghai Administration of Radio,
    Film, and Television, 98
Shanghai Morning Post, 156
Shanghai Satellite TV, 108
Shanghai Securities News, 82
Shanghai Security Daily, 78
Shanghai Television, 93
Shanxi Brick Kilns event, 214–15, 222,
    223
Shen Gui Tonic Wine, 94
She Xianglin, 150–51, 157, 162
Shi Tao, 30
Sichuan Daily, 53

and foreign affairs, 229
and foreign policy, 238
and government transparency, 23
and Internet censorship, 206, 208,
    233, 236
and Internet portals, 14–15
and monitoring of local officials, 21
and public opinion, 240
and Shanxi Brick Kilns case, 215
State Environmental Protection
    Administration (SEPA), 119, 120,
    122, 125
state-owned banks, 83–84
Stockmann, Daniela, 8, 9, 23
stock markets, 79–80, 88
Strategy and Management, 243
Strong China Forum, 241
Strong Country Forum, 135
Strong Nation Forum, 246
student demonstrations, 2, 23, 184,
    230, 235
subscription quotas, 134
subsidies, 8–9, 42–43, 94
substantive justice, 170
Sun Zhigang, 17–18, 62–66, 159–60,
    161–63, 165
Sun Zhongtong, 131
Super Girl, 97, 100–102
Supreme People's Court (SPC), 151, 159,
    162, 164–66, 168
Supreme People's Procuratorate, 152
synchronization of news content,
    185–86, 188, 191–93

tabloids, 51, 53, 78, 102–5, 239
Taiwan
    and Chinese foreign policy, 184–85,
        225–26, 228, 238, 247–48
    and the Great Chinese Firewall, 211
    and Internet news sources, 188
    and military journalism, 129
Taiwan Strait, 141, 183, 228
Ta Kung Pao, 141

Tang Jiaxuan, 243
Tang Wenfang, 197
Tan Zuoren, 24
"Tear Down This Firewall" campaign,
    220
television
    and advertising, 93–96, 103, 111, 230,
        231–32
    and BAS study, 187
    and censorship, 97–98, 98–99, 236
    classification of stations, 91–92
    and commercialization of media, 2
    and competition, 92–96, 111
    and conformity pressures, 96–102
    and court journalism, 165, 170
    and economic reforms, *179*
    and foreign policy, 230–32
    and government controls, 11, 98–100
    influence of, 201n28
    and media reform, 8–9
    and official news, 105–8
    and relaxation of party control, 1
    and tabloid news, 102–5
    and watchdog role of the media,
        108–11
Television Department, 92
Teng Biao, 65
territorial disputes, 35n26, 142, 234, 245.
    See also Taiwan Strait; Tibet
textbooks, 183
text messaging, 68–69
Three Closenesses, 43, 104
Three Gorges Dam project, 85, 166
Tiananmen Square
    and Beijing Olympic Games
        protests, 3
    and business journalism, 80
    and CCP media strategy, 16, 39,
        71–72n4
    and commercialization of media, 2
    and economic news, 12
    and government censorship, 208,
        209, 237